Overreaching in Paradise

United States Policy in Palau Since 1945

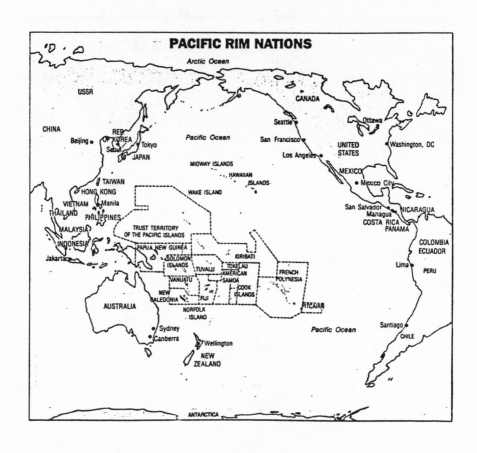

PACIFIC RIM NATIONS

Arctic Ocean

USSR

CANADA

CHINA

Seattle

Ottawa

REP.
OF KOREA
Beijing
Seoul
Tokyo
JAPAN

Pacific Ocean

San Francisco

UNITED
STATES

Washington, DC

Los Angeles

MIDWAY ISLANDS

MEXICO

TAIWAN

HAWAIIAN
ISLANDS

Mexico City

HONG KONG

WAKE ISLAND

VIETNAM
Manila
THAILAND

San Salvador
NICARAGUA
Managua
COSTA RICA
PANAMA

PHILIPPINES

MALAYSIA

TRUST TERRITORY
OF THE PACIFIC ISLANDS

INDONESIA

COLOMBIA
ECUADOR

Jakarta

PAPUA NEW GUINEA

KIRIBATI

SOLOMON
ISLANDS

Lima

PERU

TOKELAU

TUVALU

VANUATU

AMERICAN
SAMOA

FRENCH
POLYNESIA

NEW
CALEDONIA

FIJI

COOK
ISLANDS

AUSTRALIA

NORFOLK
ISLAND

PITCAIRN

Santiago

Pacific Ocean

CHILE

Sydney

Canberra

Wellington

NEW
ZEALAND

ANTARCTICA

Overreaching in Paradise

United States Policy in Palau Since 1945

Sue Rabbitt Roff

THE DENALI PRESS

Denali, derived from the Koyukon name *Deenaalee*, is the native name for Mount McKinley. Mount McKinley, the highest mountain on the North American continent, is located in Denali National Park. The lowlands surrounding this majestic mountain provide a diverse wildlife habitat for a variety of animals including grizzly bears, wolves, caribou and moose.

Copyright © 1991 by Sue Rabbitt Roff

Published by The Denali Press
Post Office Box 021535
Juneau, Alaska USA 99802-1535
(907) 586-6014

Library of Congress Cataloging-in-Publication Data

Roff, Sue Rabbitt.
    Overreaching in paradise : United States policy in Palau since 1945.
        p. cm.
    Includes bibliographical references (p.) and index.
    ISBN 0-938737-22-8 :
    1. Palau--Politics and government. 2. Palau--Foreign relations--United States.   3. United States--Foreign relations--Palau. 4. United States--Foreign relations--1945-   I. Title
    DU780.R64   1991
    327.730966--dc20   90-3608
                                                                          CIP

∞ The paper in this book complies with the Permanent Standard issued by the National Standards Organization. This book is printed on recycled paper.

For my father, Lloyd Clayton Rabbitt
and for Bedor Bins—two Pacific men who
would have understood each other and who
died within weeks of each other. And for
Bernie Keldermans and Roman Bedor who
have had to pay such a high price.

Contents

Acknowledgements

It is a commentary on the events of the past decade that I do not feel it would be wise to name all those Palauans who have helped me in preparing this study. But in Koror, New York and Washington many people of courage have helped me to understand the tensions of their homeland.

It is also a commentary on the health of the American political process that I have no reservations about naming those United States-based people with whom I was privileged to share information throughout the 1980s—Glenn Alcalay, Stuart J. Beck, Walden Bello, Elizabeth M. Bounds, Mary Beth Braun, William J. Butler, Roger S. Clark, Gary Gamer, Barbara Glendon, Sebia Hawkins, James Heddle, Victor Hsu, Ingrid Kircher, Glen Peterson, Susan Quass, David G. Richenthal, Anne E. Simon, Charles Scheiner, Michelle Syverson, M. D. Taracido, B. David Williams, Lynn Wilson, Chris Wing, Paulette Wittwer and Lyuba Zarsky.

There were also those who supported this work with grants over that decade. I much appreciated the advice of Vincent McGee in directing me to support for the Palau project of Minority Rights Group. The grants made by the Samuel Rubin Foundation, the Tides Foundation, the Ploughshares Fund, the J. Roderick MacArthur Foundation, National Community Funds, National Council of Churches, the Pro Publico Bono Fund, the Hunt Alternatives Fund and Mr. and Mrs. Ferry were important moral as well as financial support.

Helen Wasti and Sarah Roff both brought bibliographical and word processing skills to the preparation of the study and Alan Edward Schorr has been the most uncomplaining of editors.

Most of the library research was done in the excellent holdings of the Columbia University Libraries and the document archive for the study is now held by Columbia Law Library's Special Collections for those who may wish to consult it.

If William R. Roth had lost faith in my work during the past decade I would have found it very hard to continue to argue an analysis that made me decidedly unpopular in several quarters. But he didn't and as always his integrity is my lodestar in this enterprise.

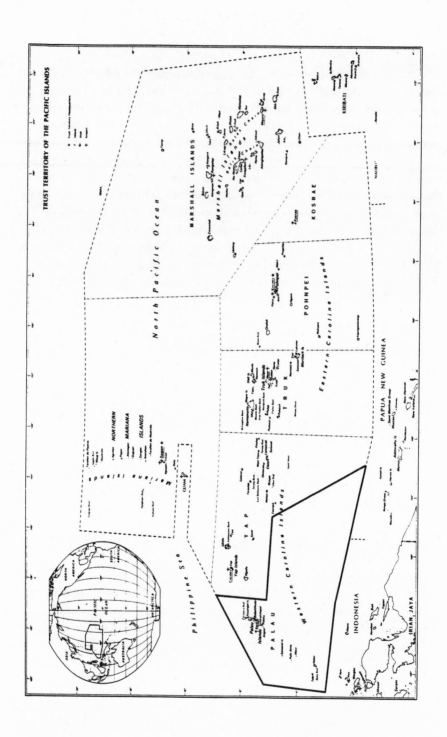

TRUST TERRITORY OF THE PACIFIC ISLANDS

Preface

In little more than a decade the nine thousand registered voters of Palau have voted ten times on the question of whether or not they should ban nuclear substances from their islands. They voted to have a nuclear-free constitution in 1979 and under pressure from the United States as administering authority of the Trust Territory of the Pacific Islands they twice reaffirmed their commitment to that constitution. The United States then proposed a Compact of Free Association which was incompatible with the constitution because it would permit nuclear substances into Palauan territory. Seven times since 1983 variations of that Compact of Free Association have been submitted to plebiscite as required in the constitution—and seven times the Palauan electorate has refused to override the anti-nuclear provisions of their constitution.

In the process of insisting on the "ratification" of what by 1986 had become a non-negotiable Compact the United States has overreached its rights as administering authority under the Trusteeship Agreement for the Trust Territory of the Pacific Islands which it entered into with the United Nations Security Council in 1947.[1] Simultaneously, every United States administration since that of President Kennedy has worked on a strategy for the unilateral termination of the Trusteeship Agreement because it was aware that the process of determining the future political status of the territory would not stand close scrutiny outside the narrow confines of the Trusteeship Council, much less the Security Council.

As Roger S. Clark noted in a letter to the *American Journal of International Law* in reviewing the twenty years of Micronesian status negotiations

> These events can only leave the impression that something is being swept under the carpet. There are serious issues at stake as to whether the United Nations norms for the proper exercise of self-determination have been met. . . .[2]

First we will define what these United Nations norms for the proper exercise of self-determination are and then we will review events to establish to what extent United States policy in Palau has constituted overreaching.

The process of self-determination in Palau has been marred in the 1980s by three violent deaths—the assassination of the first President of the Republic of Palau, Haruo Remiliik in 1985; the murder of the father of leading opponents of the Compact in 1987; and the suicide of the second president, Lazarus Salii, in 1988. These would be sad events for any community; for the fifteen thousand people of Palau they are a tragic reminder of the pressures that have ravaged their island paradise over the past decade. The Palauan people voted overwhelmingly for a constitution whose anti-nuclear clauses could not be amended with less that a 75 percent consensus in a referendum called specifically on the issue. In Palau, the two thousand voters who have consistently refused to accept nuclear substances are respected as exercising a legitimate right conceded to them in the constitution. The resort to pressure culminating in physical intimidation testifies to external pressures which Palau has been unable to escape.

It is to be hoped that in the 1990s there emerges a solution by consensus, a process that would be in the best traditions of both Palau and the United States. The courage of those two thousand voters and their leaders—and the fact that of this writing there are still no nuclear substances in Palau—is a beacon to all of us who want to work our way out of the global nuclear mindset.

[1] For the text of the 1947 Trusteeship Agreement see Appendix A.

[2] *American Journal of International Law* 81 (1987): 934.

Chapter One

Decolonization Principles and Norms: Forty Years of United Nations Policy and Practice

More than forty years of United Nations policy and practice have clearly established the limits to the rights of former colonial powers to influence the process of self-determination in non-self-governing territories. To suggest that the United States has overreached those rights in parts of the Trust Territory of the Pacific Islands is to argue that a superpower has felt it necessary to try to get the better of a very small community by artifice or cunning, has tried to outwit the Palauan people and cheat them of their right to self-determination in the modern world. It may also be to suggest that in so doing the United States has strained itself and defeated its own purposes by trying too hard to control a situation and its outcome.

Contemporary international law is constitutive and consensual. When everyone agrees, it works well. When one state disagrees or violates the consensus, the other states have the choice of rallying round to enforce the consensus, changing the basis of their consensus to accommodate the interest of the violating state, or agreeing— explicitly or implicitly—to tolerate the dissension. In some cases, the violator refuses to accept the choice of the other states and remains in aggressive violation of international law. This pushes the dispute to a more dangerous level of disagreement, but the international community in the twentieth century—especially since the acquisition of nuclear capabilities—is very loathe to admit outright confrontation. It will try to localize the conflict in order to contain it.

Maintaining consensus through continuing consent is the major purpose of the United Nations and why 159 nations states maintain expensive delegations. But it can also be an important testing ground for dissent from the consensus that has evolved over its four decades of policy and practice which have created the precedents which now constitute the *jus cogens* of international law.

It is important to establish just what are the norms of international law covering decolonization in order to assess whether or not the

United States has overreached them in the nascent Republic of Palau—
a South Pacific archipelago that visitors often describe as paradise.

The Rhetoric of Self-Determination

Franklin D. Roosevelt wrote to Myron C. Taylor in September 1941
that

> The self-determination of boundaries and forms of
> government was the most substantial contribution made by
> the Versailles Treaty . . . i.e. the plebiscite method, which, on
> the whole, was successful. [1]

This perception pervaded the rhetoric of the second major postwar
settlement of the century. The very term "United Nations" was
proposed by Roosevelt and first used in the Declaration by United
Nations signed by the representatives of the twenty-six nations
fighting against the Axis aggressors in Washington on January 1, 1942,
in which they undertook to cooperate in winning the war and not to seek
a separate peace. The signatories of the Declaration by United Nations
also committed themselves to the principles of the Atlantic Charter
drafted by Churchill and Roosevelt on August 14, 1941 in which they
asserted that

> their countries seek no aggrandizement, territorial or other;
> . . . desire to see no territorial changes that do not accord with
> the freely expressed wishes of the peoples concerned; . . .
> [and] respect the right of all peoples to choose the form of
> government under which they will live; and they wish to see
> sovereign rights and self-government restored to those who
> have been forcibly deprived of them.

On October 30, 1943 the Foreign Ministers of Britain, the United
States, and the Soviet Union together with the Chinese ambassador in
Moscow issued the Moscow Declaration recognizing

> the necessity of establishing at the earliest practicable date a
> general international organization based on the principle of
> the sovereign equality of all peace-loving States, and open to

membership by all such States, large and small, for the maintenance of international peace and security. [2]

Umozurike Oji Umozurike notes that there was no mention of self-determination in the Dumbarton Oaks proposals of 1944. [3] In February 1945 at Yalta, Churchill, Roosevelt and Stalin called a meeting of the "United Nations," all those who had declared war on Germany or Japan and had signed the Declaration by United Nations, for April 1945. At this meeting in San Francisco the term 'United Nations' was unanimously adopted.

In San Francisco the Soviet delegation pressed the issue of the right to self-determination. [4] Ofuatey-Kedjoe points out that

> in the final stages of World War One the groups which were agitating for self-determination and independence were the European nationalities. . . . Therefore, the question of self-determination was posed as 'national self-determination'. . . . After World War Two, it was not the European nationalities that were in revolt, it was the overseas colonies. . . . .Thus the answers have been provided in relation to colonial peoples— self-determination of peoples. [5]

Chapter XI of the United Nations Charter was the Declaration Regarding Non-Self-Governing Territories drafted at San Francisco. Article 73 asserted that

> Members of the United Nations which have or assume responsibilities for the administration of territories whose people have not yet attained a full measure of self-government recognize the principle that the interests of the inhabitants of these territories are paramount, and accept as a sacred trust the obligation to promote to the utmost, within the system of international peace and security established by the present Charter, the well-being of the inhabitants of these territories, and, to this end:
>
> (a) to ensure, with due respect for the culture of the peoples concerned, their political, economic, social, and educational advancement, their just treatment, and their protection against abuses;
>
> (b) to develop self-government, to take account of the political aspirations of the peoples, and to assist them in the

progressive development of their free political institutions, according to the particular circumstances of each territory and its peoples and their varying stages of advancement.

This was a much more equivocal formulation of the right to self-determination than the proposed Soviet formula that "Every people and every nation has the right to national self-determination." [6] References to sovereignty and independence had given way to "self-government" and "advancement" of territories in which the political aspirations of the people would be "taken account of."

These modified goals were to be implemented by Article 73(e) which required the administering members

> to transmit regularly to the Secretary-General for information purposes, subject to such limitation as security and constitutional considerations may require, statistical and other information of a technical nature relating to economic, social and educational conditions in the territories for which they are respectively responsible. . . .

The victorious powers were able to agree to create a second international mechanism for the oversight of dependent territories. All territories which had been held under mandate from the League of Nations, together with territories which were to be detached from enemy states as a result of the Second World War, together with some territories voluntarily placed u:.der the system by states responsible for their administration were placed under the International Trusteeship system created by Article 75 of the United Nations Charter. [7] The purpose of the trusteeship system was to further international peace and security and

> to promote the political, economic, social and educational advancement of the inhabitants of the trust territories, and their progressive development towards self-government or independence as may be appropriate to the particular circumstances of each territory and its peoples and the freely expressed wishes of the peoples concerned, and as may be provided by the terms of each trusteeship agreement.

Article 82 provided for the designation in any trusteeship agreement "a strategic area or areas which may include part of all of the trust territory." Article 83 provided that "All functions of the

United Nations relating to strategic areas, including the approval of the terms of the trusteeship agreement and of their alteration or amendment, shall be exercised by the Security Council" which could "avail itself of the assistance of the Trusteeship Council to perform those functions."

S. Hasan Ahmad points out that the principles and obligations of the Declaration Regarding Non-Self-Governing Territories were the same as those for the Trusteeship System, "but unlike the latter, no international machinery was provided for the implementation of its provisions." San Francisco, suggests Ahmad, was "the hour of trust." [8] The Charter of the United Nations was declaratory; the rhetoric had been carefully wrought to persuade the victors that they would not have to concede too much, while yet promising a new *postbellum* world for the dependent peoples. Forty years of practice would be needed to substantiate the principles involved in the doctrine of self-determination. Those battles have been described as between the strict and broad constructionists,[9] between the group that wished to implement the principle fully and quickly and those who wished to obstruct its implementation. [10]

1945-1950: Defining the Terms

The British Information Services sought to explain *Britain and Trusteeship* in a 1947 publication. Trusteeship

> is not a new word. It has been used for more than a century and a half to denote the restraining and humanizing influence in colonial affairs. It has always meant a moral obligation on the part of advanced nations towards backward peoples. [11]

The doctrine of trusteeship was born of the humanitarian movement of the late eighteenth and early nineteenth centuries, centered for many years in its attack upon slavery. It moved from an ethical to a political aspect in the mid-nineteenth century with the political emergence of Canada, Australia, New Zealand and South Africa "as entirely autonomous states." The main principle of political trusteeship, according to this British government publication, is the development of self-government (not independence) and it is this principle which "is now, on British initiative, an integral part of the United Nations Charter." [12] The latest official summing up of "British colonial policy" was the statement by the Secretary of State for the Colonies in the House of Commons in July 1946 in which he said that

> it is our policy to develop the colonies and all their resources so as to enable their peoples speedily and substantially to improve their economic and social conditions, and, as soon as may be practicable, to attain responsible self-government.

According to the Secretary of State for the Colonies, this limited goal of "responsible self-government"

> in no way differs from the principles contained in the trusteeship chapters of the United Nations Charter. [13]

While the British were trying to confine the goals of Chapter XI to self-government, the French, Belgian and Netherlands delegations to the newly-created Ad Hoc Committee to the Fourth Committee were working to have their colonies removed from the oversight established by Article 73 and its reporting requirement in section (e).[14] They opted for an intriguing strategy to achieve this end.

The French delegate pointed out that

> The term 'Non-Self-Governing Territory' was not defined in the Charter and did not necessarily refer to the Colonial Territories alone. [15]

The Belgian delegate elaborated what became known as the "Belgian thesis"

> All under-developed peoples of the world were entitled to expect Members of the United Nations to proclaim their acceptance of a sacred mission with regard to them, similar to that which Belgium has accepted in regard to the Belgian Congo. Some non-self-governing peoples lived in territories, some in reservations; areas which they inhabited were in some cases within or adjacent to the frontier of a State, while in other cases they were separated by the sea. From a legal point of view, whether the area inhabited by non-self-governing peoples was within the frontiers of a State or

outside them, the better-developed State had certain rights over that area. [16]

The Belgian delegate then pushed his point home by suggesting that it would be useful for all member States to report on the underdeveloped peoples within their frontiers, giving as examples the Indians of Central, South and North America and the Negritos of the Philippines.

As Ahmad reports, the delegations of Bolivia, Brazil, Cuba, India, Indonesia, Iraq, the Philippines, Mexico, Syria and others of the "implementationist" or "broad constructionist" group emphatically rejected this Belgian thesis of the scope of Chapter XI and Article 73 since they were all plural societies. [17] The Belgian delegation pressed its point remorselessly. Ahmad summarizes the debate:

> the representative observed that to claim that the colonies and protectorates were the only territories whose peoples were not yet fully self-governing was tantamount to claiming that the indigenous primitive or semi-primitive peoples of America, Asia or Malaya were already self-governing within the meaning of the Charter. But in fact they were so backward that, where they did not altogether escape the administration of the State to which they belonged, they were placed under a specified legal or administrative constitutional system, just like the people of the colonies. Furthermore, they were totally different, not only by the reason of their primitive character but also race, language, and culture, from the peoples from whom the government administering the State emanated. These peoples, who could be counted in their millions, were almost completely isolated from the centers of government, separated generally from them by vast stretches of almost impenetrable jungle. It was true that they were an integral part of the State on whose territory they dwelt, but the same was true, for instance, of the peoples of the Congo, the Belgian Congo being also an integral part of the Belgian State. [18]

The "implementationist" group was forced into the uncomfortable position of arguing against this extension of the scope of Chapter XI and Article 73 because of the implications for themselves and their minority communities. Ahmad suggests that this Franco-Belgian theory was "intended only to divert the Committee from its main task," but it was in fact far more substantive. On April 29, 1949 the French government notified the United Nations that it would not voluntarily transmit information on its non-metropolitan territories as required by Article 73 (e) because

> the determination of territories whose peoples have not yet attained a full measure of self-government lies exclusively within the competence of the States which have the responsibility for the administration of such territories. [19]

This unilateral decision not to transmit information on its territories to the Fourth Committee of the United Nations was supported by Australia, Belgium, the Netherlands and Britain. [20] With this one stroke, France implemented the Belgian thesis that better-developed States have certain rights over less-developed peoples even in non-contiguous areas, while at the same time refusing to report on the progress towards self-government of those peoples.

While the British were promoting self-government as a sufficient goal for dependent territories, the Belgians were arguing that their sacred mission was to civilize non-contiguous territories such as the Congo, and the French were defining their State as both its metropolitan and non-contiguous territories, the "implementationist" and "broad constructionist" groups were trying to strengthen Article 73 (e). As written, it carefully did not specify the transmission of political information—and all other socioeconomic information was "subject to such limitation as security and constitutional considerations may require."

The Soviet bloc was vociferous in urging the reporting of political information—having protected its own dependent territories from scrutiny by having them accorded membership of the United Nations itself, an irony rarely remarked upon in the contemporary discussions in the literature. The United States and the Netherlands were prepared to voluntarily transmit political information on their territories; the British were adamantly opposed. However Resolution 146 (VI) of November 3, 1947 established the Special Committee on Information Transmitted Under Section 73 (e) of the Charter, to receive information on the 74 territories enumerated as non-self-governing in Resolution 66 (I) of December 14, 1946. In the first instance the Special Committee on Information was established for a year but was given a three-year mandate by Resolution 332 (VI) of the General Assembly on December 2, 1949. On the same day, the General Assembly recommended in

Resolution 327 (VI) that the transmission of political information to the Special Committee no longer be optional but mandatory. The Committee was renamed the Committee on Information from Non-Self-Governing Territories in 1955, and the new title was significant in reflecting that by the mid-fifties it was beginning to receive information not only from administering powers but also from inhabitants of the territories.

Under the Trusteeship System, Australia, Britain, France, Belgium and New Zealand had been successful in having trusteeship agreements approved for eight Territories in 1946. The General Assembly recommended that the Mandated Territory of South West Africa be placed under the trusteeship system and invited the Union of South Africa to propose a trusteeship agreement. But South Africa argued that the majority of the inhabitants of the territory wished to be incorporated into the Union, an interpretation which the General Assembly rejected. In 1947 the United States secured a strategic trusteeship agreement for the Territory of the Pacific Islands, the only strategic trust created. In the same year Australia, New Zealand and Britain proposed an agreement for Nauru. The first visiting missions of the International Trusteeship System visited Ruanda-Urundi and Tanganyika in 1948. In 1949 South Africa informed the Secretary-General that it would submit no further reports on its administration of South West Africa. The General Assembly asked the International Court of Justice for an advisory opinion on the international status of South West Africa and the obligations of South Africa in regard to the Territory. In its Advisory Opinion of July 11, 1950 the World Court

> was of the unanimous opinion that the Union of South Africa acting alone was not competent to modify the international status of the Territory of South West Africa. Such competence to determine and modify the international status of South West Africa rested with the Union acting with the consent of the United Nations [21]

because

> the obligations imposed on South Africa by the Mandate were still in force and the General Assembly was competent to discharge the necessary supervisory functions previously exercised by the League of Nations. [22]

This Advisory Opinion thus explicitly joined the jurisdiction of the League of Nations to that of the United Nations and established both a theoretical and historical continuity in the doctrine of self-determination in international law in the twentieth century.

By the end of 1950, then, the United Nations Trusteeship System and Committee on Decolonization had established the requirement of administering powers to submit to international scrutiny of their wardships of nearly 80 territories. France and South Africa had withdrawn from participating in this system of international scrutiny; the Soviet Union had never submitted to it. Britain was trying to limit the expectations of its dependent territories to self-government while Belgium and the Netherlands were arguing a modified form of the French thesis that their States extended beyond their metropolitan territories. The United States had fulfilled its wartime promise to the Philippines but had no intention of allowing Hawaii, Alaska, Puerto Rico or the Pacific Islands to become independent.

The Fifties: Codifying the Factors

In 1947 Britain had ceased transmitting information on Malta, arguing that constitutional developments there made it no longer appropriate to do so. France was no longer transmitting information on its Overseas Departments and Territories or the "associated states" of Vietnam, Laos and Cambodia. The United States considered that a Panamanian statement claiming sovereignty over the Panama Canal Zone released it from transmitting information on this territory until the issue was settled by consultations between the two countries. [23]

The General Assembly worked energetically in 1952 and 1953 to strengthen the right to self-determination in the face of the avoidance tactics of the administering powers. Resolution 637 (VII) of the 403rd plenary meeting on December 16, 1952 called on the administering powers to actively facilitate the exercise of the right according to

> the freely expressed wishes of the peoples concerned, the wishes of the people being ascertained through plebiscites or other recognized democratic means, preferably under the auspices of the United Nations; . . .

and urged that information regarding the political progress towards self-determination be transmitted under Article 73 (e). In order to ensure international respect for the right of peoples to self-determination, the same General Assembly in its Resolution 648 (VII) began to codify the "Factors which should be taken into account in deciding whether a Territory is or is not a Territory whose people have not yet attained a full measure of self-government."

The factors indicative of independence, other separate systems of self-government and of the free association of a Territory on equal basis with the metropolitan or other country as integral part of that country or in any other form were reaffirmed the next year in Resolution 742 (VIII). However on the same day, November 27, 1953, the General Assembly adopted Resolution 748 recognizing that the people of the Commonwealth of Puerto Rico had achieved a new constitutional status of mutually agreed association with the United States which left the Puerto Rican people

> invested with attributes of political sovereignty which clearly identify the status of self-government attained by the Puerto Rican peoples as that of an autonomous political entity.

As Roger S. Clark comments,

> Curiously, the General Assembly did not see fit to try to apply in any detail to the case of Puerto Rico its list of 'Factors Indicative of the Attainment of Independence or of other Separate Systems of Self-Government' [24]

adopted earlier in the day.

The second half of the decade saw continued attempts by the administering powers to distinguish particular cases from the general principles codified in Resolutions 648 and 672. The Netherlands Kingdom sought to "reconstruct" itself in a new relationship with Surinam and the Netherlands Antilles in which the territories would have some areas of autonomy but in others would submit to the authority of the Netherlands. The territories did not have the right to unilaterally terminate the arrangement with the Netherlands as required by Resolutions 648 and 742. There was no plebiscite to ascertain the peoples' will. There was considerable doubt about the substance of the autonomy accorded the territories under the arrangement. Nevertheless, General Assembly Resolution 945 declared

> on the basis of the information before it as presented by the Government of the Netherlands, and as desired by the Government of the Netherlands, cessation of the transmission of information under Article 73 (e) of the charter in respect of the Netherlands Antilles and Surinam is appropriate.

Again, as in the case of Puerto Rico, the Factors had not been applied in the face of the clear determination of the administering power to ignore them. [25]

In Resolution 849 (IX) of November 22, 1954 the General Assembly had accepted the petition of the peoples of Greenland to be incorporated into the Kingdom of Denmark. In that case, Ahmad notes,

> resolution 849 (IX) specifically took into consideration the recommendation in resolution 742 (VIII) that the documentation was to be studied in the light of the list of Factors. [26]

Greenland was, Ahmad suggests, "an exemplary case" and the application of the Factors did not endanger the outcome desired by the administering power. Before the end of the decade the United States would secure full integration of two of its territories, Hawaii and Alaska, on the same terms.

But if in the first half of the decade the list of Factors was more honored in the breach than the observance, the states supporting the fullest implementation of the principles of self-determination were rallying at Bandung in 1955. The Final Communique of the 29 African and Asian nations issued from Bandung on April 24, 1955 declared "its support of the cause of freedom and independence for all dependent peoples." The Bandung conference did not equivocate about its commitment to direct support for full independence of those suffering from alien subjugation by which they meant the colonialism of the previous four hundred years.

Meanwhile, two French Associates States—Laos and Cambodia—and two French Protectorates—Morocco and Tunisia—had attained independence under De Gaulle's dispensation and become member States of the United Nations. The British territories of the Gold Coast and

Togoland were emerging as Ghana, and the Federation of Malaya was admitted to the United Nations in 1957. By the end of the decade, French Guinea, French Togoland and the French Cameroons had all moved to independence and full membership. The non-aligned movement was forming in its meetings in Accra in 1958, Monrovia in 1959 and Addis Abbaba in 1960. Burma, Ceylon, Indonesia, Libya, Pakistan, the Philippines, Israel and Jordan were members by 1955; in 1960 an additional 17 new nations became members, of which 16 were African. In all 33 new nations joined the United Nations in its first fifteen years. David A. Kay notes that this new bloc of members wrought "changes so substantial that they altered the nature of the political process of the Organization." [27] Their priorities were decolonization and economic aid for development.

These new nations did not trust the goodwill of the administering powers as reflected in the political process of the United Nations in the 1950s. The administering powers had always advocated working through committees, on which they sought a preponderance. The new nations broke this system by using their numbers to work in "committees of the whole" in the 1960s. They needed to strengthen the supervision system over the non-self-governing territories because by 1960 they realized that the machinery of the Trusteeship System set up by Chapter XI was much more effective in protecting the right to self-determination than the Declaration Regarding Non-Self-Governing Territories.

The Changing Balance of Power in the Sixties

The administering powers still considered it their constitutional right to ascertain which territories were considered non-self-governing, rather than this determination resting with the General Assembly of the United Nations. However, the balance would be altered within the decade. On September 23, 1960 Prime Minister Kruschchev proposed a Resolution on the Granting of Independence to Colonial Countries and Peoples which, when it was adopted as Resolution 1514 (XV) in December 14, 1960, represented, according to el-Ayouty an important advance in the evolution of the Assembly's competence in the determination of NSGTs. [Non Self Governing Territories] [28]

The Declaration's language reflected some of the frustration of the non-Western states that had built up in the fifteen years since the drafting of Chapter XI of the Charter. In 1960 the General Assembly

Recognizing the passionate yearning for freedom in all dependent peoples and the decisive role of such peoples in the attainment of their independence,

Aware of the increasing conflicts resulting from the denial of or impediments in the way of the freedom of such peoples, which constitute a serious threat to world peace. . . .

Believing that the process of liberation is irresistible and irreversible and that, in order to avoid serious crisis, an end must be put to colonialism and all practices of segregation and discrimination associated therewith

declared *inter alia* that

Inadequacy of political, economic, social or educational preparedness should never serve as a pretext for delaying independence

and insisted that

Immediate steps shall be taken, in Trust and Non-Self-Governing Territories or all other territories which have not yet attained independence, to transfer all powers to the peoples of those territories, without any conditions or reservations, in accordance with their freely expressed will and desire, without any distinction as to race, creed, or color, in order to enable them to enjoy complete independence and freedom.

There was only one reservation in the Declaration, which asserted in its sixth paragraph that

Any attempt at the partial or total disruption of national unity and the territorial integrity of a country is incompatible with the purposes and principles of the Charter of the United Nations.

The last paragraph reaffirmed the principle of

non-interference in the internal affairs of all States, and respect for the sovereign rights of all peoples and their territorial integrity.

The conjunction of "national unity *and* the territorial integrity of a country" was to prove as problematic in the next two decades as the conjunction of respect for "the sovereign rights of all peoples *and* their territorial integrity." But the next day, December 15, 1960, the General Assembly passed Resolution 1541 (XV) which codified the Principles that should guide Members in determining whether or not an obligation exists to transmit the information called for under article 73 (e) of the Charter. This elevated the factors annexed to General Assembly Resolution 742 (VIII) of November 27, 1953 into principles of obligation to transmit information under Article 73 (e) of the Charter which

constitutes an international obligation and should be carried out with due regard to the fulfillment of international law.

This Resolution 1541 (XV) worked harder to specify the situations it covered than did the previous day's Resolution 1514 (XV). Principle I argues that

The authors of the Charter of the United Nations had in mind that Chapter XI should be applicable to territories which were then known to be of the colonial type. An obligation exists to transmit information under Article 73 (e) of the Charter in respect of such territories whose peoples have not yet attained a full measure of self-government.

Resolution 1541 (XV) held as Principle IV that

Prima facie there is an obligation to transmit information in respect of a territory which is geographically separate and is distinct ethnically and/or culturally from the country administering it.

Additional elements of

inter alia an administrative, political, juridical, economic or historical nature

should also be assessed to see if

they affect the relationship between the metropolitan State and the territory concerned in a manner which arbitrarily places the latter in a position or status of subordination.

The decade of the sixties would see the newly-emerged states working hard to extend these principles to all such territories; the seventies and eighties would see them trying desperately to confine these principles only to the territories dependent on the western colonial powers.

Resolution 1541 (XV) was much less prolix than Resolution 742 (VIII) had been in stating the conditions when a non-self-governing territory can be said to have reached a full measure of self government. There were three conditions:

(a) Emergence as a sovereign independent State
(b) Free association with an independent State; or
(c) Integration with an independent State.

Sovereign independence was thought to be self-explanatory. Principle VII stated

(a) Free association should be the result of a free and voluntary choice by the peoples of the territory concerned expressed through informed and democratic processes. It should be one which respects the individuality and the cultural characteristics of the territory and its peoples, and retains for the peoples of the territory which is associated with an independent State the freedom to modify the status of the territory through the expression of their will by democratic means and through constitutional processes.

(b) The associated territory should have the right to determine its internal constitution without outside interference, in accordance with due constitutional processes and the freely expressed wishes of the people. This does not preclude consultations as appropriate or necessary under the terms of the free association agreed upon.

Principle VIII insisted that

> Integration with an independent State should be on the basis of complete equality between the peoples of the erstwhile Non-Self-Governing Territory and those of the independent country with which it is integrated. The peoples of both territories should have equal status and rights of citizenship and equal guarantees of fundamental rights and freedoms without any distinction or discrimination; both should have equal rights and opportunities for representation and effective participation at all levels in the executive, legislative and judicial organs of government.

According to Principle IX,

> Integration should have come about in the following circumstances:
>
> (a) The integrating territory should have attained an advanced stage of self-government with free political institutions, so that its peoples would have the capacity to make a responsible choice through informed and democratic processes;
>
> (b) The integration should be the result of the freely expressed wishes of the territory's peoples acting with full knowledge of the change in their status, their wishes having been expressed through informed and democratic processes, impartially conducted and based on universal adult suffrage. The United Nations could, when it deems it necessary, supervise these processes.

Principles X, XI and XII addressed the reservation in Article 73 (e) making transmission of information subject to "such limitations as security and constitutional considerations may require." Principle X insisted that while this may limit the information provided by an administering power it "cannot relieve a Member State of the obligations of Chapter XI." It related only to the "quantum" of information to be transmitted. Principle XI made clear that

> The only constitutional considerations to which Article 73 (e) of the Charter refers are those arising from constitutional

relations of the territory with the Administering Member. They refer to a situation in which the constitution of the territory gives it self-government in economic, social and educational matters through freely elected institutions.

This Principle clearly undercut the basis of the British refusal to transmit information on Southern Rhodesia because, the United Kingdom delegation maintained, it had attained constitutional self-government and therefore did not need or wish to transmit information via the British government.

The final Principle of Resolution 1541 (XV) maintained that

Only in very exceptional circumstances can information on economic, social and educational conditions have any security aspect. In other circumstances, therefore, there should be no necessity to limit the transmission of information on security grounds.

Resolution 1541 (XV) was passed 89: 0 with nine abstentions—Australia, Belgium, the Dominican Republic, France, Portugal, Spain, the Union of South Africa, the United Kingdom and the United States.

In 1961 the General Assembly established a Special Committee of 17 members to examine the application of the Declaration, enlarged the next year to 24 members hence its name as the "Special Committee of 24 on Decolonization." The General Assembly empowered the Special Committee to establish its own procedures, and to meet away from United Nations headquarters whenever required. The Trusteeship Council, the Committee on Information from Non-Self-Governing Territories and the specialized agencies were requested to cooperate with the Committee of 24. [29]

Over British and American opposition, the Committee of 24 quickly flexed its procedural powers to review the status of individual territories rather than contenting itself with regional reports. It showed a willingness to hear from petitioners from the territories themselves, and it looked for increased political reporting by the administering powers.

Writing in 1970, King-Yuh Chang commented:

The creation and the functioning of the Special Committee indicates that the balance of forces within the United Nations has changed. In order to accommodate the administering powers, the composition of the Trusteeship Council and the Committee on Information was based upon equality of membership between the administering and the non-administering states. In the composition of the Special Committee, the General Assembly recognized the numerical superiority of the anti-colonial states within the Organization. These anticolonial countries intended to use the new organ to achieve their political objective: to enable the dependent-peoples to become self-governing or independent in the shortest period of time. [30]

By 1971 all the administering powers had withdrawn from the Special Committee of 24.

The first action under the Declaration of the Granting of Independence to Colonial Countries and Peoples was Resolution 1542 (XV) which declared that the Territories under Portuguese administration were non-self-governing within the meaning of Chapter XI of the Charter and that Portugal was obliged to transmit information on them. The Portuguese position was that

> When Portugal was admitted as a Member of the United Nations, it was not a territory that was admitted but a sovereign State as constituted at the time. The Constitution of the Portuguese State was known to the United Nations and there could be no doubt as to the territorial extension and political structure of that State. As a sovereign State, Portugal comprises the territory also called Portugal, the archipelagos of Azores, Madeira and Cabo Verde, the S. Tome and Prince islands, Portuguese Guinea, Angola, Mozambique, the Portuguese State of India (Goa and its dependencies), Macau and Timor. The sovereign State known as Portugal should not be confused with the European territory called by the same name. . . . The territorial extension and basic structure of Portugal as a sovereign State is over four centuries older than United Nations. [31]

This same argument had prevailed when the French in their letter of April 29, 1949 refused to transmit information on their overseas territories. But the General Assembly of the 1960s was a far different political calculation and was prepared to press the issue until the dependent peoples could claim their sovereignty in the 1970s.

The Trusteeship Council employed the plebiscite very actively in the 1960s to ascertain the wishes of the peoples in the Trust Territories of the British Cameroons, Western Samoa and Ruanda-Urundi. Britain informed the Assembly in 1961 that full internal self-government had been attained in Tanganyika, which subsequently joined with Zanzibar to become Tanzania and take its place as a Member.

Southern Rhodesia proved a more difficult case. The British position was that it had granted internal self-government to Southern Rhodesia in 1923, retaining only specific reserved powers involving African interests and constitutional amendments. These reserved powers were abolished by the white Southern Rhodesia electorate in 1961, and were replaced by provisions that clearly disenfranchised the black majority. The General Assembly in 1962 affirmed that Southern Rhodesia was a non-self-governing territory within the meaning of Chapter XI and called on the United Kingdom to suspend the 1961 constitution and call a constitutional conference that would fully represent the majority of the people in order to prepare for independence. [32] The United Kingdom maintained that since Southern Rhodesia was a self-governing colony since 1923, it could not intervene in the internal affairs of the territory. Although the situation remained in stalemate for nearly two decades, El-Ayouty aptly points out that

> Southern Rhodesia. . . . illustrates how the Assembly, under pressure from the Afro-Asian bloc, applied its test of factors and principles to a Territory fifteen years after the United Nations had accepted the original United Kingdom listing of 1947. [33]

When the British asked why the General Assembly had not queried the omission of Southern Rhodesia back in 1947, the Iraqi delegate answered

> Because at that time, the General Assembly had not yet decided upon the factors which should be taken into account in determining whether a Territory had attained a full measure of self-government. [34]

The possibility of retrospective inscription or re-inscription onto the list of non-self-governing territories to come under the scrutiny of the Fourth Committee did not please any of the administering powers, least of all France. Spain bowed to the inevitable and agreed to transmit information on its dependencies. In 1962 the International

Court of Justice found that, on the basis of Article 7 of the Mandate for South West Africa, the Court did have jurisdiction in the cases brought by Ethiopia and Liberia against South Africa concerning its performance as a Mandatory Power.

Pressure on Portugal continued with the 1963 decision by the Security Council that the situation in the territories under Portuguese administration constituted a serious disturbance of the peace and security in Africa. While Northern Rhodesia became independent as Zambia and Nyasaland as Malawi after a brief attempt at federation, the Southern Rhodesian government issued a unilateral declaration of independence on November 11, 1965. The United Kingdom rejected the unilateral declaration and declared itself to be the only legal government of Southern Rhodesia, a reversal of its dependence on the 1923 partial transfer of powers.

In mid-1965 the Legislative Assembly of the Cook Islands resolved that

> the Cook Islands shall be self-governing in free association
> with New Zealand

reserving foreign affairs and defense responsibilities to New Zealand but retaining the right to modify this relationship unilaterally. The necessary constitutional amendments were approved in an election held under United Nations supervision which, as Roger S. Clark points out,

> marked the first time that an administering power had
> agreed to United Nations participation in elections other
> than those in trust territories. [35]

The free association of the Cook Islands and later Niue with New Zealand became

> the only 'approved' examples in United Nations usage since
> 1960 of decolonization by means of free association. [36]

The territories can enter into international agreements in their own right without necessary approval of New Zealand, and have the potential right to apply for United Nations membership if they seek full sovereignty. In its Resolution 2064 accepting the arrangement, the General Assembly took care to reaffirm the responsibility of the United Nations, under General Assembly Resolution 1514 (XV), to assist the people of the Cook Islands in the eventual achievement of full independence, if they so wish, at a future date.

The British attempt to fulfill the decolonization expectations of Antigua, Dominica, Grenada, St. Kitts-Nevis-Anguilla, St. Lucia and St. Vincent with a variation on associated statehood in 1967 was less successful. The British government sought wider powers of definition of what constituted matters relating to defense, external affairs, nationality or citizenship, or succession to the throne, in a manner reminiscent of the Netherlands proposed arrangements with Surinam and the Antilles the previous decade. The British were not sufficiently responsive to the new mood in the United Nations, and sought to bring these arrangements to the General Assembly as a *fait accompli* without adequate involvement of the United Nations in the process of consulting the West Indies electorate. [37] The legislature that approved the arrangements in the West Indies had been elected under the colonial system; the United Kingdom refused to allow a United Nations observer team to ascertain the wishes of the people.

Perhaps most important was the failure of the British to clearly offer the peoples of the West Indies options other than associated statehood. King-Yuh Chang explains the differences between the Committee of 24's responses to the Cook/Niue proposals and those of the British for the West Indies territories:

> First, the peoples of the Cook Islands had been offered four alternatives: complete independence, integration with New Zealand, internal self-government, and federation with the Polynesian groups. The choices were not available to the people of the Caribbean Territories. Only association with the Administering Power was offered to their representatives. Secondly, the people of the Cook Islands participated in a general election with their future political status as the central issue and their elected representatives approved the new political status. In the Caribbean Islands, only the Legislatures, elected when the Territories were mere colonies, had a say in the new arrangements. The peoples did not specifically exercise their right of self-determination. [38]

Margaret Broderick suggests that another area of concern was the method devised for the Associated States to achieve complete independence. Delegates opposed the required two-thirds majority in the legislature plus a two-thirds majority of the electors in a referendum before the termination of association could come into effect. They felt that this left the way open for a conservative minority to obstruct the true aspirations of the majority of the people, and they favoured a simple majority. [39]

More happily, the small but resource-rich island of Nauru attained independence in 1968, though it opted not to undertake the financial burden of membership of the United Nations. By the end of the decade all the A [40] and B [41] Mandates—Iraq, TransJordan, Palestine, Syria and Lebanon, British and French Cameroons, British and French Togoland and Ruanda-Urandi—had become independent on their own or by joining other states, although not all their peoples, e.g., the Palestinians, regarded themselves as having been decolonized.

Of the C Mandates (those territories taken from the defeated Axis powers), Nauru and Western Samoa had attained independence, although the latter had signed a grant of powers back to New Zealand to act as its agent in some matters of external affairs and neither could afford to join the United Nations. Papua New Guinea would become independent in 1975. The former Japanese territories in the South Pacific islands were administered as a strategic trust by the United States and South Africa had refused to relinquish its mandate over Southwest Africa.

The Mandate over South West Africa was terminated on October 27, 1966 by the General Assembly because South Africa had failed to fulfill its obligations and in fact disavowed the Mandate. This decision was taken despite the International Court of Justice's reversal of its 1962 Judgement that individual League Members could bring legal action against a Mandatory Power under Article 7 of the Mandate. In 1966 the International Court of Justice denied the petition of Ethiopia and Liberia to institute action in regard to the administration of a Mandate. [42] The United Nations took the territory under its jurisdiction by establishing a 14-member Ad Hoc Committee for South West Africa to recommend practical means by which the Territory should be administered so as to enable its people to exercise their right to self-determination. The next year this committee became the Council for

Namibia. In 1969 the Council recognized the legitimacy of the struggle of the Namibian people against the illegal presence of the South African authorities. In 1970 the Security Council sought an Advisory Opinion of the International Court of Justice on the legal consequences of South Africa's continued presence in South Africa.

The administering powers naturally looked askance at the rapid rate of decolonization promoted by the supporters of the 1960 Declaration on Granting Independence to Colonial Peoples. In the mid-sixties, the United States in particular began to propose the notion of some form of associate membership of the United Nations for very small territories that might be decolonized. They were supported in this proposal by Britain in particular and by the Secretary-General of the United Nations, U Thant, who was concerned about the logistical problems of managing a membership that might approach 200.

The Secretary-General urged "a thorough and comprehensive study of the criteria for membership in the United Nations, with a view to laying down the necessary limitations on full membership which would benefit both the 'micro-States' and the United Nations." A Committee of Experts was convened by the Security Council to consider the issue, but it was no more successful in resolving the deep political problems than was a Panel on Participation of Ministates in International Affairs convened by the American Society of International Law in 1968.

In that discussion, the American experts such as Roger Fisher of Harvard Law School saw the Committee of 24 as "a sort of international lobby for absolute independence regardless of the consequences." [43]

In addition to the difficulties of defining which states should be excluded from membership in the United Nations, because they were "mini," "micro" or "diminutive," there was the problem of applying this determination retrospectively to the fourteen members of the United Nations, 11 percent of the total in 1967, that had populations under one million [44] While Jacques G. Rapoport of UNITAR held that

> the two major concerns of the United Nations are that the choice would be *free*; and that the choice should be informed[45]

Moshen S. Esfandiary, Delegate of Iran to the Committee of 24, insisted that

> On the basis of the practice of the United Nations . . .
> decolonization has come to mean effective transfer of
> powers. [46]

The United States and the Secretary-General continued to press the Security Council to come to grips with the issue before the anticipated next wave of applications for membership from small states. [47] In a desultory fashion, the "Ministate Committee" did report two substantive proposals in 1970. [48] The United States proposed a category of associate membership that would give such states access to the General Assembly, Security Council, Economic and Social Council and Specialized Agencies of the United Nations but no voting rights. Such associate members would be exempted from the financial assessments of other Members. The British proposal reflected their long-standing view of the nature of the desirable relationship between newly decolonized territories and the dominant powers—they should voluntarily renounce certain rights and obligations after admission as full members of the Organization. [49]

But there was no will in the United Nations to confront these proposals at the end of the sixties. Faced with South African intransigence in Namibia and competing claims to sovereignty in the Western Sahara, together with the loss of British control over Southern Rhodesia to its white minority, the General Assembly in Resolution 2625 issued a Declaration on Friendly Relations Between Countries in 1970. Lee C. Buchheit saw this as attempting

> a fairly explicit elaboration of seven primary norms of
> international conduct expressly stated or implicit in the
> Charter, including the principle prohibiting the use of force,
> the principle of non-intervention, the principle of equal rights
> and self-determination of peoples. [50]

This Declaration would set the tone for the procedural debates over the decolonization processes of the next decade.

The intransigence of South Africa provoked the Security Council to seek an Advisory Opinion of the International Court of Justice on the question

What are the legal consequences for States of the continued presence of South Africa in Namibia, notwithstanding Security Council resolution 276 (1970)?

The majority of the Court found that

> The Mandates System established by Article 22 of the Covenant of the League of Nations was based upon two principles of paramount importance: the principle of non-annexation and the principle that the well-being and development of the peoples concerned formed a sacred trust of civilization. Taking developments of the past half-century into account, there can be little doubt that the ultimate objective of the sacred trust was self-determination and independence. [51]

The Mandatory was to observe a number of obligations; the Council of the League was to see that they were fulfilled. The rights of the Mandatory as such had their foundation in those obligations. Those obligations survived the dissolution of the League of Nations, which was merely the supervisory organ. Mandates survived the demise of the League. Moreover the Court found

> the entry into force of the United Nations Charter established a relationship between all Members of the United Nations on the one side, and each Mandatory Power on the other, and that one of the fundamental principles governing that relationship is that the party which disowns or does not fulfill its obligations cannot be recognized as retaining the rights which it claims to derived from the relationship. [52]

Therefore States Members of the United Nations are under obligation to recognize the illegality and invalidity of South Africa's presence in Namibia and to refrain from lending it any assistance or support in reference to that occupation,

> The Mandate having been terminated by a decision of the international organization in which the supervisory authority was vested. [53]

The implications of the termination of this Mandate were not lost on the United States. A month later the United States notified the Chairman of the Special Committee on Decolonization of

> its view that the Special Committee lacked competence to consider the United States administration of the strategic Trust Territory of the Pacific Islands. Article 83 of the Charter clearly provides that all functions of the United Nations relating to this Territory should be exercised by the Security Council which in turn has delegated responsibility to the Trusteeship Council. [54]

More than a jurisdictional or procedural dispute, we shall see that this was an attempt by the United States to avoid having the principles of international law pertaining to decolonization as developed in the previous twenty-five years of United Nations practice applied to the Trust Territory of the Pacific Islands.

The obligations of Members in situations where fellow Members were defying the United Nations were further spelled out in General Assembly Resolution 3103 of December 13, 1973, setting out The Basic Principles of the Legal Status of the Combatants Struggling Against Colonial and Alien Domination and Racist Regimes. Following the tone of successive resolutions relating to the Territories Under Portuguese Domination of the past few years, these Basic Principles included the responsibility of Member States to lend moral and material aid to national liberation movements.

The Contradictions of the Seventies

In its first twenty five years, the membership of the United Nations had more than doubled. Most of the new members were beneficiaries of the process of decolonization that was implemented over and against the wishes of the administering powers from the old colonial era. The great majority of these new states-members were themselves plural societies. Their territories were usually defined by the colonial boundaries of the previous four decades. They were clearly successor states not necessarily to pre-colonial geopolitical realities but to the more recently determined political boundaries of their colonial predecessors.

This uncomfortable reality had compelled the newly-emerged states' acceptance of the Belgian thesis that minorities within continental borders of a nation-state were not necessarily entitled to self-determination, although they were not willing to accept the extension of that thesis to non-contiguous areas such as Belgium, France and the Netherlands together with Portugal and Spain tried to argue. At the same time, the new states were very sensitive to charges of 'neocolonialism' in their relations with their minorities. As Gerard Chaliand expressed it, they blurred the traditional ambiguity in the principle of self-determination:

> the right of peoples not constituted in States and the right of peoples already constituted into States to self-determination.[55]

In the sixties, the Afro-Asian countries were unanimous in their condemnation of the secession of Katanga because they saw it as an attempt by Belgium to annex the resource-rich part of the Congo. The Organization of African Unity meeting in Kinshasha in 1967 repudiated the Biafran secession and declared it an internal affair. Emperor Haile Selassie of Ethiopia said at the Lagos meeting of the Organization of African Unity on November 22, 1967 that "the national unity and territorial integrity of member states in not negotiable." [56] But Biafra was recognized as legitimate by Tanzania, Gabon, Ivory Coast, Zambia and Haiti as an attempt by the Iboes to assert their right to self-determination. However the only successful secession in the seventies was that of Bangla Desh from Pakistan, further demonstrating the artificiality of the old colonial construct of India.

At the same time, Indonesia insisted on the incorporation of West Irian as part of its territory. Ironically, the Republic of Indonesia itself represented the first successful challenge of the Belgian Thesis that colonial states were constituted of their non-contiguous dependent territories as well as their continental territory. In asserting its claim over the western half of the island of Irian Indonesia claimed long standing historical connections between Java and the ethnically distinct people of west Irian. There was no substantial evidence of tribute ever having been paid by the west Irianese to the medieval kingdoms of Java, so the arguments rested basically on indications of a trading route by Muslim traders—themselves incomers—in the archipelago. The Indonesians could not demonstrate any linguistic or cultural connections. Even the racial stock of the two peoples are clearly different. The basic connection was the Dutch colonial experience.

At no time in the debate over West Irian did the Indonesians ever extend their arguments to the people of the eastern portion of the island, who had been under German, British and Australian colonial jurisdiction for the same period that West Irian had been in Dutch hands. Nor did the Indonesians ever make the same claims for the eastern portion of the nearby island of Timor, which had been split between the Dutch and the Portuguese spheres of influence four hundred years earlier.

After six years of administration, during which President Sukarno took Indonesia temporarily out of the United Nations, the Indonesian administrators convened a series of local councils which met on the issue of the future political status of the territory. As is carefully documented in the *Report of the Secretary-General Regarding the Act of Self-Determination in West Irian* presented to the twenty-fourth session of the General Assembly at the end of 1969, there was a limited education campaign prior to the council meetings and many critics of the option of incorporation into Indonesia were detained as political prisoners. [57] The Indonesian military suppressed incidents of agitation against the only prospect presented to the councils, annexation by Indonesia. Mr. Ortiz Sanz, the United Nations representative, received nearly two hundred petitions against the process, as did individual journalists covering the events. The United Nations observer was able to see only 20 percent of the elections of 1,025 representatives to the consultative councils. Voting in the end was by consensus, an Indonesian tradition, rather than by one person one vote. No observer considered that this process constituted a plebiscite. [58]

Yet on November 19, 1969 the General Assembly voted 84:0 to accept incorporation of Irian by Indonesia. Earlier, Ghana had argued that the events of 1969 did not constitute an act of free choice and 30 (mainly African) countries abstained from the vote. The Ghanaian attempt to have a second act of free choice was defeated 60:13 with 39 abstentions.[59]

What became known popularly as "the act of no choice" in West Irian is, as Roger S. Clark, notes, "a stain on the U.N.'s record." [60] Keith Suter argues that Resolution 2504 (XXIV) took note of rather than endorsing the outcome of the events of 1969. [61] Certainly the indigenous people did not happily accept annexation by Indonesia. In September 1975, Papua New Guinea attained its independence and the last trusteeship (other than the Strategic Trust of the Pacific Islands) was terminated. At the same time, Indonesian troops were massing on the western border of East Timor preparatory to the invasion of December 6, 1975. [62] Repeated United Nations resolutions over the next decade condemned the naked use of force by Indonesia in the *de facto* annexation of the Portuguese territory of East Timor. [63]

Clearly the Indonesians could not claim any colonial ties with East Timor as they had with West Irian, and therefore they could not argue that the Republic of Indonesia as the successor state to the Netherlands East Indies was also entitled to the Portuguese-held territory of East Timor. The Indonesian government therefore tried to argue that pre-colonial ties within the archipelago entitled them to possession of East Timor. Even if the use of armed force had not been at issue, the United Nations would have been reluctant to accept this argument since in October 1975 the International Court of Justice had handed down its decision on the claims of Morocco and Mauritania to the Western Sahara. The Court decided that the evidence presented to it did not "establish any tie of territorial sovereignty between the territory of Western Sahara and the Kingdom of Morocco or the Mauritanian entity" such as might affect the application of resolution 1514 (XV) or of the principle of self-determination through free and general expression of the will of the peoples of the Territory. [64] The Court also found that the territory of the Western Sahara at the time of its colonization by Spain was not a *terra nullius*, belonging to no-one.

By implication, then, the Western Sahara Opinion of the International Court of Justice not only denied that there were ties of territorial sovereignty between the pre-colonial states of Morocco and Mauritania but treats the "tribes living in the territory of the Western Sahara" as peoples sufficiently politically organized to have been capable of such relations—and therefore their heirs are entitled to self-determination, as claimed by POLISARIO. [65] Unfortunately, the aftermath of the International Court's opinion was the Madrid

Agreement whereby Spain ceded the territory illegally to Morocco and Mauritania.

Thomas M. Franck (Editor in Chief of the *American Journal of International Law*) emphasizes another holding by the International Court of Justice in the Western Sahara Case:

> Asked by Spain and Morocco to determine whether, before its colonization by Spain, the Western Sahara had belonged to the Moroccan empire (or, even, to the Mauritanian 'entity'), the Court found those questions of historic title largely irrelevant. Instead, the judges asserted the supremacy of the norm developed by U.N. resolutions and by the practice of decolonization: the Sahrawi population was entitled to self-determination within the perimeters of the existing colonial entity. During the past fifty years, the large majority of judges said, self-determination had become the rule, trumping such earlier concepts as "historic title." In declaring self-determination the absolute right of colonial peoples as the *sine qua non* of decolonization the Court reaffirmed the same principle enunciated three years earlier in its advisory opinion of Namibia. In the Western Sahara Case the ICJ cited with approval U.N. General Assembly revolution 1514 of 1960 which decreed that a colony could become independent as part of a neighboring state only as a 'result of the freely expressed wishes of the territory's peoples acting with full knowledge of the change in their status, their wishes having been expressed through informed and democratic processes, impartially conducted and based on universal adult suffrage.' The Court explicitly rejected the notion that there were between the Western Sahara and Mauritania or Morocco such ties of historic title 'as might affect the application of Resolution 1514 in the decolonization of Western Sahara and, in particular, of the principle of self-determination through the free and genuine expression of the will of the peoples of the Territory.' In other words, it is the will of the people of the colony at the moment of its liberation from colonialism which must determine their future status. [66]

At the same time, in 1976, the General Assembly expressed support for the armed struggle of the Namibian people and recognized the South West People's Organization (SWAPO) as the sole and authentic representative of the people of Namibia. [67] Given the continued intransigence of the South African government, the United Nations constituted a Council for Namibia and instructed it to develop a

Nationhood Programme that would guide it to independence. In 1977 the United Nations strengthened sanctions against the illegal regime in Southern Rhodesia and committed itself to support the struggle for Zimbabwe. In 1979 Britain was able to inform the United Nations of the progress achieved at the Lancaster House conference. The first general election under universal suffrage took place in February 1980 and Zimbabwe attained independence under majority rule in April 1980.

It was of course in relation to South Africa itself that the United Nations made its strongest statement of what could not be accepted as legitimate acts of self-determination and decolonization. From 1970 onwards, all major organs of the United Nations repeatedly repudiated the so-called "bantustans" or "homelands" as

> a violation of the principles of self-determination and prejudicial to the integrity of the State and unity of its people.[68]

The bantustans or homelands, 13.7 percent of South Africa's territory in which 8.5 million Africans were compelled to live, emerged from the Native Lands Act, No. 27 of 1913, the South African Bantu Trust of 1936, the Bantu Authorities Act, No. 68 of 1951, the Transkei Constitution Act, No. 48 of 1963 (which declared the Transkei a "self governing territory within the Republic of South Africa"), and the Status of Transkei Act, No. 100 of 1976. The South African government claimed to foster the evolution of self- government sufficient to prepare the people of the bantustans for independence. But most observers agreed with Roger J. Southall that in fact

> various factors—notably an increasing rural population, little industrial investment, and a greater outflow of migrant labour—indicate a growing dependence on the white-dominated economy [69]

rather than increased self-sufficiency.

The South African government sponsored general elections in the Transkei in 1963, 1969, 1973 and 1976. According to Southall,

> it was not until 1973 that the Transkei National Independence Party was able to secure a majority—55.2%—of the popular vote, and even this was gained only in conditions of declining participation and voter apathy. [70]

The final Transkei voter participation was 43.4 percent, meaning that barely 20 percent of the people accepted bantustan status. The attempt by South Africa to have the Transkei and other bantustans accepted as sovereign entities was repudiated by 134 members of the United Nations on October 26, 1976. The United States was alone in not joining in the otherwise universal condemnation of what the rest of the world perceived as the ultimate step in the policy of *apartheid*—the stripping of Africans of their citizenship in the state of South Africa and therefore their claim on its resources, while coralling them in fragmented pieces of territory that could never hope for economic viability and forcing them to work as a migrant labor force controlled by the passlaws.

The bantustans did not meet any of the standards for sovereignty. Apart from the sham governments that were established, the South African government retained substantial control over the territories by a series of supplementary agreements covering a wide range of governmental functions. Henry J. Richardson, III expressed an almost-universal point of view when he argued that

> This system of supplementary agreements is a focus of major concern and differing expectations for both the South African government and the Transkei officials and people, as reflected in the South African parliamentary debates on the act. In a position striking international chords, opposition members argued that these agreements established controlling arrangements far beyond the mere implementation of a consensus-based public order within the Transkei and that they were of real and pervasive constitutive significance such as to render the Transkei impermissibly controlled by and dependent on South Africa. These agreements apparently govern major values of power, wealth, skills transfer, and other sources of authority and influence in such a way as to leave major value allocations still remaining with South African government officials, notwithstanding the Transkei's change of status. Moreover, South African government speakers joined in confirming the value significance of these agreements, not only because they maintained a 'status quo' beyond the Transkei's change of status but also because of the need for continuing interdependence between South Africa and the Transkei in the areas of labor, agriculture and food, as well as the need

for common policies to enable South Africa to supply the Transkei with 'knowledge' and the 'methods' of production. [71]

The United States spent the last half of the 1970s moving the Strategic Trust Territory of the Pacific Islands towards self-government. The Trusteeship Council spent seven weeks in the islands observing preparations for a referendum on a draft constitution for the proposed Federated States of Micronesia and the Marshall Islands in 1978. The Marshalls and Palau rejected the proposed constitutions and set about drafting their own. The Council returned in 1980 because the United States had set a target date of 1981 for the termination of the Trusteeship Agreement. In the event, it was to take more votes than had occurred in the Transkei to get the peoples of Micronesia to accept virtually the same status as the bantustans.

The Agenda for the Eighties

In thirty-five years, the membership of the United Nations tripled. Only one major state, Switzerland, declined to become a member although it remained an active observer and contributed in material ways to the humanitarian work of the organization. One country, Indonesia, withdrew for eighteen months in protest against the refusal of the international community to accept its claims on Malaysia. The mainland China government prevailed over Taiwan in its claims to China's seat. One country, South Africa, stood in contempt of the organization.

More than 70 nations whose people were formerly under colonial rule had joined the United Nations as sovereign independent states. Thirty of them had gained their independence prior to the December 1960 Declaration on the Granting of Independence to Colonial Countries and Peoples. Forty nations gained their independence in the next twenty years. Several of the nations that gained independence in the lifetime of the United Nations had not been among the 74 territories enumerated by the eight colonial powers—Australia, Belgium, Denmark, France, the Netherlands, New Zealand, the United Kingdom and the United States—in 1946.

Twenty years after the adoption of Resolution 1514 (XV), the General Assembly adopted resolution 35/118, the Plan of Action for the Full Implementation of the Declaration on the Granting of Independence to Colonial Peoples in order to hasten the process of decolonization of the twenty island peoples still on the List of Territories with which the Special Committee is Concerned and the peoples of southern Africa.

The General Assembly no longer equivocated about the obligation of member states to support the liberation struggles of people under colonial oppression; Article 2 required them to render "all necessary moral and material assistance." Article 6 required them to "continue to wage a vigorous and sustained campaign against activities and practices of foreign economic, financial and other interests operating in colonial Territories which are detrimental to the interests of the population." Other articles enumerated ways in which member states could and should support the struggles for self-determination of all peoples, particularly those in South Africa.

The Plan of Action also significantly extended the definition of who was entitled to the right of self-determination. Article 17 emphatically reasserted the principle that

> Questions of territorial size, geographical isolation and limited resources should in no way delay the implementation of the Declaration.

Moreover, political statuses short of complete independence could only be transitional according to Article 17 since

> Where General Assembly resolution 1514 (XV) has not been fully implemented with regard to a given Territory, the Assembly shall continue to bear responsibility for that Territory until all powers are transferred to the people of the Territory without any conditions or reservations and the people concerned have had an opportunity to exercise freely their right to self-determination and independence in accordance with the Declaration.

Article 8 sought to protect the integrity of peoples of dependent territories by requiring member states to adopt the necessary measures to discourage or prevent the systematic influx of outside immigrants and settlers into Territories under colonial domination, which disrupts the demographic composition of those Territories and may constitute a major obstacle to the genuine exercise of the right to self-determination and independence by the people of those Territories.

This would appear to leave the way open for reconsideration of several cases, among them West Irian where Indonesian transmigration policies threatened to render the indigenous Melanesian people a minority in their own land by 1990 [72] and New Caledonia, where the Kanak people were rendered a minority in their territory by French immigration during the nickel boom of the early seventies. Article 17 clearly leaves open the possibility for any non-independent peoples to reopen the issue of their future political status whenever they have the political will to do so.

The 1980 Plan of Action, then, is a major revision of many of the assumptions of the administering powers as expressed in their statements of the first ten or fifteen years of the United Nations. The issue is how far the "third world" countries are prepared to extend the right of self-determination. Despite the dangerous implications for themselves as plural societies and sometimes neo-colonial states, there is evidence that the Afro-Asian nations are prepared to tolerate a wider definition of "people" than when they joined ranks to repudiate the Belgian thesis that extended that notion to "all non-self-governing peoples" no matter where located.

The battle lines are still drawn much as they were in 1945 inasmuch as the six countries that voted against resolution 35/118 in 1980 were Belgium, France, the German Federal Republic, Luxembourg, the United Kingdom and the United States. The twenty abstaining countries were also predictable: Australia, Austria, Canada, Denmark, Finland, Greece, Guatemala, Iceland, Ireland, Israel, Italy, Japan, Malawi, Mauritius, the Netherlands, New Zealand, Norway, Portugal, Spain and Sweden. But a great deal of decolonization had taken place in the interim, and in the process what Djura Ninci called the "antinomy between domestic jurisdiction and self-determination, between Articles 2/7 and 1/2 of the Charter . . . tended to be resolved along the lines of a greater assertion of the right to self-determination." Certainly the "colonial variant of domestic jurisdiction was compelled to withdraw before the advance of self-determination." [73]

Ian Brownlie points to the paradox of the process of the first forty years of postwar decolonization that may have to be resolved before the end of this century:

> In the modern period of significant European political expansion a major paradox is present. No doubt the British and others were prepared to make treaties with tribal societies like the Basuto and Somalis. The fact remains that before European penetration such societies were to a degree cut off from participation in international diplomacy. Having been colonized, they became part of the world of general diplomacy—but lost their separate personality. However, and herein lies the paradox, European ideas of nationhood and self determination were adopted and resulted eventually in a programme of statehood, and not a desire for a simple restoration of the traditional *status quo ante*. Colonialism, and other external influences provided a very radical element in African and Middle Eastern affairs. The outcome has been that various societies have been brought, however precariously and artificially, into the orthodox system of diplomacy and statehood. [74]

The United Nations organs through which this new international law was developed were the Fourth Committee and its Special Committee of 24 on Decolonization and the Trusteeship Council. We have seen how the administering powers that came together in San Francisco in 1945 resisted the pressures to decolonize their territories under Article 73 of the Charter. But the process proved inexorable especially after the decolonized member states outnumbered the founding states of the United Nations by the mid-sixties. The broad constructionist/implementationist group prevailed in drafting resolutions 1514 (XV) and 1541 (XV). Some of the administering powers sought to restrict the interpretation of those resolutions (Rhodesia/Namibia/Western Sahara) in the seventies, and the first of what will probably be several cases of neocolonialism broke out in West Irian and East Timor as Indonesia sought to manipulate the resolutions to its own territorial advantage.

But the states that wished to implement the decolonization resolutions as broadly as possible held firm on the central issue of the new international law of sovereignty—that those communities that

Chapter One: Decolonization Principles | 39

wished to assert their sovereignty should be encouraged to do so. Even small communities such as Cook and Niue could aspire to sovereignty. The realities of their geopolitical and economic limitations were reflected in the concept of "associated statehood" with their former administering power, New Zealand. But the case of the West Indian Federated States confirmed that the United Nations membership would not tolerate a sham transfer of powers to window dress continuing *de facto* colonization. Specific conditions were set to the two extant cases of associated statehood.

The case of the bantustans again clearly established what the new international law considered to be insufficient transfer of powers to constitute sovereignty, and the international community refused to consent to the proposals of the administering power, whose government it has also declared illegitimate on the grounds that the people of the territory are not fully enfranchised.

The case of Namibia indicates the refusal of the international community to agree to unilateral termination of the League of Nations Mandate transformed into a Trusteeship. The transformation of Rhodesia into Zimbabwe indicated that administering powers could not rely on resolutions that did not really have the consensus of the international community remaining static.

We will now examine whether or not the United States was willing to accept these canons of international law in the devolution of power in the Strategic Trust Territory of the Pacific Islands. Or whether it was going to attempt unilateral termination of a strategic trusteeship on the South African model in Namibia.

Notes

1 W. Ofuatey-Kedjoe, "The Principle of Self-Determination in International Law." Ph.D. diss., Columbia University, 1970, 194.

2 *Yearbook of the United Nations 1947-48*, 3.

3 Umozurike Oji Umozurike, *Self-Determination in International Law* (Archon Books, 1972), 44.

4 *Self-Determination in International Law*, 44

5 "The Principle of Self-Determination in International Law," 271.

6 *Self-Determination in International Law*, 44.

7 Article 77 of United Nations Charter.

8 S. Hasan Ahmed, *The United Nations and the Colonies* (New York, Asia Publishing House, 1974), 35.

9 Yassin El-Ayouty, *The United Nations and Decolonization: The Role of Afro-Asia* (The Hague, Martinus Nijhold, 1971).

10 *United Nations and the Colonies*, 35.

11 British Information Services, *Britain and Trusteeship* (February 1947), 3.

12 *Britain and Trusteeship*, 4.

13 *Britain and Trusteeship*, 6.

14 For the formation of this Ad Hoc Committee, see *United Nations and the Colonies*, 77 ff.

15 See *United Nations and the Colonies*, 273.

[16] Official Records, 4th Committee, 124th meeting (1949), 180 quoted in *United Nations and the Colonies*, 274.

[17] *United Nations and the Colonies*, 275.

[18] *United Nations and the Colonies*, 279. The full debate is reported at GA (VIII), Plenary Meeting, 459th, 312 ff.

[19] Quoted in *Yearbook of the United Nations, 1948-49*, 731.

[20] *Yearbook of the United Nations, 1948-49*, 731.

[21] *Yearbook of the United Nations, 1950*, 810.

[22] *Objective: Justice* XVII: 1 (June 1985): 12.

[23] Roger S. Clark, "Self-Determination and Free Association: Should the United Nations Terminate the Pacific Islands Trust?," *Harvard International Law Journal* 21: 1 (1980): 40.

[24] Clark, "Self-Determination," 42.

[25] Clark, "Self-Determination," 46-49.

[26] *United Nations and the Colonies*, 310.

[27] David A. Kay, *The New Nations within the United Nations, 1960-67* (New York: Columbia University Press, 1970), 2.

[28] *The United Nations and Decolonisation*, 187.

[29] *Objective: Justice*, 19.

[30] King-yuh Chang, "The United Nations and Decolonization 1960-68: The Role of the Committee of Twenty Four." Ph.D. diss., Columbia University, 1971, 59-60.

[31] Ministry of Foreign Affairs, Portugal Replies in the United Nations (1972), Lisbon, 4.

[32] Resolution 1747 (XVI) June 28, 1962.

[33] *United Nations and Decolonisation,* 202.

[34] United Nations and Decolonisation, 203 from ORGA, Sixteenth Session, Fourth Committee, 889.

[35] Clark,"Self-Determination," 54-55.

[36] Clark, "Self-Determination," 54.

[37] Clark, "Self-Determination," 63.

[38] King-yuh Chang, "United Nations and Decolonization," 77.

[39] Margaret Broderick, "Associated Statehood—A New Form of Decolonization," *International and Comparative Law Quarterly* 17 (1968): 393.

[40] The provisional independence of these former Turkish provinces was guaranteed and by 1949 all Class A mandates had achieved full independence.

[41] The establishment of military and naval bases in Class B territories by the mandatories was forbidden by the League of Nations; commercial equality with other nations and native rights were guaranteed. Upon the formation of the United Nations all former mandated territories became trusteeships.

[42] *Objective: Justice,* 21.

[43] *American Society of International Law Proceedings* (1968): 168. Fisher was at the time an adviser to Anguilla.

[44] P.W. Blair, *The Mini State Dilemma.* Carnegie Endowment for International Peace (*Occasional Paper* No. 6) 1967, 2.

[45] *Proceedings* (1968): 157.

[46] *Proceedings* (1968): 175.

[47] M. H. Mendelson, "Diminutive States in the United Nations," *International and Comparative Law Quarterly* 21 (1972): 609.

[48] 25 UN SCOR, Supp. (April-June 1970) 211, UN Doc. S/9836, Annex 1, 1970.

[49] M. M. Gunter, "What Happened to the United States Ministate Problem?," *American Journal of International Law* 71 (1977): 113. See also S/9836 Annexes I and II for U. S. and U. K. views.

[50] Lee C. Buchheit, *Secession—The Legitimacy of Self-Determination* (Yale University Press, 1978), 32.

[51] Reported in Report of the Secretary-General on the Work of the Organization, 16 June, 1970-15 June, 1971, GAOR, 26th Session, Supplement No. 1 (A/8401) at page 226.

[52] See note 54, page 227.

[53] See note 54, page 228.

[54] *Objective Justice*, 26.

[55] Gerard Chaliand, "Les Minorities dans le Monde a la Age de l'Etat-Nation," in Chaliand and others, *Les Minorities a l'age de l'Etat-nation.* (Paris, Fayard, 1985), 13.

[56] Quoted in *Secession*, 169.

[57] Document A/7641, 15 August 1969.

[58] Keith Suter, *East Timor and West Irian* (London, Minority Rights Group, 1979 and 1982); J.M. van der Kroef, *Indonesia After Sukarno* (University of British Columbia Press, 1971).

[59] Thomas M. Franck and Paul Hoffman, "The Right to Self-Determination in Very Small Places," in *New York Journal of International Law and Politics* (1976): 337, footnote 19.

[60] Roger S. Clark, "The 'Decolonization' of East Timor and the United Nations Norms on Self-Determination and Aggression," *Yale Journal of World Public Order* 7: 1 (Fall 1980): 15, footnote 66.

[61] Suter, *East Timor and West Irian*, 11.

[62] See Sue Nichterlein, "The Struggle for East Timor: Prelude to Invasion," *Journal of Contemporary Asia* (December 1977) for the events leading to the invasion.

[63] See Clark, "Self-Determination" for review of United Nations responses to Indonesian attempts to legitimise the annexation.

[64] International Court of Justice, Western Sahara Advisory Opinion, 16 October, 1975.

[65] See Tony Hodges, *The Western Saharans* (London, Minority Rights Group *Report* No. 40) 1984.

[66] Thomas M. Franck, "The Theory and Practice of Decolonization: the Western Sahara Case," paper presented to Conference on Western Sahara, Oxford University, Refugee Studies Program, March 21-22, 1986.

[67] *Objective: Justice*, 32.

[68] Resolution 2671 (F) (XXV) 8 December 1970.

[69] Roger J. Southall, "Beneficiaries of Transkeian 'Independence'," *Journal of Modern African Studies* 15 (1977): 2.

[70] "Beneficiaries of Transkeian," 8.

[71] Henry J. Richardson, III, "Self-Determination, International Law and the South African Bantustan Policy," *Columbia Journal of Transnational Law* 17 (1978): 209-10.

[72] See Sue Rabbitt Roff, "Playing for Time," *Australian Society* (August 1985): 34-36.

[73] Djura Ninci, *The Problem of Sovereignty in the Charter and Practice of the United Nations* (The Hague, Martinus Nijhoff, 1970), 234.

[74] Ian Brownlie, "The Expansion of International Society: The Consequences for the Law of Nations," in Hedley Bull and Alan Watson (eds.) *The Expansion of International Society* (Oxford, 1984), 364.

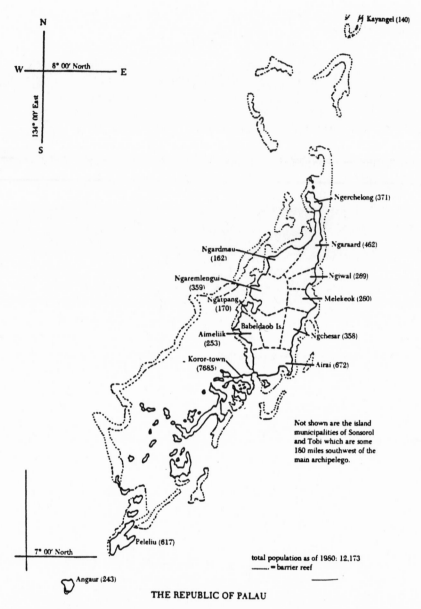

N

W ———— 8° 00' North ———— E

134° 00' East

S

Kayangel (140)

Ngerchelong (371)

Ngaraard (462)

Ngardmau
(162)

Ngiwal (269)

Ngaremlengui
(359)

Melekeok (260)

Ngatpang
(170)

Aimeliik
(253)

Babeldaob Is.

Ngchesar (358)

Koror-town
(7685)

Airai (672)

Not shown are the island
municipalities of Sonsorol
and Tobi which are some
160 miles southwest of the
main archipelego.

7° 00' North

Peleliu (617)

total population as of 1980: 12,173
———— = barrier reef

Angaur (243)

THE REPUBLIC OF PALAU

Reprinted from Donald R. Schuster, "More Constitutions for Palau" in
*Proceedings of the 1982 Politics Conference: Evolving Political Cultures
of the Pacific Islands* (Laie: Brigham Young University, Institute for
Polynesian Studies, 1982)

Chapter Two

From Roosevelt to Carter

The three archipelagos of the Marshalls, the Carolines and the Marianas are a multitude of small atolls with a total land area only slightly larger than Rhode Island spread over an area of ocean equal to that of the mainland of the United States. The westernmost island, Palau, is several hundred miles closer to both the Philippines and Indonesia than is Guam, the southernmost island of the Marianas group which has been administered by the United States since it was seized from Spain in 1898. Palau is the northern boundary of a deep sea trench that stretches down through the Omba-Wetar Straits between Timor and Flores, affording access for submerged vessels between the Pacific and Indian Oceans. Palau also sits astride the major seatrade route of the Lombok Straits. East of Palau lie the Yap, Ponape and Kosrae groups of islands, and northeast of them the Marshalls which include the largest atoll in the world, Kwajalein. The northmost islands in the Marshalls are Bikini, Enewetok, Rongelap and Rongerik.

The Micronesian peoples—an amalgam of Mongoloid, Polynesian and Melanesian immigration from Southeast Asia[1]—have nine major languages, all mutually unintelligible but a broadly similar ethnography based on a matrilineal hierarchical system of extended families congregated in chiefdoms. There is an extensive literature on the Micronesian peoples dating to the first European contacts in the early sixteenth century. Magellan sighted Guam, Saipan and Rota in the Marianas in 1521. In 1565 the Spanish claimed the Marianas, although it was another century before the first Spanish colonizers arrived in the person of Jesuit missionaries. Like successor colonizers, the Spanish forcibly relocated the indigenes moving most of the Chamorro population to Guam. The first American missionaries arrived in the 1850s in the Carolines, and the Protestant and Catholic emissaries began to compete for the allegiance of the Micronesians. The Germans established themselves in the Marshalls in 1885 and bought the rest of Micronesia (except for Guam) from Spain after 1898. However, the Japanese seized the German possessions in 1914.

Between 1921 and 1935 Micronesia was a League of Nations Mandate under Japanese administration. The Japanese invested considerable effort in developing the economic and military infrastructure of the territory, and by 1938 the Japanese settlers outnumbered the indigenes, being 58 percent of the population.[2] In 1931 exports were 214 percent of imports.[3] After Japan withdrew from the League of Nations—perhaps even before 1935—it had engaged in extensive militarization of the islands. In her official history, *United States Naval Administration of the Trust Territory of the Pacific Islands*,[4] Dorothy E. Richard reports that

> the Marshalls, Carolines and Marianas had been fortified in defiance of the terms of the League of Nations Mandate. When the United States Navy crashed the barrier it discovered that between the years 1934 and 1941 that the Japanese had built a chain of airfields and seaplane bases stretching from Saipan to the Palaus and from Truk to Woltje. The militarization of Truk and the Marshalls had begun more than year before the attack on Pearl Harbor. At least 40 vessels were constantly employed in carrying men and materials from Japan to the islands.[5]

Kwajalein was the headquarters of the Japanese Fourth Fleet and was also the port for part of the Sixth (Submarine) Fleet that left in December 1941 for the attack on Pearl Harbor, and the expeditionary force attack on Wake Island.

The battle for the Micronesian islands was horrendous. "Never in the history of human conflict has so much been thrown by so many at so few," wrote the historian of *The Marines at War*, F. Pratt.[6] Whatever had been achieved in economic development in the first twenty years of Japanese occupation had been devastated by first the demands of the Japanese garrisons on the fragile ecology of the islands and then by the fearful bombing and burning of the American invasion. The official United States naval historian writes,

> The condition of the Marshallese when the United States forces landed on enemy occupied islands was evidence of the suffering which they had endured during the latter years of the Japanese administration and an indication of the problems, other than military, which existed in areas of the Mandated Islands yet to be occupied. The people were ill and dazed, hungry, and clad in tatters. Even the sails of their

canoes were threadbare. Many of them were homeless, displaced from their islands to make way for Japanese garrisons and military installations. Others had been forcibly removed to enemy held areas to work as laborers. Their economy was ruined and they had no trade goods nor money. Their diet was barely a subsistence one. There was no market for their copra and their coconut trees were deteriorating from lack of care.[7]

It was difficult even to determine how many people were in the islands. The Japanese, Korean and Okinawan populations were easier to count because they were placed in prisoner of war camps while repatriation was organized. There were a total of 147,314 "displaced Oriental people" in the Japanese Mandated Islands according to the Navy's count in 1945—24,832 in the Marshalls and 122,482 in the Marianas. There were 104,218 Japanese, 31,619 Okinawans and 11,308 Koreans.[8] The Micronesians proved harder to count. Richard reported:

> Determination of population figures proved difficult and at no time during this period of administration (1945-47) was it possible to do more than approximate the number of Micronesians in the islands. . . . The greatest discrepancies appeared in reports from the Caroline Islands where the population was more scattered and education had been least available in the pre-World War II era.[9]

The official figures for August 1945 included 9,046 people in the Marshalls, 34,580 in the Carolines, 4,525 in the Northern Marianas or a total of 48,151 indigenes.[10] The Navy was faced with a massive task in repatriating the Oriental people and resettling the Micronesians, a great many of whom were forcibly removed from their home villages over the past decade. And once it completed that task, the naval administration prepared Micronesia for a future which involved not Japan but the United States of America.

From Naval Administration to Strategic Trusteeship

Naval responsibility for the administration of the Japanese Mandated Islands from the period of the Japanese surrender until the formation of the Strategic Trust of the Territory of the Pacific Islands in July 1947 represented a political victory for the Secretaries of War and the Navy over the Secretary of State. Secretary of War Henry L. Stimson argued in a memorandum dated January 23, 1945 that the Pacific Islands were not really 'colonial areas.'

> Acquisition of them by the United States does not represent an attempt at colonization or exploitation. Instead it is merely the acquisition by the United States of the necessary bases for the defense of the security of the Pacific for the future world. To serve such a purpose they must belong to the United States with absolute power to rule and fortify them. They are not colonies; they are outposts, and their acquisition is appropriate under the general doctrine of self-defense by the power which guarantees the safety of that area of the world.[11]

The State Department however was worried that this would lead to

> reservations of other territories by other nations until the non-aggrandizement plan of the Atlantic Charter would become a mockery.[12]

At Yalta in February 1945 a form of internationalization of such critical security issues was achieved by the agreement to form a Security Council consisting of the five major postwar powers. It was agreed that the notion of trusteeship should be applied to existing mandates of the League of Nations, territories to be detached from enemy states after the war, and any other territory that might voluntarily be placed under trusteeship. It should be remembered that the Soviet Union was as much concerned about the Kurile and other islands to the north of Japan as the United States was about the Micronesian atolls to the south.

Secretary of the Navy James V. Forrestal reported what he perceived as President Roosevelt's thinking after a meeting on March 9, 1945:

> The President made some observations about his conception of the trusteeship idea as applied to territory taken from the enemy, with particular reference to the Pacific Ocean Area. He said that his idea, which he advanced to Stalin and Churchill, was based on the concept of what he called multiple sovereignty—that is, sovereignty would be vested in all of the United Nations, for example, of the Pacific Islands,

but that we would be requested by them to exercise complete trusteeship for the purpose of world security. He further said that the Australians had advanced the thesis that they would take by direct acquisition everything south of the equator, leaving to us those islands north of that line. This he said was unacceptable. I said there were a number of places that we ought to have for our naval security—Kwajalein, the Marianas, Truk, etc. He also included Manus in this category and said that he would even be inclined to have military rights on Noumea while leaving to the French the economic accruals from New Caledonia. The Secretary of War expressed the hope that if the trusteeship idea was adopted the basis of our exercise of powers under it would be very clearly stated so that there could be no misunderstandings in the future.[13]

But two weeks before the San Francisco Conference opened on April 25, 1945, President Roosevelt died. The State Department was still disturbed at the notion of annexation and military government of acquired territory. Meetings were held at Hyde Park after Roosevelt's interment, and State, according to Forrestal,

> agreed to a directive which made it clear that while the general question of a trusteeship system might be raised at San Francisco there was to be no discussion of trusteeing any particular areas, and that any general system should include provisions permitting the maintenance of full American military and strategic rights at appropriate points.[14]

While the nature of a trusteeship was being developed, the United States Navy administered the territory it had fought so hard to conquer. By September 1945 there were 800 officers and 3,750 enlisted men in the service of the United States Naval Administration of the Pacific Islands.[15] This period of military government lasted from July 1, 1944 through July 17, 1947. In those three years the Navy spent more than $7,000,000 on relief aid, of which 78.5 percent went to the Northern Marianas and 8.7 percent to the Marshalls.[16]

The United States Navy, according to its official historian, knew its governance of the territory to be temporary and agreed that

> abandonment of any considerable population to the social and economic distortions of permanent military government is believed to be alien to American ideas.[17]

However, there was considerable difficulty in preparing the way for civilian government. The official policy of reconstruction was "to restore the islands to their normal degree of self-sufficiency." But the first task was the repatriation of the prisoners of war and those Micronesians who had been displaced from their home atolls. Malnutrition was apparent among the 200,000 people in the islands—on the atoll of Lib the Americans found seven blind people among 52 inhabitants, and yaws was widespread.

By 1947 the naval administration could look beyond the immediate problems of rehabilitation and consider the prospects for economic development for the future. In retrospect, it seems a major failing of the United States administration at this time that it did not begin to develop the indigenous economy. The Micronesians were weary and depressed after years of occupation and war in which their subsistence economy had been exploited beyond its capacity to withstand. The Navy brought medical and dental treatment and food, but the naval administrators never came to understand the culture of the people despite a massive ethnographic and anthropological survey of Micronesia in these years. The fault may have been with the training that the officers of the occupation received in the United States. For example, courses at Columbia and Yale did not prepare them for Truk and Ponape as the following reflections of a "Military Governor Upon a Lonely Isle" indicate

> They took me off the ocean
> And they sent me back to school
> To teach me island customs
> And the proper way to rule.
> They taught me economics,
> Sanitation, public health;
> They put in law and safety
> And a course in island wealth.
> They taught me 'Pigin English'
> And a little Japanese;
> And they dwelt upon the customs
> Of the local Marshallese.
> Then they put me in a transport
> And they sent me far away;
> To cash in on my learning

And to make my schooling pay.
On the voyage to the island
I reviewed the things I knew,
And then began to figure out
Exactly what I'd do.
I said I'd take the biggest house
And hang my shingle out.
I'd have them know who was the boss,
Of that, there'd be no doubt.
I'd set up all my offices
And start a government
With pomp and ceremony
At the village monument
I'd open up the banks and set
A monetary rate;
To encourage trade and barter
For their economic fate.
The things the school had taught me
I in turn would try to teach;
But—that was on the voyage and
Before I hit the beach.
They didn't teach me how to dig
A fox hole in the ground
But I soon learned to do it
What with bullets whizzing round.
They didn't teach me how to shoot
A carbine from the hip,
I learned it from a soldier when
He yelled 'That guy's a Nip.'
They didn't tell me what to do
With all the buildings gone,
Nor how to handle natives by
The thousands—come each dawn.

There was not a single building
Not a bank, a house or store,
They all had been demolished
By the fire from ships off shore.
I didn't have a blessed thing
To start a government
And all my dreams collapsed around
My village monument.

I threw 'the book' into a pile-
And started in a rule
Of Military Government
I wasn't taught at school.

'Twas tough and hard and difficult
But yet a lot of fun
With a lot of satisfaction
At the way the jobs were done.
And soon the things I learned at school
Began to find their place
In questions and in problems that
I'd daily have to face.

I'm a Military Governor,
Upon a lonely isle,
But I'm glad I found the book
I had thrown into that pile. [18]

But there was a certain readiness to blame the victim for his or her inability to keep Navy time. According to Dorothy Richard,

> A general labor situation which might be considered to constitute a problem was the continual struggle to persuade many of the people to observe regular working hours and stay at their jobs over a period of time. The Micronesians were accustomed to work where and if they desired and a five day week and an eight hour day of specific hours was beyond their ability to understand and appreciate. It was a problem the Navy never solved. [19]

Two extraordinary consequences of this failure of communication and understanding was the loss of the indigenous fishing and boatbuilding industries. Richard writes,

> The administration gradually become convinced that the natives would not and could not carry on a commercial fishing industry. Security regulations forbade the use of Japanese fisherman in the area. The only solution, therefore, was to allow approved non-indigenous fishing companies to perform fishing operations.[20]

Richard places the blame on the Japanese:

their administrators for thirty years had allowed them no participation in business and managerial tasks, and only minor participation in the type of economy indigenous to the area. As a result, the islanders not only failed to acquire new skills but lost, through disuse, native skills, notably deep sea fishing.[21]

In fact, the Navy developed its own trading agency, the United States Commercial Company, which in 1947 became the Island Trading Company of Micronesia. During the period of Naval administration these companies traded 95 percent of the foreign merchandise brought into the territory.

The Navy did not have much more success (or interest) in promoting self-government among the people. In the first years, the territory was clearly under military administration which only gradually developed a civilian administrative infrastructure. The Navy's primary concern was security—having fought for the islands it was not going to relinquish them again to Japanese, Korean or Chinese pressures. Even as hostilities were developing in Korea, the Joint Chiefs of Staff entered on the nuclear testing program at Bikini Atoll, chosen because

> it met the Joint Chiefs of Staff's requirement that the location be at least 500 miles distant from all sea and air routes and have steady directional winds for better control of the atomic cloud.[22]

The 167 inhabitants were taken off their island, the first of several forced removals. These removals were conducted under military authority with only minimal understanding and consultation with the people involved and their chiefs. A further insight into the nature of the naval administration from 1945 to 1951 is indicated by the fact that

> the administering authority, at the close of the period of naval administration, had custody of about 434 square miles, including public domain and land which had been controlled or owned by the Japanese government or its agencies, or by Japanese corporations or private individuals, and then under custody of the Alien Property Custodian.[23]

The indigenous population as of June 30, 1951 owned about 250 square miles of land in the Trust Territory, most of which was held under collective systems of clan or lineage ownership. Census taking had improved since 1947 and in 1951 there were 56,178 people in the territory, not counting the naval personnel.[24] The Navy's official historian notes that

> The decision by the United States to place the ex-Japanese Mandated Islands under trusteeship and to accept the trust was made after many months of study by interested governmental agencies. The further decision to give the United States Navy interim authority for the administration of the Trust Territory was arrived at after long and, at times, bitter discussions between military and civilian officials.[25]

The Soviet Union had secured the southern Sakhalin and Kurile Islands at Yalta, and it was difficult for many Americans to accept the degree of internationalization of the Micronesian islands proposed in the Trusteeship Agreement. Others, most particularly Secretary of the Interior Harold L. Ickes, were vociferously critical of the Navy's military administration of the territory, which he likened to the command of a battleship—"a rule of authority, color distinction and the ignoring of the problems of and striving toward democratic living."[26] The Navy saw the islands primarily as bases and successfully sought congressional appropriations for fiscal year 1946 for bases on Saipan, Tinian, Eniwetok, Kwajalein, Truk, Palau and Majuro.[27] The State Department however was under pressure from Americans and members of the United Nations who thought that the future political status of the people of Micronesia was as least as important as the potential of their atolls as military bases. President Truman resolved this dilemma by proposing a "strategic trusteeship" for the former Japanese Mandated Islands. The difference between this strategic trust and the ten other trusts to be created under the Trusteeship Council was that, as Secretary of the Navy Forrestal noted in his diary, the former would be "upon terms to be stated unilaterally by the United States."[28]

R. N. Chowdhuri points out that the Trusts differed from the League of Nations Mandates in requiring the administering authorities to develop political institutions with a view to the achievement of self-government or independence, and on a stronger protection of the rights of the inhabitants (which he suggests was a term used to encompass indigenes and settlers) over the land of the territory. He sees the principle of the 'open door' that characterized the A and B mandates subordinated to the interests of the inhabitants and the consideration of international peace and security in the trusteeships. The administering authorities of both trusts and strategic trusts retain the full power to establish bases, erect fortifications, station armed forces and raise voluntary contingents in the trust territory. Chowdhuri further points out that it was envisaged that some trusts might become strategic trusts:

> In some Trust Agreements, the distinction between the strategic and non-strategic types depends entirely upon the discretion of the Trustee. Article 17 of the Trusteeship Agreements for the Cameroons, Togoland and Tanganyika under the administration of Britain; and Article 17 of Ruanda-Urundi under Belgian administration; and Article 11 for the French Cameroons and Togoland expressly reserve the right of the Administering Authority to propose 'at any future date,' the designation of 'the whole or part of the Territory as a strategic area' in accordance with Articles 82 and 83 of the Charter.[29]

Article 83 provides that "All functions of the United Nations relating to strategic areas, including the approval of the terms of the trusteeship agreements and of their alteration or amendment, shall be exercised by the Security Council" which may "avail itself of the assistance of the Trusteeship Council to perform those functions of the United Nations under the trusteeship system relating to political, economic, social and educational matters in the strategic areas."

In fact, in the forty years of the trusteeship system, there has only been one strategic trust, that of the Trust Territory of the Pacific Islands. The essential feature of a strategic trust is the right of the administering authority not to submit information about such a territory to the United Nations—the Trusteeship Council or the General Assembly—on "any areas which may from time to time be specified by it as closed for security reasons."[30]

The United States as administering authority of the strategic trust is nevertheless under the same obligation as other trustees to promote "the development of the inhabitants of the trust territory toward self-government or independence," to promote the "economic advancement and self-sufficiency of the inhabitants," in this case particularly by the development of fisheries, agriculture and industries; and to promote the social and educational advancement of the people as well as to protect their health.[31] Chowdhuri reports that it was the Soviet Union which insisted that the phrase "or independence" be inserted in Article 6 of the Trusteeship Agreement for the Pacific Islands although the United States delegate said he did not think it could be achieved "in any foreseeable future."[32] The Soviet Union also forced the deletion of reference to the territory as "an integral part of the United States" which would have made clear the annexationist intent of the United States despite the State Department's attempts to avoid charges of hypocrisy.

However, the Soviet Union did not succeed in rewriting Article 15 to require Security Council action for amendment or termination of the Agreement, and Article 15 reads

> The terms of the present agreement shall not be altered, amended or terminated without the consent of the administering authority.

It remained to be seen how Article 15 of the Trusteeship Agreement could be reconciled with the assertion of Article 83 of the Charter of the United Nations that "All functions of the United Nations relating to strategic areas, including the terms of the trusteeship agreements and of their alteration or amendment, shall be exercised by the Security Council." There was extensive debate at the time about the implications of the ambiguities of Article 83 for the ongoing administration of the trusteeship system. The Soviet Union persisted in seeing the Security Council as the ultimate locus of authority while Australia, France, Belgium, Britain, Colombia, Brazil and the United States argued that Article 83 was "mandatory" in requiring the Security Council to avail itself of the assistance of the Trusteeship Council to oversee the trusts.[33] In the event, this view prevailed.

The advantage of Article 13 to the United States was apparent in April 1954 when various petitioners complained to the Trusteeship Council about the explosion of a hydrogen bomb by the administering authority which destroyed two islands and contaminated 236 inhabitants. Clearly in violation of Articles 6 and 7, it nevertheless was possible for the United States to invoke Article 13 in its refusal to explain itself or permit international inspection of the testing sites.[34]

The 1950s were a period of stagnation for the territory. Indeed the number of Micronesians employed actually fell by 14 in the years 1949-53 while the number of United States employees increased by 129.[35] The United Nations Visiting Mission in 1953 received 1,080 complaints in regard to land, concerning 63 percent of the total land area. A Land and Claims Administration was established to examine these complaints.[36] There was progress in education, with 90 percent of school age children and adolescents enrolled by 1953, and the population had increased to 58,000 by mid-decade. Most significantly, a start had been made on reconstructing local government at the municipal level as a preparation for a territory-wide legislature. By 1953 there were 117 municipalities, with 97 magistrates.

The process of chartering these municipalities began in 1957. The first advisory legislative body was the Palau Congress which was established just prior to the Trusteeship Agreement. The Marshall Islands Congress was formed in November 1949; the Yap Islands Congress in 1951 (although the people from Yap's outer islands were not represented in it until 1968); and the Ponape Islands Congress in 1952. But at the same time the islands of Saipan and Tinian in the Northern Marianas were placed back under the administration of the Department of the Navy on January 1, 1953 for security reasons. The first territory-wide organ of self-government, the Inter-District Advisory Committee to the High Commissioner, was instituted in August 1956 and became the Council of Micronesia on September 15, 1961.

Carl Heine, the son of one of Micronesia's early postwar leaders, Dwight Heine, suggests that the early forms of municipal self-government sponsored by the American administration in the 1950s were "more a sanction of the remnants of the traditional systems, rather the establishing of the Western form of local government."[37] Most of the magistrates at this stage were also hereditary chiefs, depending more on their traditional authority than that lent by the United States administration. In some areas such as Ponape and many other districts, according to an American social scientist,

> there were no traditional socio-political institutions on the district level. Much less were there any such institutions on

the territorial level. Therefore, self-government on the district and territorial levels could not very well be within the framework of Micronesian institutions and traditions since no political institutions and traditions existed on these levels.[38]

Writing in the late sixties, this observer commented that

> Perhaps the most intriguing elected leadership role on Ponape is that of Micronesian Congressman. The speed and thoroughness with which this role has been accepted on a non-traditional basis is remarkable.[39]

The development of self-government institutions was a deliberate policy of the sixties. If Micronesia's interests had been subordinated to the security requirements of the atomic bomb testing program and the military operations in Korea in the fifties, there was in the Kennedy Administration an apprehension that the United States would be left as the last Trustee as Nauru and Papua New Guinea were clearly moving to termination.

The Kennedy Administration and the Solomon Game Plan

John F. Kennedy was elected President of the United States even as the fateful 1960 General Assembly was taking place in New York, with Prime Minister Krushchev introducing what was to become Resolution 1514, the Declaration on the Granting of Independence to Colonial Countries and Peoples. The 1961 Visiting Mission to the Pacific Islands was particularly critical of the slow pace of development in what was becoming known as the "Rust Territory." This criticism was all the more telling because in fact that Visiting Mission was not dominated by anti-American or newly independent countries.[40] At much the same time Micronesia experienced a polio epidemic which particularly offended President Kennedy in an age when vaccines were available.

On April 18, 1962 the president issued National Security Action Memorandum (NSAM) 145 establishing an interagency task force for Micronesia. A subsequent NSAM, 243, of May 9, 1963 established a mission to be headed by Harvard economist Anthony N. Solomon to visit the territory and report on economic, social, educational and political developments and to "Make recommendations leading to the formulation of programs and policies for an accelerated rate of development so that the people may make an informed and free choice as to their future, in accordance with United States responsibilities under the Trusteeship Agreement."

The Solomon Survey Mission went to Micronesia in the summer of 1963 and delivered its report to President Kennedy a month before his assassination. The "Solomon Report" has remained classified, but parts of it were published in a University of Hawaii student newspaper in 1969 and a typescript copy of much of the report (but not including the section relating to military matters) has circulated for two decades. One of these *samizdat* copies is the source for the following discussion. The report was no doubt classified in the first instance because it detailed a plan for effective incorporation of the territory which has in the main been implemented. By the 1970s, however, the report also appeared offensive in its paternalism and condescension towards Micronesians, and manipulative of the newly emerging political elite in the territory.

The Solomon Report noted that the population had risen to 81,000 but

> in the almost twenty years of United States control, physical facilities have further deteriorated in many areas, the economy has remained relatively dormant and in many ways retrogressed while progress towards social development has been slow. The people remain largely illiterate and inadequately prepared to participate in political, commercial and other activities of more than a rudimentary character.

Per capita Micronesian income was almost three times higher before the war than in 1963, when the territory was in a state of "aimless drift." The limited progress made towards self-government was imbalanced leaving the outer islands feeling "outdistanced and overwhelmed by the district center." The Trust government and United States agencies employed 65 percent of all Micronesians who worked for wages. The relocation program had resulted in "a barren, dirty slum" on the atoll of Ebeye in order to vacate Kwajalein for the missile base.

The Report notes that

> In recognition of the problem, the President, on April 18, 1962, approved NASM No. 145 which set forth as United States policy the movement of Micronesia into a permanent

relationship with the United States within our political framework. In keeping with that goal, the memorandum called for accelerated development of the area to bring its political, economic and social standards into line with an eventual permanent association.

The mission therefore addressed itself to the following questions:

a. What are the elements to consider in the preparation for, organization, time and favorable outcome of a plebiscite in Micronesia and how will this action affect the long-run problem that Micronesia, after affiliation, will pose for the United States?

b. What should be the content and cost of the minimum capital investment and operating program needed to ensure a favorable vote in the plebiscite. . . ?

These questions would have to be answered with due concern for the "unique elements in the delicate problem of Micronesia" which included the fact that the United States would be

moving counter to the anti-colonial movement that has just about completed sweeping the world and will be breaching its own policy since World War I of not acquiring new territorial possessions if it seeks to make Micronesia a United States territory.

Of all the eleven trusteeships, Micronesia will be

the only one not to terminate in independence or merger with a contiguous country, but in territorial affiliation with the administering power.

Solomon and his colleagues reported that "the Washington policy, adopted last year, of having the Trust Territory affiliate permanently with the United States" had not had an observable effect on the Trust Territory government which appeared to be still "thinking in terms of independence for Micronesia as an eventual, distant goal." The mission was most concerned that "there appears to have been little attempt to direct Micronesia toward thinking about eventual affiliation with the United States." They perceived political power among the Micronesians as being a "triumvirate" of the traditional clan chiefs, the educated younger bureaucracy working in the Trust Territory government, and the small but powerful group of businessmen operating trading companies. The primary worry of the traditional chiefs centered on land alienation, while the bureaucrats feared losing their jobs to expatriate Americans and the businessmen also feared competition which would result in their losing status "as the Hawaiians did."

The Solomon mission was appalled that

> Only after tedious and delicate questioning could most Micronesians be led to frame for themselves the possibility of changing the status of the Trust Territory and then it was obvious, except for the Saipanese and very few elite Micronesians, that the chance of becoming part of the United States had simply not entered into any rational analysis.

It was essential that the indigenous political forces be mobilized to make that possibility apparent and acceptable to the people of Micronesia—and the sooner the better as the United States was in danger of becoming the last Trustee before the end of the decade. The mission was convinced that if the plebiscite was held as soon as possible there was no chance that the people would vote for independence; all they needed was to be educated about the possibility and advantages of affiliation with the United States and they would overwhelmingly embrace that option. But at the same time the mission argued that it was essential to have an effective capital investment program before the plebiscite "to give the Micronesians a sense of progress." However

> it is the Mission's conclusion that those programs and the spending involved will not set off a self-sustaining development process of any significance in the area. It is important, therefore, that advantage be taken of the psychological impact of the capital investment program before some measure of disappointment is felt.

Although the mission "would go so far as to say that even if a plebiscite were held today without preparation, the total vote for independence would probably be only from 2 to 5 percent" it recommended that the plebiscite be held in 1967 or 1968 after the political leadership had been cultivated by sponsored visits to the United States and careful attention to the school system including the "introduction in the school system of United States oriented curriculum changes and patriotic rituals." The mission urged that young Micronesians be given scholarships to study in the United States, that basic pay scales between the Micronesian and expatriate communities be equalized, and that Social Security be extended to the islands. The extension of United States nationality was considered an important inducement, as was the opening of free immigration into the United States from the islands. The mission spelled out the implications of this proposal:

> It is worth pointing out that the extension of the status of United States nationals appears to the Mission, although questioned by State, to be legally possible under the trusteeship agreement which permits the extension of all the administering authority's laws to the Territory, and that this could be the first in a series of steps that could make the trusteeship agreement an academic issue, even if the Security Council were not willing to terminate the trusteeship agreement.

The mission recommended:

> As the practical solution to this many-pronged dilemma . . . a government organization for the Territory of Micronesia that gives, on the one hand, a reasonable appearance of self-government through an elected Micronesian legislature and a Micronesian Chief Executive nominated by and having the confidence of the legislature, but on the other hand retains adequate control through the continuation of an appointed United States High Commissioner.

Independence was ruled out as an option because it would

> only be possible . . . on the unreliable and undependable basis for both parties of an arrangement involving continuing United States subsidies on the one hand and 'permanent' ceding by Micronesia of exclusive defense and military use rights to the United States on the other.

—which in the event turned out to be a pretty fair description of what happened.

It was clear to the mission that a plebiscite was essential to gain the acceptance of the United Nations, and the group insisted that it should be held as soon as possible.

> There is no important hard core of resistance to affiliation with the United States either among the leaders or the people of Micronesia. If the people of Micronesia were offered a simple choice between self-government in affiliation with the United States or independence, we believe an overwhelming majority would favor self-government in affiliation with the United States.

The Solomon Report clearly acknowledged that

> the Security Council will have jurisdiction over the formal termination of the trusteeship agreement

and warned that

> if such a termination is vetoed there, the United States might have to decide to proceed with a series of actions that would make the trusteeship agreement a dead issue, at least from the Micronesian viewpoint.

The report was not very specific about these actions except to say that

> The question of additional steps to make the trusteeship agreement a dead issue (such as the discontinuance of reporting to the UN completely or by reporting to the Committee on Non-Self-Governing Territories rather than the Trusteeship and Security Councils) is one that can only be decided at the appropriate time given the over-all situation at that time.

Clearly the Solomon Mission was prepared to envisage a situation in Micronesia similar to that in Namibia.

The recommendations of the Solomon Report were immediately put into practice. The Council of Micronesia which had been constituted out of the predecessor Inter-District Advisory Committee in 1961 was given actual legislative authority, although the High Commissioner had the power of veto (Secretary of the Interior Order No. 2882, September 28, 1964) and renamed the Congress of Micronesia. But in the process a new political elite was confirmed in Micronesia. A long-time observer of and adviser to the Congress of Micronesia, Norman Meller, commented that

> The Congressional elections marked the emergence of a new political elite, young, American-educated and trained, and in good part dependent upon government employment for a livelihood. . . . A greater proportion of the House had obtained political prominence through prior membership in territorial legislative bodies rather than through service in district legislatures or municipal offices. They were more familiar with Territory-wide political institutions and their potential policy-making and public-opinion forming functions.[41]

The median age of the new legislators was 33. They were more cosmopolitan than their fathers, having had access to American education in Hawaii and the continental United States and also military service in Europe and other places.

In 1967 the Congress of Micronesia adopted Senate Joint Resolution 25 creating a "Future Political Status Commission" which worked for two years to review the options for the islands, in the process visiting the Virgin Islands, Puerto Rico, Washington, American Samoa, Western Samoa, Fiji, Papua-New Guinea, Nauru and the Cook Islands. The Commission reduced the "desirable alternatives to two, and from among these two" chose one:

> that the Trust Territory of the Pacific Islands be constituted as a self-governing state and that this Micronesian state—internally self-governing and with Micronesian control of all its branches, including the executive—negotiate entry into free association with the United States.

This recommendation recognized

> two inescapable realities: the need for Micronesian self-government and the fact of long-standing American interest in this area.

In language that could have been written by the Solomon Mission the Micronesian Commission reported one item of material value which Micronesians can offer the United States—an item which is most precious in Micronesia and to Micronesians: the use of their land. Micronesians recognize that their islands are of strategic value, that the United States may require the use of some areas for purposes of military training and defense. We have seen the strategic value of these islands, have seen them conquered in historic battles, have seen them used for nuclear experiments and missile testing. Our experience with the military has not always been encouraging. But as a self-governing association in free association with the United States, we would accept the necessity of such military needs and we would feel confident that we could enter into responsible negotiations with the military, endeavoring to meet American requirements while protecting our own interests.[42]

The other option, independence, was weakly listed as "the only road left to us" if negotiations with the United States failed.

The Constitutional Convention and the Fragmentation of Micronesia.

The reaction against this statement in Micronesia was intense. As one Micronesian observer, Carl Heine, wrote in 1970,

> it seems to me that the Status Commission left out one very important commodity: the people.[43]

Speaking nine different regional languages and with very little communication of any sort except among the new political elite which met at the Congress, the 81,000 people of Micronesia were not at all in agreement with this decision to surrender, virtually without protest, their land to the military needs of the United States. Instead of forcing the fusion desired by the administering authority, the statement of the Congress of Micronesia sparked the fission of Micronesia that took place in the next decade. The critical ingredient of the Solomon proposals had been omitted: the holding of the plebiscite before the Micronesians had become sufficiently politically educated to analyze the proposals being offered them.

Even as President Nixon was enunciating the "Guam doctrine" which in effect began the withdrawal of United States land forces from Asia and the Pacific and marked a new need for staging bases for American forces on the islands of the Pacific and Indian Oceans, the mood changed in Micronesia. As the Congress of Micronesia was about to enter negotiations with the United States on the future political status of the territory, it issued a Joint Resolution (No. 87, 1970) which set forth the Four Principles which would guide the Micronesian negotiators. They were substantially different in tone and content from the previous year's Status Commission Report.

> 1. That sovereignty in Micronesia resides in the people of Micronesia and their duly constituted government;
>
> 2. That the people of Micronesia possess the right of self-determination and may therefore choose independence or self-government in free association with any nation or organization of nations;
>
> 3. That the people of Micronesia have the right to adopt their own constitution and to amend, change or revoke any constitution or governmental plan at any time; and
>
> 4. That free association should be in the form of a revocable compact, terminable unilaterally by either party.[44]

The problem was that all four of these principles were unacceptable to the Department of Defense which was locked in battle with both State and Interior for control of the territories in the 1970s. The institutional issue was resolved by the creation of an interagency Office of Micronesian Status Negotiations on July 28, 1971 in which all the senior officials were taken from the Pentagon, and "the overriding role of Defense is evident."[45] The Micronesians and the Americans entered on a series of negotiations in the next few years in which the central issues posed by the Principles could not be resolved. The military was in no hurry to divest itself of the total control without scrutiny afforded by Article 13 of the Trusteeship Agreement, and was completely uninterested in the State Department's need to windowdress *de facto* annexation in the language if not the substance of decolonization.

Donald F. McHenry, when a Fellow with the Carnegie Endowment for International Peace during the Republican years of the seventies (he later succeeded Andrew Young as Ambassador to the United Nations in the Carter Administration), wrote a critical analysis of the experience of Micronesia in the Nixon and Ford years. It was as polemical as its title, *Micronesia: Trust Betrayed*, suggests. It is however a very useful analysis of the negotiations which McHenry suggests "appeared to be between hostile countries rather than close associates."[46] The ultimate sticking points from the beginning were control over land—and by implication the application and scope of the power of eminent domain by the United States military in the territory—and the Micronesian insistence on the power to unilaterally terminate the arrangements, as were vested in Cook and Niue in their relationship with New Zealand. The power of eminent domain is that "superior dominion of the sovereign power over all the property within the state which authorizes it to appropriate all or any part of thereof to a necessary public use, reasonable compensation being made." (*Webster's New International Dictionary*, Second Edition)

The continuance of United States power of eminent domain in the territories, whatever their future political status, would clearly constitute an erosion of whatever sovereignty they might have. It would however permit the former administering authority—the United States—to build military bases at will in the territories in perpetuity.

When the Congress of Micronesia's negotiating team was given a renewed mandate in 1972, it was also required to negotiate for independence. At the same time, the United States began serious separate negotiations with one of the six districts of Micronesia, the Northern Marianas. Preoccupied with the Vietnam War, the Nixon and Ford Administrations nevertheless continued to implement the recommendations of the Solomon Mission in the social and educational spheres. The chief agent of Americanization in the seventies was the Peace Corps which "saturated" Micronesia so that at its high point there was one volunteer teacher or community development adviser or health technician for every 800 Micronesians. Appropriations in 1969 were $39 million; they jumped rapidly and by 1971 were $59.8 million. Some progress was made in promoting Micronesian business enterprises, aided by the creation of Air Micronesia and better communications systems within the territory.

A new echelon of Micronesian administrators and teachers were coming out of the secondary schools and the University of Hawaii and mainland colleges. Their entry into the government administration is usually referred to as "Micronization"[47] but in fact it was an attempt to ensure that American values and styles of government should prevail in the future political status. The problem was that the more educated these young Micronesians became on the west coast and Hawaii in the early 1970s, the more they aspired to substantive self-government or even independence. The "Micronesia Club" at the University of Hawaii was as significant as such organizations have been in other nationalist struggles in increasing the new elite's understanding of the possibilities—and their aspirations.

At the same time, the Trust Territory administration deliberately promoted the "districtization" or decentralization of the six districts of Micronesia. There was virtually no support from the Micronesians for a centralized government on Saipan or any other major island because there had been no history of such centralization and each district was jealous of its own power to govern and protect its cultural heritage. But a Micronesian observer argued that "districtization" was itself disturbing of the old order because it confirmed the transition from traditional styles of leadership to the new elite of young graduates disbursing appropriations from the external Trust Territory administration

> The process of districtization has been the strongest factor in breaking the ties of the Micronesians to their traditional modes of life. It has produced a new elite society that dominates the politics of the various districts in Micronesia. Indeed, the territorial politics of the districts is largely limited to those within the centers. And as the most Westernized elements of the society, members of this elite are the most responsible for shaping future policies and hence the future development of Micronesia.[48]

The disruption of traditional life had been occurring since the arrival of the Japanese, but the rate of change intensified in the early seventies. That it was dysfunctional for those many young Micronesians in particular who were left out of the new elite is indicated by the fact that suicide became the most frequent cause of death for adolescent males, and the territory's population was spending one million dollars annually on alcohol despite not yet being fully within the money economy.[49]

Carl Heine notes that the fragmentation of Micronesia was hastened if anything by the emerging commercialization which

> has, in general, accelerated the process of districtization, secularization and expansion in scope of the political community. [50]

While the State Department looked askance at these fissiparous tendencies within the Trust Territory, the Department of Defense probably encouraged them. There has been no intensive analysis of the events leading to the separation of the Northern Marianas, but Donald McHenry devoted a full chapter to it in his 1975 study. The United Nations *Decolonization* report depends heavily on McHenry. The trigger seems to have been a territory-wide tax bill passed by the Congress of Micronesia which would have taxed the Northern Marianas to the benefit of the poorer districts. D. Michael Green notes that in a parallel situation

> The internal St. Christopher-Nevis-Anguilla dispute centered around allegedly neglectful economic policies towards the latter on the part of the other two of that state's three constituencies [51]

and the problem was certainly not made easier by having twice as many constituent areas.

But the Northern Marianas, site of a major Central Intelligence Agency base in the early sixties and still an important staging post to East Asia, was considered strategically critical by the Pentagon and McHenry points out that

> The 'commonwealth' arrangement would make the Marianas a territory over which the United States has sovereignty. A military base on sovereign United States territory would present fewer problems than a base where the United States does not have sovereignty—such as the other Micronesian districts in free association with the United States.[52]

Legal scholars were dubious about the propriety of fragmenting the Trust Territory of the Pacific Islands in this way, and particularly about the adequacy of the Covenant as a future political status for part of the territory in United Nations terms.[53] The problem would be deferred until the rest of the territory had settled upon its future—in the event, division into three more separate entities. Certainly the United States willingness to deal with the Northern Marianas as a separate entity boded ill for the Constitutional Convention of the Congress of Micronesia in 1975.

Over the objections of the Congress of Micronesia, the United States began negotiating separately with the Northern Marianas in February 1971 and four years later signed a "Covenant to Establish a Commonwealth of the Northern Marianas in Political Union with the United States of America" which was ratified by the electorate of the Northern Marianas on June 17, 1975. In a voter turnout of 93 percent, 3,945 voted in favor and 1,060 opposed. The Covenant was approved by the United States Congress on March 24, 1976, and the Secretary of the Interior issued an Order separating the Northern Marianas District administratively from the rest of Micronesia. It was left to the State Department to field criticism in the United Nations, which was as disturbed by the fragmentation of the Trust Territory as it had been by the division of Togoland and the Cameroons.

As the Director of Territorial Affairs in the Department of the Interior, former Texas businessman Fred M. Zeder, pointed out at the time, approval of the Covenant would mean

> the Marianas will no longer take part in the Congress of Micronesia. This will permit the Congress to concentrate on the affairs in the interest of other districts. The Congress will, of course, lose the revenue which is generated in the Marianas.[54]

Ten years after the Constitutional Convention of 1975 which drafted the basic proposals for the Federated States of Micronesia, one of its technical staff advisors, Norman Meller, wrote a close history of the 90-day life of the Convention. Meller emphasizes the role of the Palauan delegation's confrontational style under Delegate Lazarus Salii, typified by their presentation of seven non-negotiable demands early in the Convention.

> The seven points are: 1) The central government would have only those powers given to it by the constitution, and the

districts would have all the others. 2) A unicameral (single house) legislature with equal representation from each district. 3) The district controls ownership and use of land. 4) Foreign aid would be divided and shared equally by the districts and the national government. 5) The Districts would contribute equally to the national government. 6) Each district would have the right to withdraw from the union for a certain period of years, and 7) The seat of government would be in Palau.[55]

The Palauan Delegation threatened to wreck the Constitutional Convention if they did not get their way. In fact, at the eleventh hour of the 90th day session, compromises were reached that enabled the Convention to report out a draft constitution to be placed before the people. Meller notes almost in passing that

> All during the long weeks of sparring over the major issues of the Convention, less inflammable matters were also being brought before the delegates and adopted without engendering extended controversy. 'Radioactive, toxic chemical, or other harmful substances' are not to be 'tested, stored, used, or disposed of' within Micronesia without the express approval of the national government (Art. XIII, Sec. 2), a provision destined to raise the hackles of the United States representatives at the future status negotiations. Agreements for indefinite-term use of land are barred, and all existing agreements voided after five years (Art. XIII, Sec. 5). The national government is directed to seek renegotiation of land use agreements to which the United States is a party (Art. XIII, Sec. 6) Amendment of the constitution can be by convention, popular initiative, or Congressional act, but ratification will require the extraordinary majority of a three-quarters vote in three-quarters of the states (Art. XIV).[56]

Meller's account stresses the fragility of the Convention and the fissiparous pressures on it—the danger of a walkout by the traditional chiefs or by the Palauan delegation in their practice of confrontational politics. But as much as the divisive tendencies inherent in trying to federate such a widely disparate group of people, there was the clearly stated unwillingness of the United States to accept all of the above elements of the draft constitution. The United States response was to delay the referenda necessary to ratify the draft constitution. Meller comments,

Whether or not by sheer ineptitude, the United States so delayed the termination of the Trusteeship of the Pacific islands that the regional cleavages inherent in the artificiality called 'Micronesia' were encouraged to reassert themselves.[57]

Perhaps the United States design was to isolate the intransigents of Palau. At this time in Micronesian political history one close observer at least—Norman Meller—saw the Palauan "firebrand" Lazarus E. Salii as the architect of the notion of Micronesia as a freely associated state. But after an eight month review of the draft constitution United States Ambassador Hayden Williams rejected it as incompatible with the Compact of Free Association simultaneously being drafted for presentation to the peoples of Micronesia as their future political status. The incompatibility lay in the fact that

Free Association as envisioned by the compact is clearly inconsistent with the sovereign independent status called for by the draft Constitution. . . . Free Association . . . is a free and voluntary and terminable relationship between a self-governing territory with a fully independent state. Free Association by definition is not a relationship between two independent states.[58]

Meller's emphasis on the role of the Palauan delegation in the Constitutional Convention would seem to be misplaced, then, since the draft constitution that emerged was more that of a sovereign independent state than of a freely associated state. If Salii was an architect of free association in 1975, his views did not prevail in the Constitutional Convention of the Congress of Micronesia. The centrifugal tendencies prevailed probably because the United States was unwilling to risk ratification of this strongly sovereign constitution, complete with its ban on nuclear substances and use of eminent domain by the central government. In the process, Lazarus Salii became the chief negotiator for Palau in the Compact negotiations that were to stretch over another decade precisely because the same issues mentioned above were considered non-negotiable by the Palauan people in determining their future political status.

The Ford Administration ended ingloriously in Micronesia with the revelation by Watergate reporter Bob Woodward of Central

Intelligence Agency bugging of the negotiations held in Saipan. Woodward noted that in the latter half of 1976 "the Micronesians have taken a harder line and seek full independence sooner, while the United States has sought to dissolve the trusteeship more gradually."[59] It was the professed intention of Director Zeder that the trusteeship should be terminated by 1980 or 1981.

The Carter Administration: From the Hilo Principles to the Compact of Free Association

Despite the strictures of Donald McHenry on the developments sponsored by the Ford and Nixon administrations, the Democratic appointees of the Carter period found themselves locked into the same dilemma. As Roger S. Clark pointed out at the end of that period,

> There is no case of a trust territory maintaining a continued constitutional relationship with the former Administering Authority.[60]

and

> the Marianas arrangement does not appear to satisfy any of the tests that are likely to be applied by the United Nations.[61]

The Carter Office of Micronesian Status Negotiations entered on "two tier" talks with the Congress of Micronesia and its Political Status Commission representing the four central districts of Yap, Truk. Ponape and Kosrae, while the Marshall Islands Political Status Commission and the Palau Political Status Commission were separately represented.

> The talks proceeded on two levels, one contemplating some kind of future all-Micronesia entity, the other dealing with the separate interests of the individual Micronesian entities.[62]

However in April, 1978 a meeting at Hilo in Hawaii produced a "Statement of Agreed Principles of Free Association" among all parties. Most significant was Principle 7 which provided that

The agreement will permit unilateral termination of the free association political status by the processes through which it was entered and put forth in the agreement and subject to the continuation of the United States defense authority and responsibility as set forth in Principle 5, but any plebiscite terminating the free association political status will not require United Nations observation.

This was compatible with Principle 4 of the Political Status Commission

That free association should be in the form of a revocable compact, terminable unilaterally by either party.

As the legal advisor to the President's Personal Representative for Micronesian Status Negotiations, Arthur John Armstrong, noted in a 1979 law journal commentary:

The Cook Islands free association is based . . . on a principle similar to the one stated in the Hilo Agreement in that either government may unilaterally dissolve the political relationship.[63]

Even though Armstrong noted that

Lacking independence, Namibia cannot be considered a 'sovereign country'[64]

and acknowledged that

Whether the other states of the world will recognize the international personality of the Micronesian governments will depend on their assessment of the Micronesian capability to comply fully and in good faith with its international obligations as well as their perceptions of Micronesian integrity and independence from the United States.[65]

"In the final analysis," the legal advisor under the Carter Administration somewhat blithely suggested, "these perceptions are more important than a splitting of fine definitional hairs over words such as 'sovereign country.'"[66]

The official United Nations description of the Hilo Principles noted that "the Micronesians shall enjoy full internal self-government" while the United States will maintain "full authority and responsibility for security and defense matters" for a period of at least fifteen years, subject to renegotiation. The administering Power recognized the right of unilateral termination by either side and the "authority and responsibility (of the Micronesians) for their foreign affairs including marine resources." Unilateral termination by the Micronesians was tempered, however, by the provision that should the relationship be terminated other than by the United States or by mutual consent the United States "shall no longer be obligated to provide the same amount of economic assistance . . . initially agreed upon." [67]

The rump of the Trust Territory (excluding the Northern Marianas) voted in a referendum on July 12, 1978 under United Nations observation to approve a constitution for the Federated States of Micronesia on the understanding that this constitution would not take effect in those districts in which it was rejected by a majority of voters. The constitution was affirmed by the districts of Yap, Truk, Ponape and Kosrae which thus became the Federated States of Micronesia, while Palau and the Marshall Islands opted for separate political status. This result was confirmed when the Secretary of the Interior issued an order in September 1978 which dissolved the Congress of Micronesia and called into being three separate interim legislatures. Elections took place in 1979 to the Congress of the Federated States of Micronesia, the *Nitijela* of the Marshall Islands and the *Olbiil Era Kelulau*, the bicameral legislature of Palau. Each of these legislatures ratified Constitutions for their districts in 1979 and thus the Micronesians entered fully into self-government which, as the United Nations official description points out,

> pending the termination of the Trusteeship Agreement, [is] under the general supervision of the United States Secretary of the Interior, acting through the Trust Territory's High Commissioner, who retains a veto power over legislation.[68]

By January 1980 a Compact of Free Association had been drafted, ostensibly on the basis of the Hilo Principles, to be presented to the three legislatures of the Federated States, the Marshalls and Palau for ratification. Legal advisor Armstrong noted that this first 1980 proposed Compact

> establishes a new political status known as 'free association' which has no precise precedent either in international practice or in United States constitutional law. . . . The political relationship has no fixed termination date and continues in effect until terminated by agreement or unilaterally. A freely associated state, however, may terminate unilaterally only after a plebiscite has demonstrated the freely expressed will of the people.[69]

The United States strategy at the end of the Carter administration was clear from Armstrong's statement that

> The one critical international legal criterion for a political status is that it be chosen freely by the former non-self-governing peoples. The most widely recognized forms of self-government are independence, integration with an independent state, and free association, which itself has a variety of forms. The Compact of Free Association establishes relations between the United States and the freely associated states that, in some aspects, are analogous to the relations between independent states and, in other aspects, are analogous to the relation between the United States and its territories.[70]

The United States, it was apparent, was offering some sort of hybrid future political status to the Micronesians on the calculation that acceptance by the Micronesian electorates would overwhelm international reservations about the actual terms of an arrangement that might not add up to the sum of any of its parts. Indeed, the Carter appointees of the Office of Micronesian Status Negotiations hoped to complete this process before they had to leave office in early 1981. There was one major obstacle to the United States efforts to gain the consent of the Micronesian people to the first 1980 Compact of Free Association: it was incompatible with the constitution that the people of Palau had ratified, over intense United States pressure, in 1979.

President Carter's Personal Representative for Micronesian Status Negotiations, Peter R. Rosenblatt, took the somewhat unusual step of introducing the Summer 1981 issue of the *Brooklyn Journal of International Law* which was devoted to an examination of the Free

Association concept being proposed for Micronesia. Clearly he and his staff associates such as Arthur Armstrong, who contributed to the issue, wanted to delineate their concept and strategy for the forthcoming Republican administration, even as they moved into private law practices in Washington, much of whose work was to be concerned in the next eight years with issues arising from the Micronesian situation. Ambassador Rosenblatt foresaw that the "many unique characteristics of the Compact" would be closely examined not only by lawyers but also historians, and that the *travaux preparatoires* of these agreements would be a subject of considerable interest since "organic dispute resolution provisions rely heavily on voluntary accommodation within the framework of the unique free association relationship," all the more so since "the document will also be offered to Congress for adoption as a joint executive-legislative agreement rather than as a treaty" and would thus be "both an international agreement and a United States domestic statute." [71]

President Carter's Ambassador to Micronesia referred quite explicitly to the interagency differences in the drafting of the first 1980 Compact and admitted that

> The unfortunate concomitant was that the higher the level of the officials who were required to decide interagency differences, the more the ultimate United States position which emerged from the process became substantially non-negotiable with our Micronesian negotiating partners. The give and take of negotiations could have destroyed the carefully constructed compromise upon which the internal United States consensus was founded.[72]

Armstrong spelled out the assumptions of this "carefully constructed compromise" by arguing that

> Free association differs from independence in that one of the parties to the bilateral agreement willingly binds itself, by its own constitutional process—whether by delegation or otherwise—to cede to the other a fundamental sovereign authority and responsibility for the conduct of its own affairs. Specifically, this distinction is exemplified by the reservation to the United States of plenary defense authority (as contrasted with treaty rights to exercise certain defense functions), and the ensuing limitation on Micronesian freedom of action. Free association is distinguished from

integration into a metropolitan power by the retention by the freely associated government of the power to assert itself domestically and internationally without reference to the legal authority of another state.[73]

The goal of the Compact is to provide "a political order which allows independence of action within the framework of their interdependence" between the parties, but the Compact

> must also offer an economic order that will foster development in the freely associated states without an endless drain on the United States treasury.[74]

Armstrong noted that by the end of the 1970s United States federal expenditure in Micronesia averaged $125,000,000 per annum, or about $1,000 per inhabitant.[75]

It is the defense relationship set forth in the Compact and its Agreements which most clearly distinguishes free association from independence because the United States has three major objectives in the security and defense relationship:

> — Denial of the area to the armed forces of foreign nations, to ensure that present or potential adversaries do not establish a foothold in the area and thereby compromise the defense posture of the United States in the Pacific;

> — Access for United States military forces to the harbors and airfields of the freely associated states on an occasional or emergency basis . . . ;

> — Mechanisms for obtaining use of and operating rights in specified land and water areas in the freely associated states.[76]

Specifically, in addition to "establishing full defense responsibility and authority for fifteen years" the United States sought continuing use of the Kwajalein Missile Range in the Marshall Islands and use and operating rights in Palau for its national defense, which of course is a nuclear defense.

> In Palau, there are several sites which the United States wishes to be able to activate at its option, either routinely or as a hedge against unforeseen circumstances. They include a

potential exclusive-use area adjacent to Palau's major commercial harbor, two existing airfields for possible joint use and a potential non-exclusive-use training area in the sparsely inhabited central portion of Palau's largest island, Babelthaup. The activation of the training area would also require activating a small, exclusive-use support facility.[77]

Armstrong did not note that this described more than 40 percent of Palau's total land area. He did note that

The interests of the United States and the freely associated states would be ill-served by a political relationship which lasted only until the first opportunity for either party to terminate it. . . . The maintenance of a political relationship with Micronesia which serves essential United States security interests must be drafted to minimize political friction between governments, especially with respect to foreign affairs.[78]

Armstrong thought that the proposed Compact resolved the issue of sovereignty for the Micronesian entities because

Sovereignty, as a principle of international law, describes the totality of powers which a State may exercise under international law

and from the point of view of the United States

the sovereignty issue has three components: (1) the negotiators for the peoples of the Trust Territory must have apparent authority prospectively to bind their peoples; (2) the constitutions of the freely associated states must be compatible with the Compact to the extent that there is no *de jure* proscription on their negotiators' authority to agree to the elements of free association; and (3) the United States must secure a sufficient degree of *de facto* 'sovereignty' in the freely associated states to be able to exercise plenary security and defense authority and responsibility in the area for at least fifteen years.[79]

Armstrong did not consider that the Micronesian entities had to experience a "scintilla moment" of sovereignty in order to be able to enter into agreements which would result in free association; he argued that this could be achieved by a 'government to government' form of the agreement . . . by which the peoples of the Trust Territory, having progressed toward self-government by instituting their own constitutions and electing their own leadership, can enter into an agreement on their future political status which, absent evidence of coercion by the Administering Authority during the negotiations, should survive termination of the Trusteeship Agreement.[80]

This would result in a form of sovereignty which was less than complete independence, but Armstrong was able to cite only one authority for the existence of such a form of sovereignty, a representative from Truk to the Congress of Micronesia.[81] He clearly acknowledged that

if the relationship is to be 'freely chosen' its content must be fully disclosed to the inhabitants.[82]

Another commentator in this 1981 symposium was less sanguine than the United States negotiator about the acceptability of the proposed compact of free association given the resistance of the United Nations and third world countries to statuses other than independence. J. Ross Macdonald noted that

This dilemma is exacerbated in that the Trust Territory is a strategic trust, under the responsibility of the Security Council. Other problems for free association include the resistance of the international system to a status other than sovereign statehood and the necessity of adapting concepts and precedents for purposes other that those for which they were originally intended.[83]

Macdonald pointed out that

Neither free association nor integration are such clear examples of self-determination (as independence) and, consequently, there is some justification for the United Nations and recently decolonized countries to fear overreaching by an administering country in the absence of some international supervision.[84]

While the Compact of Free Association "hews closely to the model adopted by the Cook Islands and Niue," there are "two small differences"—the Micronesians will not become United States citizens as the Cook and Niue islanders attained New Zealand citizenship, and

> Second, while New Zealand is largely in charge of foreign relations for the Cook Islands and Niue, the United States has agreed that the Micronesians should have full control of their external relations except so far as such control impinges upon United States security and defense concerns.[85]

Macdonald somewhat disingenuously argued that

> this reveals an even more independent status than that given to the Cook Islands and Niue, since the area of power reserved by the United States is appreciably smaller than that correspondingly reserved by New Zealand.[86]

Macdonald was more than disingenuous in stating that

> the political free association status is terminable at any time under Principle 7 of Hilo and sections 441-43 of the Compact.[87]

In fact, Section 441 provides for termination by any one of the Governments of Palau, the Marshall Islands or the Federated States of Micronesia by mutual agreement, rather than the unilateral termination option held by Cook and Niue. The United States Government under Section 442 attains the right to unilateral termination. Article 452 provides for the survival of the crucial defense agreements for fifteen years after any such 'termination' of the compact, and Section 451 restricts any continued economic assistance from the United States after such 'termination' to "mutually agreed upon terms."[88] Macdonald acknowledged that

> In light of section 311 of the Compact, it is not plausible to maintain that the freely associated states will be fully sovereign or independent states [89]

since section 311 declares that

> The Government of the United States has full authority and responsibility for security and defense matters in or relating to Palau, the Marshall Islands and the Federated States of Micronesia.

Thus

> The Micronesian associated states will clearly not be states *stricto sensu*. Principle I of Hilo states that the relationship shall be that of free association as distinguished from independence. Yet they will clearly possess some measure of personality.[90]

This was not however, spelled out with any precision by Macdonald beyond the possession of "some legal capacities." Macdonald agreed with Armstrong that it was not necessary for the Micronesian entities to enjoy a "scintilla moment of sovereignty" in order to enter into the compact of free association; this could be done by their duly constituted legislatures acting with the clear consent of the majority of the populations.

The other part of the 'termination equation' is the correct procedure to be followed in the United Nations. Donald McHenry had stated clearly at the outset of the Carter administration his conviction that

> On balance . . . the language of the Charter, procedures followed in the termination of other trusteeships, and explicit recognition by the United States of a United Nations role in the termination process support a conclusion that the United States has a legal duty to obtain Security Council approval for termination of the Trusteeship Agreement.[91]

Article 15 of the Trusteeship Agreement requires that

> The terms of the present agreement shall not be altered, amended or terminated without the consent of the administering authority.

The United States had successfully resisted a Soviet attempt to make alterations and termination dependent upon decision of the Security Council, and in the process, according to McHenry, submitted a text which proposed that the terms of the agreement "shall not be altered, amended or terminated except by agreement of the administering authority and the Security Council," which in turn was unacceptable to the Soviet Union. McHenry however pointed out that

> Nonetheless it reflected an understanding on the part of the United States that the approval of the Security Council would be required for termination of the Trusteeship Agreement. Moreover, at the same meeting of the Council, the United States representative Warren Austin said, 'The United States wishes to record its view that the draft trusteeship agreement is in the nature of a bilateral contract between the United States on the one hand and the Security Council on the other.' As a bilateral contract, he added, the Trusteeship Agreement could not be amended or terminated without the approval of the Security Council.[92]

Article 83 of the United Nations Charter states that

> All functions of the United Nations relating to strategic areas, including the approval of the terms of the trusteeship agreements and of their alteration or amendment, shall be exercised by the Security Council.

The lack of specific reference in either the Charter or the Trusteeship Agreement about the exact procedures required for terminating the only Strategic Trust permits some United States officials to float the argument that

> the extent of the United States obligation is only to *submit* the question of termination to the Security Council and does *not* include any requirement to secure the Council's approval of termination of the trusteeship.[93]

At any commonsense level of interpretation, this would seem to be a misstatement of the possibility that the United States might simply inform the Security Council of the *fait accompli* of termination without considering itself bound to seek Security Council approval of the terms of termination. McHenry envisaged a situation where the United States first secured the approval of the Trusteeship Council (which under Article 83 (3) has been performing the "functions of the United Nations under the trusteeship system relating to political, economic, social and educational matters in the strategic area" for the past forty years) and then simply forwarding Trusteeship Council acceptance of the termination as a matter of information to the Security Council, if necessary vetoing any resolution affirming continuation of the Trusteeship Agreement. As McHenry noted in 1976, "it is doubtful that the procedure is politically feasible or legally correct;"[94] it is however the procedure that was followed a decade later. Macdonald agreed in 1981 that

> the only lawful way to terminate the trusteeship is by action of both the United Nations Security Council and the United States.[95]

But he envisaged the possibility of the United States circumventing the possibility of a Soviet veto of the Compact of Free Association as the terms of termination by the presentation of the matter as a procedural one rather than a substantive one, requiring the concurrence of the permanent members. Specifically,

> The United States could propose a resolution stating that the Trusteeship Council had overseen the plebiscites in the associated states, that it was satisfied that self-determination had been accomplished and that it recommended that the Security Council terminate the trusteeship. While this resolution might be classified as procedural in that it was simply acknowledging a report from one organ to another, in practice, its possible consequences have extended ramifications. Such a resolution, if considered procedural and passed over a negative vote by a permanent member, might be held up subsequently as proof that the conditions of self-determination had been complied with in the event of a veto on the main trusteeship termination resolution. Such a resolution, despite its apparent procedural nature, might then serve to legitimate the United States-Micronesian status despite the fact that legal termination had not occurred.[96]

The technical success of this strategy would probably depend on having a sympathetic Security Council chairperson to rule the resolution procedural. Macdonald, however warned that

> it seems justified to question the wisdom of manipulating the rules in so brazen a manner. Expediency such as this leads to the breakdown of rules and the establishment of troubling precedents.[97]

Because

> if there is a perception that the United States is attempting to avoid its legal obligations to the trust territory or to manipulate the termination process for its own selfish strategic or geopolitical ends, the associated states will arrive on the international scene stillborn.[98]

All observers seem to agree with the impossibility of unilateral United States termination of the trusteeship agreements. While the April 1980 issue of *Decolonization* is unable to give much guidance on the actual procedures for termination, it emphatically endorses the opinion expressed by Roger S. Clark [99] that the 1950 Advisory Opinion of the International Court of Justice unanimously rejecting the view that South Africa could unilaterally terminate the League of Nations mandate over South-West Africa bound the United States in reference to Micronesia.[100]

The same source notes that when in 1971 the United States chose to repudiate the jurisdiction of the Special Committee on the Declaration of the Granting of Independence to Colonial Countries and Peoples which had placed the Trust Territory of the Pacific Islands on its list of Territories in 1962 it did so on the grounds that

> under the Charter all United Nations functions relating to strategic Trust Territories are exercised by the Security Council.[101]

But the Special Committee has continued to concern itself with the conditions in the Trust Territory, and it is not at all clear that it would rubberstamp terms for termination agreed upon by a Trusteeship Council composed of Britain, France, the United States and the Soviet Union alone.

By 1980, then, on the eve of the Reagan administration, Micronesia had been under United States control for thirty-five years. The United States carefully negotiated the terms of the Trusteeship Agreement in the late forties to leave unclear the process for termination of the Agreement—particularly the role of the Security Council in the termination process. Both the United States and the Soviet Union have veto powers in the Security Council; this could be a double-edged sword.

The strategy for determining the future political status of the islands was devised by the Solomon Commission during the Kennedy Administration. It was left intact during the Johnson, Nixon and Ford administrations and the Carter administration was committed to implementing it.

But it meant fostering the development of self-government in American terms without allowing it to become too independent-minded in any sense of the word. The Solomon Commission warned that it was important to seize the moment. But while limited self-government was encouraged in the Congress of Micronesia, the Americans were not able to contain the divergent tendencies of the seventies. By the end of the Carter Administration the dilemma was as the writers in the *Brooklyn Journal of International Law* noted—to negotiate a deal with a sufficiently sovereign group of Micronesians to limit their sovereignty, preferably without them noticing it, and then to have that deal accepted by the United Nations as freely associated state status even if it meant bypassing the Security Council and in effect terminating the trusteeship unilaterally as South Africa had tried to do in Namibia.

This was the strategy the Carter administration officials bequeathed to the Reagan administration. However, the Carter administration officials dealing with Micronesia's future political status seem to have missed the lessons emerging from the relationship between New Zealand and the Cook Islands in the 1970's.

The intention of the American administrators was clearly to keep the Micronesian territories within the United States sphere of influence, as tightly under American control as they could manage in order to protect access to the nuclear weapons testing sites and to deny access to hostile powers. They made the mistake of thinking that freely associated state status would serve those goals.

In fact, even in the far less fraught geopolitical situation between New Zealand and the Cook Islands, problems had arisen in the first decade of the relationship. On the one hand, the Cook Islands government was finding it difficult to get recognition of their sovereignty in several international fora. On the other hand, the external affairs of the Cook Islands government under Prime Minister Sir Albert Henry were sometimes at variance with the policies of New Zealand. In 1973 New Zealand Prime Minister Norman Kirk initiated an exchange of letters to clarify the relationship. The formulation was markedly un-legalistic in the view of the New Zealand Government there are no legal fetters of any kind upon the freedom of the Cook Islands, which make their own laws and control their own Constitution. . . . the relationship between the our two countries has been simply one of partnership, freely entered into and freely maintained. The Cook Islands Constitution Act, and the Constitution itself, provide guarantees and guidelines for the conduct of this partnership; but in the final analysis everything turns on the will of each of our countries to make the arrangement work.[102]

On delicate questions of differing views on internal political issues in the Cook Islands, the New Zealand Prime Minister referred carefully to

an expectation that the Cook Islands will uphold, in their laws and policies a standard of values generally acceptable to New Zealanders.

As the Cook Islands became more active in regional and international affairs, the issue of recognition became more pressing. C. C. Aikman, Director of the New Zealand Institute of International Affairs, noted in 1982 that by the end of the seventies—the end of the Carter administration in the United States and Micronesia—

the New Zealand Government has taken the view—and made this generally known—that the Cook Islands Government is competent to take the executive and legislative action required to enter into international obligations on behalf of the Cook Islands. New Zealand concedes, however, that capacity at international law depends on recognition and that the Cook Islands can enter into international obligations only if other party or parties to the proposed obligation are prepared to recognize that the Cook Islands has the necessary attribute of sovereignty to enter into the obligation. Should such recognition not be forthcoming New Zealand has the competence by virtue of the executive authority of Her Majesty the Queen in right of New Zealand—also the Head of State of the Cook Islands— to enter into the obligation on behalf of the Cook Islands. It would nevertheless be necessary for the Cook Islands Parliament to take any legislative action that might be required to implement that obligation.[103]

In other words

> the New Zealand Government cannot proceed to ratification
> or accession without obtaining the views of the Cook Islands
> Government and satisfying itself that the Cook Islands has
> enacted any necessary legislation. The prospect is a
> forbidding one. The need to obtain a decision from the Cook
> Islands (and Niue) Government and to ensure in appropriate
> cases that legislative action has been taken before the New
> Zealand Government itself can take action is likely to lead to
> frustrating delays.[104]

By the late eighties it was apparent that the Cook Island government was capable of pursuing a foreign policy in direct contradiction of New Zealand's. The former Prime Minister of New Zealand, David Lange remarked in April 1990 on the "extraordinary situation . . . where President Bush has seen Cook Island's Prime Minister Geoffrey Henry in Washington but will not see the Prime Minister of New Zealand." [105]

This was the corner into which the American negotiators were painting themselves at the end of the Carter administration in Micronesia. The main virtues of the freely associated state status to the Americans was the fact that it obviated accession to full sovereignty by the territories (at which point they might become independent-minded as well) and left the United States in effective control of the territories without continuing United Nations supervision. But the American negotiators failed to notice that the Cook Islands/New Zealand relationship evolved in the direction of loose principles of continuing cooperation rather than tight control by the former colonial power. Every difference of opinion in the seventies was resolved in favor of loosening the degree of New Zealand control of the situation (culminating in diametrically opposite responses by the two governments to the issue of United States nuclear vessels in the early eighties.) Yet the United States persisted in seeing freely associated statehood status as the best option for controlling the Micronesian entities and was prepared to go to considerable lengths to achieve it.

Notes

[1] "On the Trust Territory of the Pacific Islands," *Decolonization* (United Nations, April 1980): 4.

[2] *Decolonization.*, 7.

[3] *Pacific Islands Yearbook*, 1942, 95 quoted in Roger W. Gale, *The Americanization of Micronesia: A Study of the Consolidation of U.S. Rule in the Pacific* (University Press of America, 1979), 37.

[4] Office of Chief of Naval Operations, 1957, 3 volumes; hereafter cited as *U.S. Naval Administration.*

[5] *U.S. Naval Administration*, I, 101. For the Japanese period, see also P. Clyde, *Japan's Pacific Mandate*, 1935 (reissued by Kennikat Press 1967); Ramon H. Myers and Mark R. Peattie, *The Japanese Colonial Empire, 1895-1945* (republished 1987); and Tadao Yanihara, *Pacific Islands Under Japanese Mandate*, (Oxford Unversity Press, 1940). Also Dirk Anthony Ballendorf, "Secrets Without Substance: U.S. Intelligence in the Japanese Mandates, 1915-1935," *Journal of Pacific History*, 19 (April 1984).

[6] (New York, 1948), 144. Quoted in *U.S. Naval Administration*, I, 120.

[7] *U.S. Naval Administration*, 329. See also Douglas L. Oliver (ed.), *Planning Micronesia's Future: A Summary of the United States Commercial Company's Economic Survey of Micronesia* (University Press of Hawaii, 1951). Facsimile edition, Harvard University Press, 1971.

[8] *U.S. Naval Administration*, II, 26.

[9] *U.S. Naval Administration*, II, 305.

[10] *U.S. Naval Administration*, II, 305.

[11] Quoted in James N, Murray. Jr., *The United Nations Trusteeship System* (University of Illinois Press, 1957), 29.

[12] *United Nations Trusteeship System.*

[13] James V. Forrestal, *The Forrestal Diaries*, 33; quoted in *U.S. Naval Administration*, II, 63.

[14] *Forrestal Diaries*, 44; quoted in *U.S. Naval Administration*, II, 65.

[15] *U.S. Naval Administration*, II, 132.

[16] *U.S. Naval Administration*, II, 344.

[17] *U.S. Naval Administration*, II, 60.

[18] CNO Military Government *Bulletin* (April 16, 1945); quoted in *U.S. Naval Administration*, II, 65-67.

[19] *U.S. Naval Administration*, III, 657.

[20] *U.S. Naval Administration*, III, 780.

[21] *U.S. Naval Administration*, III, 836.

[22] *U.S. Naval Administration*, III, 507. The following 63 pages provide a very useful account of the relocation programs for the earliest atomic tests. Their effects on the displaced people over the next two decades is comprehensively reported in Robert C. Kiste, *Kili Island: A Study of the Relocation of the Ex-Bikini Marshallese* (University of Oregon, 1968); *The Bikininians: A Study in Forced Migration* (Cummings Publishing Co., 1974); and "The Relocation of the Bikini Marshallese" in Michael Lieber (ed.), *Exiles and Migrants in Oceania* (University Press of Hawaii *ASAO Monograph* no.5, 1977). See also Jack Adair Tobin, "The Resettlement of the Enewetak People: A Study of a Displaced Community in the Marshall Islands," Ph.D. diss. (Berkeley: University of California, 1967).

[23] *U.S. Naval Administration*, III, 505.

[24] *U.S. Naval Administration*. III, 417.

[25] *U.S. Naval Administration*, III, 3.

[26] Address to Institute of Ethnic Affairs and the Insitute of Pacific Relations, Washington, May 29, 1946; quoted in *U.S. Naval Administration.*, III, 19.

[27] *U.S. Naval Administration*, III, 20.

[28] *Forrestal Diaries*, 215; quoted in *U.S. Naval Administration*, III, 23.

[29] R.N Chowdhuri, *International Mandates and Trusteeship Systems; A Comparative Study* (The Hague: Martinus Nijhoff, 1955), 97; hereafter cited as *International Mandates*.

[30] Article 13 of Trusteeship Agreement for the United States Trust Territory of the Pacific Islands.

[31] Trusteeship Agreement, Article 6.

[32] *International Mandates*, 122.

[33] *International Mandates*, 164-65.

[34] *International Mandates*, 210.

[35] *International Mandates*, 275.

[36] *International Mandates*, 280.

[37] Carl Heine, "Micronesia: Unification and the Coming of Self-Government," in Marion W. Ward, (ed) *The Politics of Melanesia* [Fourth Waigani Seminar] (University of Papua New Guinea, 1970), 197; hereafter cited as "Micronesia Unification."

[38] Daniel T. Hughes. "Democracy in a Traditional Society: An Analysis of Socio-Political Development on Ponape, Eastern Caroline Islands," National Health Service, Fell. I-FL-MH-25 (National Institute of Mental Health, 1968), 38.

[39] "Democracy in a Traditional Society," 122.

[40] Donald McHenry, *Micronesia: Trust Betrayed* (Carnegie Endowment for International Peace, 1975) 14; hereafter cited as *Trust Betrayed*.

[41] Norman Meller, *The Congress of Micronesia: Development of the Legislative Process in the Trust Territory of the Pacific Islands* (University of Hawaii Press, 1969), 281-82.

[42] Statement of Interest of Future Political Status Commission, Congress of Micronesia, 1969.

[43] "Micronesia Unification," 202.

[44] Reprinted in "Micronesia Unification," 46.

[45] *Trust Betrayed*, 103.

[46] *Trust Betrayed*, 105, Chapter V discusses the negotiations and Appendix II has a summary of the issues discussed. For indications of Micronesian attitudes at this time, see *Micronesian Reporter* 19 (1971), especially article by Bonifacio Basilius on "Congress '71." See also John A. Worthley, "Legislatures and Political Development: The Congress of Micronesia," *Western Political Quarterly* 26 (December 1973): 675-85.

[47] Harold F. Nufer, *Micronesia Under American Rule: An Evaluation of the Strategic Trusteeship 1947-1977* (New York: Exposition Press, 1978); discussion of this process in terms of compliance with Article 6 of the Trusteeship Agreement.

[48] "Micronesia Unification," 33.

[49] Micronesian social disequilibrium is extensively discussed in Catherine Lutz (ed.), *Micronesia as Strategic Colony* (Cambridge, Mass.: Cultural Survival, 1984) and in passing in *Micronesia Under American Rule*.

[50] "Micronesia Unification," 33.

[51] D. Michael Green, "Termination of United States Pacific Islands Trusteeship," *Texas International Law Journal* 9 (1974): 186.

[52] *Trust Betrayed*, 136. Chinese Nationalists were trained on Saipan to infiltrate mainland China in the 1950s.

[53] See, for example, D. Michael Green, "America's Strategic Trusteeship Dilemma: Its Humanitarian Obligations," *Texas International Law Journal* 9/1 (Winter, 1974) and "Termination of the U.S. Pacific Islands Trusteeship," *Texas International Law Journal* 9/2 (1974); Guy Dempsey, Note, "Self-Determination and Security in the Pacific: A Study on the Covenant Between the United States and the Northern Mariana Islands," *New York University Journal of International Law* 9/2 (1976); James A. Branch, "The Constitution of the Northern Marianas: Does a Different Cultural Setting Justify Different Constitutional Standards?," *Denver Journal of International Law and Policy* 9/1 (Winter 1980) and Peter Bergsman, "The Marianas, the United States and the United Nations: the Uncertain Status of the New American Commonwealth," *California Western International Law Journal* 6 (1976). It should be noted that all these commentators assumed that final action on termination of the Strategic Trust would rest with the Security Council rather than the Trusteeship Council.

[54] Fred M. Zeder, Interview in *Micronesia Reporter* (Fourth Quarter, 1975): 6.

[55] Norman Meller, *Constitutionalism in Micronesia* (Honolulu: Brigham Young University, Institute for Polynesian Studies, 1985), 77; hereafter cited as *Constitutionalism*.

[56] *Constitutionalism*, 55.

[57] *Constitutionalism*, 341.

[58] *Constitutionalism*, 319.

[59] Bob Woodward, *Washington Post* (December 12, 1976). See also Mike Malone, "The CIA in Micronesia," *Glimpses Magazine* [Guam] (First Quarter, 1977): 28-30.

[60] Roger S. Clark, "Self-Determination and Free Association—Should the United Nations Terminate the Pacific Islands Trust?," *Harvard International Law Journal* 21/1 (Winter 1980): 67.

[61] Clark, "Self-Determination," 75.

[62] Clark, "Self-Determination," 12-13.

[63] A. John Armstrong, "The Emergence of the Micronesians Into the International Community: A Study of the Creation of a New International Entity," *Brooklyn Journal of International Law* 5 (1979): 242; hereafter cited as "Emergence of the Micronesians."

[64] "Emergence of the Micronesians," 249.

[65] "Emergence of the Micronesians," 256.

[66] "Emergence of the Micronesians, 256."

[67] *Decolonization*, 14.

[68] *Decolonization*, 22.

[69] Arthur John Armstrong, "The Negotiations for the Future Political Status of Micronesia," *American Journal of International Law* 74 (1980): 691.

[70] See note 69.

[71] Peter R. Rosenblatt, "Introduction," *Brooklyn Journal of International Law* VII/2 (Summer 1981).

72 See Rosenblatt, "Introduction."

[73] Arthur John Armstrong, "Strategic Underpinnings of the Legal Regime of Free Association: The Negotiations for the Future Political Status of Micronesia," *Brooklyn Journal of International Law* VII/2 (Summer 1981): 183; hereafter cited as "Strategic Underpinnings."

[74] "Strategic Underpinnings," 185-86

[75] "Strategic Underpinnings," 190.

[76] "Strategic Underpinnings," 194.

[77] "Strategic Underpinnings," 195

[78] "Strategic Underpinnings," 196.

[79] "Strategic Underpinnings," 197.

[80] "Strategic Underpinnings," 200.

[81] "Strategic Underpinnings," 201 and footnote 47.

[82] "Strategic Underpinnings," 231.

[83] J.Ross Macdonald, "Termination of the Strategic Trusteeship: Free Association, the United Nations and International Law," *Brooklyn Journal of International Law* VII/2 (Summer 1981): 236; hereafter cited as "Termination."

[84] "Termination," 247.

[85] "Termination," 248.

[86] "Termination," 248.

[87] "Termination," 248.

[88] The text of the 1980 Compact of Free Association is published in the *Brooklyn Journal of International Law* VII/2 (Summer 1981).

[89] "Termination," 275.

[90] "Termination," 269.

[91] *Trust Betrayed*, 49.

[92] *Trust Betrayed*, 49.

[93] *Trust Betrayed*, 49.

[94] *Trust Betrayed*, 50.

[95] "Termination," 263.

[96] "Termination," 265.

[97] "Termination," 266.

[98] "Termination," 281.

[99] See Clark, "Self-Determination."

[100] *Decolonization*, 43.

[101] *Decolonization*, 45.

[102] This basic position was restated in 1979 in the New Zealand Ministry of Foreign Affairs Statement to Lome Council Secretariat, reprinted in Roger S. Clark and Albert P. Blaustein, *New Zealand and Associated States, Cook Islands Constitutions of Dependencies and Special Sovereignties* (New York: Oceana, 1985), 109-10.

[103] C.C. Aikman "Constitutional Developments in the Cook Islands," in P. Sack (ed.) *Pacific Constitutions: Proceedings of the Canberra Workshop, School of Advanced Legal Studies* (Australian National University, 1982).

[104] See *Pacific Constitutions*.

[105] *Washington Pacific Report 6: 21 (May 1, 1990): 4.*

Chapter Three

The First Three Plebiscites

In the *Brooklyn Journal of International Law* Arthur Armstrong, a Carter administration official of the Office of Micronesian Status Negotiations, warned the incoming Reagan administration officials that

> the constitutions of the freely associated states must be compatible with the Compact to the extent that there is no *de jure* proscription on their negotiators' authority to agree to the elements of free association [1]

yet the United States must

> secure a sufficient degree of *de facto* 'sovereignty' in the freely associated states to be able to exercise plenary security and defense authority and responsibility in the area for at least fifteen years.[2]

It soon became apparent that the pre-condition for this strategy— that the people of the territory should not become too independent-minded—was no longer present by the time President Reagan assumed office in January 1981. The problem was to become most severe in Palau—not least because Palau's harbors and large island of Babelthaup were high on the Pentagon's list of desirable fall-back base sites.

The Palau District Legislature, having rejected the constitution of the Federated States of Micronesia in July 1978, established a Constitutional Convention which in April 1979 adopted a proposed constitution for the Republic of Palau.[3] As well as declaring a 200-mile maritime zone, the constitution banned the testing or storage of nuclear substances in the territory and placed restrictions on military use of the 7.8 million square kilometer zone defined by its maritime sovereignty. The nuclear-ban provisions of the Palauan constitution could only be amended by a 75 percent majority of the electorate voting in a referendum called specifically for that purpose rather than on an intergovernmental agreement, as provided in the constitution of the Federated States of Micronesia.[4]

The United States administering authority vigorously opposed this Palauan constitution. According to the United Nations

> In June 1979, reportedly owing to United States pressure, the Palau District Legislature, at a meeting which was boycotted by 10 members supporting the draft Constitution, passed a bill nullifying the proposed Constitution and cancelling a plebiscite scheduled for July. However, due to the fact that a lawsuit was subsequently filed in the High Court of the Trust Territory by pro-Constitution forces challenging the legality of the bill, the High Commissioner of the Trust Territory did not at that time act on the measure, which had been submitted to him for approval. Instead, he allowed the referendum to be held on 9 July 1979, under the observation of a United Nations Visiting Mission with the result that the Constitution of the Republic of Palau was approved by 92 percent of the votes cast. In August 1979, however, the legislature's action abrogating the proposed Constitution was upheld by the High Court of the Trust Territory and the High Commissioner refused to certify the results of the July referendum approving the Constitution. Thereafter, the legislature, still meeting without a quorum, established a new Constitutional Drafting Commission which revised the draft Constitution so as to comply with the U.S. objections. Submitted to the people in a referendum 23 October 1979, the revised Constitution was rejected by 70 percent of the voters.[5]

In July 1980 the Palauan people in their third constitutional referendum overwhelmingly supported the original constitution and thus became the world's first potential nuclear-free state (see Appendix H.)

The attitude of President Carter's negotiators to this Palauan constitution was summed up by Arthur Armstrong in the *American Journal of International Law* in 1980:

> Approval of the Compact by Palau is complicated by the United States policy not to enter into free association with a government whose prospective constitution is inconsistent with international law and with the negotiated concept of free association. Specifically, the Palauan constitution includes a

claim of sovereignty and jurisdiction over adjacent seas incompatible both with the concepts being developed at the United Nations Conference on the Law of the Sea and with United States global foreign policy and security objectives. Also included in the draft Constitution are provisions that would have the effect of limiting the ability of the United States to perform its defense functions under free association. Third, the draft Constitution would restrict the ability of the Government of Palau to acquire land for other than local purposes.[6]

The United States High Commissioner for the Trust Territory of the Pacific Islands had not vetoed this constitution. While strictly speaking he might have been technically able to do so, such action would clearly have created alarm that the administering authority was obstructing the free expression of the peoples' wishes in the process towards sufficient self-government to be able to commit themselves to the Compact of Free Association. Instead, the United States attitude as to whose responsibility it was to resolve the dilemma was made clear from the outset by Armstrong in a formulation that has been repeatedly used by subsequent negotiators:

> The success the new Palauan leadership achieves in reconciling these constitutional issues with the Compact of Free Association will determine whether the free association relationship will extend to Palau upon termination of the Trusteeship Agreement.[7]

In his subsequent 1981 article in the *Brooklyn Journal of International Law* Armstrong elaborated this American view of the locus of responsibility for resolving the incompatibility of the expressed wishes of the people of the Palauan part of the Trust Territory and the administering authority. He quoted Ambassador Rosenblatt's statement before the Palau Legislature on April 30, 1979 in which he said:

> It is not my role or right to do more than to point out to you that, in the view of the United States Government, a problem exists; a problem of such magnitude that it threatens the foundations of the free association relationship it has been my privilege to negotiate with your representatives this past year and a half. What steps, if any, should be taken to solve

the problem are for Palauans, not Americans, to decide. We await your decision with interest and concern.[8]

Armstrong then wrote in 1981 that

> These issues with Palau and a number of similar ones involving the Federated States of Micronesia were finally reconciled by means of a series of subsidiary agreements. These agreements utilize provisions of the constitutions of Palau and the Federated States of Micronesia under which major powers of government may be delegated to the United States, or other constitutional provisions may be rendered inoperative, without derogating from the concept of sovereignty and the supremacy of the freely associated states' respective constitutions.[9]

Armstrong was thus arguing the supremacy of the Compact over the constitution of Palau or the other entities; yet he and the other United States negotiators were relying on the argument that the peoples of Micronesia would be allowed to enter into a unique and anomalous future political status by the international community because they had had ample opportunity to express their wishes freely in the process of evolution of a form of self-government that could commit itself to such an inequitable arrangement as proposed in the Compact of Free Association. He negotiated subsidiary agreements which in several aspects embodied the heart of the relationship and the most extreme elements of the derogation and alienation of such sovereignty as the Micronesian entities possessed. For example,

> All four governments have agreed in principle to the concept of long-term denial, and have further agreed that the most appropriate place for the expression of its duration is the bilateral military use and operating rights which each of the freely associated states is to enter into with the United States pursuant to Section 321 of the Compact. The precise formulation of the provision is still under negotiation with the Marshall Islands and the Federated States of Micronesia but has already been agreed in the Use and Operating Rights Agreement which the United States and Palau initialed on November 17, 1980. The relevant language states that section 311(b)—which affords the United States the option to foreclose access to or use of Palau for the military purposes

of any third country—shall remain in effect for a fifty year term.[10]

The subsidiary agreements were in many respects substantive amendments of the Compact of Free Association, not least in having elements that would survive any termination of the Compact itself. Thus it was highly misleading for a senior United States negotiator to write, as Arthur Armstrong did in 1981, that the free association concept being proposed for Micronesia

> requires either a unilateral act of termination by one of the signatories or the mutual agreement of the United States and one of the Micronesian parties, in which case termination is effected bilaterally

since the substantive subsidiary agreements had specific terms which could not be abbreviated by the Micronesian entities.

One reason that so much of substance had been placed in the subsidiary agreements (which the United States may have hoped could have been signed by the Micronesian executives without reference to referenda) was that the Micronesians had won a major victory on the issue of most critical concern to them, the disposition of nuclear weapons and substances in their territory. Roger S. Clark reports that the January 1979 Draft of the Compact of Free Association contained as Section 314 (b) the following broad statement:

> The Governments of [Micronesia] recognize that it is the policy of the Government of the United States neither to confirm nor to deny the presence of nuclear weapons in its installations, ships or aircraft, and agree that this policy will apply to [Micronesia].[11]

A year later, however, subsection (b) required the consent of Micronesians for the storage of toxic or radioactive weapons for weapons use, "amounting to a clear concession by the United States."[12]

The ball was now in the court of the Reagan administration negotiators, one of whom, Howard Hills, wrote a survey article entitled "Micronesia—Our Sacred Trust What Went Wrong?" in 1980 after spending the Carter years as a Peace Corps volunteer assigned as staff attorney in the Office of Legislative Counsel of the Congress of Micronesia and as Legislative Counsel to the Kosrae State Legislature.

Hills subsequently was employed as Assistant Legislative Counsel to the House of Representatives of the Legislature of the Commonwealth of the Mariana Islands. Hills maintained that

> It is now beyond debate that the development of the public sector and government operations in the Trust Territory has not been properly balanced with economic development. Economic resources—and consequently political power—have been concentrated in public officials and bureaucrats to such an extent that the latter are now a ruling elite without that degree of accountability to the people which is essential to representative democracy. There is also a growing recognition that it may not have been entirely humane to establish government services based on technology and operational methods that are far too costly and sophisticated for Micronesians to maintain without American assistance.[13]

Hills emphasized that the budget for the Trust Territory had always been submitted to Congress through the High Commissioner's office with the Congress of Micronesia having only the theoretical right of review and recommendation "but where these deviated from the priorities of the High Commissioner, the Department of Territorial Affairs, or the Department of the Interior, they were generally ignored."[14]

Hills maintained that the movement for self-government gained momentum much sooner than the United States had expected in the mid-1970s, and the American negotiators had been "delighted with the collapse of the Micronesians' unanimity regarding their future political status."[15] However, the Hilo Principles of April 1978 represented a "major modification" of the United States position on future political status because

> For the first time, the United States agreed to recognize the sovereignty of the Micronesian governments as long as an agreement on military rights could be reached.[16]

In Hills' interpretation,

> The basic concept of the compact that has evolved is that the United States will provide a specified amount of economic aid to the three Micronesian governments in exchange for

military control over, but not necessarily military bases, in their territory.[17]

At the end of his Peace Corps service, Hills was severely critical of the

> fuel-intensive, technology-intensive, expert-intensive, administrative services-intensive, and maintenance-intensive systems complex throughout the islands that cannot be operated by an independent Micronesia for the rest of this century[18]

that resulted in land-based rather than marine-based economic activity in which real production in Micronesia in the first half of the decade was at a rate of only one percent after government expenditures which accounted for the salaries of 62 percent of all workers in the cash economy were considered.[19]

In the last months of the Carter administration the January 1980 version of the Compact of Free Association and its subsidiary agreements were revised with clarifications concerning claims against the United States stemming from the trusteeship period, continued United States grant obligations (in which the United States pledged its 'full faith and credit' to honor the terms agreed upon) and the extent of marine sovereignty of the emerging entities which were limited to "generally accepted international law" that was being codified by the conferences on the Law of the Sea.

In his analysis of these revisions, Roger S. Clark noted that whereas the January 1980 version of Section 411 of the Compact had provided that it would come into effect "coincident with the termination of the Trusteeship Agreement and subsequent to completion of" approval by the governments of the three entities following a simultaneous plebiscite in each of the entities and approval by the government of the United States in accordance with its constitutional processes, the new Section 411 provided for the Compact to come into effect "upon mutual agreement between the Government of the United States, acting in fulfillment of its responsibilities as Administering Authority of the Trust Territory of the Pacific Islands, and the Government of Palau, the Marshall Islands or the Federated States of Micronesia." Professor Clark felt that

> The plain purpose of this language is to deal with the possibility that termination of the trusteeship will not be

approved by the United Nations Security Council, the body with appropriate jurisdiction in the case of this, the only strategic trust. The language in Section 411 permits the parties, as between themselves, to ignore United Nations procedures and to bring the whole arrangement into effect without the United Nations' blessing. Such an action would not be determinative as to the legality of termination under international law but in the long run probably the only sanction open to a concerned United Nations body would be to try to encourage states to withhold recognition from the new entities.[20]

The Marshall Islands and the Federated States initialled this new draft Compact on October 31, 1980 and the Palauan executive initialled it on November 17, 1980. In addition, the Federated States initialled a subsidiary agreement Regarding Aspects of the Marine Sovereignty and Jurisdiction of the Federated States of Micronesia and a Memorandum of Understanding with Respect to Meanings of Terms and Expressions used in Section 314 of the Compact of Free Association. Palau initialled three subsidiary agreements, regarding the Jurisdiction and Sovereignty of the Republic of Palau over its Territory and the Living and Non-Living Resources of the Sea; Radioactive, Chemical and Biological Substances and the Military Use and Operating Rights of the Government of the United States in Palau Concluded Pursuant to Sections 321 and 323 of the Compact of Free Association. The Marshall Islands had not initialled any subsidiary agreements before the end of the Carter administration.

The Reagan administration began a review of the proposed Compact and its subsidiary agreements as soon as the new president was inaugurated and a new staff (including Howard Hills) had taken over the Office of Micronesian Status Negotiations. At the same time, the Micronesian people had an opportunity to study the terms that its various executives were recommending to them as the basis for the act of self-determination that would determine their future political status. As Ambassador Rosenblatt had emphasized in 1981, upon leaving office, the Compact represented a "carefully constructed compromise" among agencies of the United States government, particularly Defense, State and Interior, which had become as early as 1980 "substantially non-negotiable" from the American point of view. If anything, the advent of the Reagan administration only strengthened Defense's resistance to any further accommodation of the wishes of the

Micronesians that might be supported in principle by State (with an eye to the international perception that would have to be dealt with in the United Nations) or Interior (which was well aware that it had not fulfilled the requirements of Article 6 of the Trusteeship Agreement requiring the administering authority to promote the economic self-sufficiency of the Micronesian communities.)

However, the various Micronesian executives found themselves under severe pressure and criticism for several aspects of the agreements, and if they were to survive as the legitimate negotiators for the Micronesian people their needs would have to be met in some measure by the Washington negotiators. And this process of accommodation would have to proceed at the same time as the United States Ambassador to the United Nations and her staff prepared the way for United Nations acceptance of the deals that had been so long in the crafting. Whereas Donald McHenry, erstwhile critic of the United States role in Micronesia, had been extraordinarily lucky in not having to handle the issue of termination during his tenure as Carter's second Ambassador to the United Nations, Reagan's Mission to the United Nations under Jeane Kirkpatrick would have to bear the brunt of international criticism of a unique form of "free association" which was distinguished from that enjoyed by Cook and Niue because "there is no limit in those arrangements of any kind of denial or a continuing military relationship after termination,"[21] provisions essential to the Department of Defense's agreement to the United States proposals for the future political status of Micronesia.

It took almost two years for the Marshall Islands electorate to accept the Compact of Free Association which was affirmed by 58 percent of those voting in a plebiscite on September 7, 1982. B. David Williams, Associate Director for Peace Issues of the National Council of Churches of Christ, USA and previously Coordinator of the Church and Society Program of the Pacific Conference of Churches, participated in the World Council of Churches mission to Micronesia in May and June 1983. He noted that opposition to the Compact was not necessarily from pro-independence groups but came at least as frequently from individuals wanting an even closer association with the United States, perhaps even Commonwealth status.

Williams noted that concern focussed on the following provisions of the Marshall Islands Compact: Section 161 which exempted the United States from any environmental standard or procedure if it is in the interests of the United States to ignore such procedures; Section 163a which restricted Government of the Marshall Islands access to United States facilities; Section 177 which relieved the United States of any further responsibility for damage to land or health from the nuclear testing program to the amount of assistance specified in the Compact which were to be held as the legal settlement of any and all claims arising out of past or future damages;[22] Section 313 which gave the United States veto power over any activity or action of the Government of the Marshall Islands including business agreements or treaties with foreign governments; and Sections 453 and 454 which appeared to extend military use by the United States beyond the fifteen years originally envisaged.[23]

Although a majority of the Marshallese voters had accepted the Compact even with these deficiencies, there were strong pockets of resistance, including the landowners of Kwajalein who were unhappy with both the terms of payment for the land alienated from them for the weapons testing base and with the fact that it was to be paid not to the individual landowners directly by the United States government but to the Government of the Marshall Islands which did not necessarily intend to pass the payments along to the affected landowners. The people of Bikini, Rongelap and Kwajalein became regular petitioners at the annual meetings of the Trusteeship Council as they tried to renegotiate the settlements by presenting their case at the United Nations. This did not necessarily mean that they opposed termination of the trusteeship; in the case of the Bikini people, for example, once they had received judgement from a United States court in principle in their favor, they became anxious to see the Compact passed so that the payments would begin to flow, even though they were dissatisfied that the same compact would stop future claims at a time when no comprehensive health survey had been carried out of their community to assess radiation-related damage to present and future generations.[24]

The Palauan negotiators initialled the first 'Reagan version' of the Compact on August 26, 1982. It therefore was ready to present to the Palauan people. It would however require not a simple majority to pass but 75 percent of the voters in a referendum on the specific issues of the amendments required in the Palauan constitution to make it compatible with the Compact and its subsidiary agreements (since it was the stated United States position that it was the constitution which would have to conform with the Compact rather than *vice versa*.) According to Patrick M. Smith, Legal Counsel to Ibedul Y. M. Gibbons, Traditional Paramount Leader of the Republic of Palau

> Since the Compact would allow the United States to introduce nuclear weapons to Palau for purposes of defense, Article II, Section III of the Palauan Constitution required that it be approved by 75 percent of the voters voting in referendum. This Constitutional requirement was clearly acknowledged by all officials of the United States and Palauan Governments prior to the February 10, 1983 referendum and plebiscite on the Compact.[25]

The First Palauan Plebiscite, January/February 1983

The first attempt to hold the plebiscite and referendum came to grief because

> It was established in a Court case in late January 1983 that the United States had improperly specified the ballot language to be used. The Court invalidated the ballot language demanded by the United States holding that it violated Palauan law and was drafted to be misleading and confusing to the voter.[26]

Sixteen thousand ballots were printed for 7,200 voters; the Interior Department provided $315,000 in direct grants to the Palau government for the political education campaign of the 7,200 voters over and above the $250,000 appropriated by the Palau National Congress.

The ballot question was in two parts. Proposition One (A) asked "Do you approve of Free Association as set forth in the Compact of Free Association?" Proposition One (B) stated: "Before the Compact can take effect Section 314 under question (B) below must also be approved by at least seventy-five percent (75 percent) of the votes cast. (B) Do you approve the agreement under Section 314 of the Compact which places restrictions and conditions on the United States with respect to radioactive, chemical and biological materials?"

On January 23, 1983 a lawsuit was filed by Micronesians challenging the wording of the ballot on the grounds that Question One (B) was misleading because in fact the Palau constitution totally bans the materials listed while Section 314 of the Compact actually liberalizes the prohibitions in the constitution and would give the United States permission to do things that are prohibited by the constitution. The plaintiffs established that this wording for the ballot came from the administering authority itself rather than the Palau legislature, in a cable dated November 11, 1982 from Ambassador Zeder to Palauan Ambassador Salii, who testified in court that the United States had insisted that this language must be used.

In his judgement in the Supreme Court of Palau in *Koshiba et al v. Remeliik et al* (Civil Action No. 17-83), Associate Justice Robert A. Hefner found on January 31, 1983 that the English version of the ballot did not comply with the relevant Palauan legislation authorizing the plebiscite and the Palauan translation of Proposition One (B) was "inaccurate and inconsistent so that it misleads and confuses the voters who must rely upon the wording to cast their vote. . . . This court finds that the plaintiffs will be irreparably harmed by being denied their constitutional right to vote if the ballot language were to remain as set forth by the defendants. . . . Since the court finds that the language of the ballot will not allow a free and impartial vote, the court is compelled to enjoin the defendants from carrying out the referendum and plebiscite with the tainted language of the present ballot." Judge Hefner found

> no basis whatsoever for the proposition that the United States can dictate the wording of the ballot . . . the Preamble and Sections 411 and 412 of the Compact as well as the Constitution of the Republic of Palau and Republic of Palau Law No. 1-43 leads to the conclusion that this is a matter to be left to the constitutional and democratic processes of the Republic of Palau. The one possible exception is Department of Interior Secretarial Order No. 3039 which states that after a law is signed by the President of Palau, the High Commissioner of the Trust Territory of the Pacific Islands has 20 days to veto or suspend the legislation. This was not done and the veto period has long expired.

Judge Hefner was quite convinced in January 1983 that the proposition (B) of the ballot question bound proposition (A), and that it required at least 75 percent to pass. Clearly in this first formulation, the ballot language, dictated by Ambassador Zeder, explicitly linked the success of Proposition (A)—passage of the Compact—with the success of Proposition (B)—which was designed to amend the Palauan constitution to bring it into conformity with the Compact. It should be noted that amendment or override of the Palauan constitution requires 75 percent of the votes cast in a referendum brought on the specific issue of amendment.

On February 10, 1983 the people of Palau were presented with a different wording of the Propositions. Question I (A) asked as before "Do you approve of Free Association as set forth in the Compact of Free Association?" Question I (B) said without any preambular reference to its requiring a 75 percent affirmation or being linked to Question I (A) except as implied by the numbering, "Do you approve of the Agreement concerning radioactive, chemical and biological materials concluded pursuant to Section 314 of the Compact of Free Association?" Sixty-two percent of the voters supported A and fifty-two percent supported B. A week later a Department of State press release declared "Palau Approves Free Association with the United States. Final unofficial results from the February 10, 1983 plebiscite in Palau represent a strong victory for the Compact of Free Association. In the yes-or-no vote, Palauans awarded the Compact of Free Association a mandate of better than 62 percent." The State Department version continued,

> The United States recognizes that the plebiscite is a valid and sovereign act of self-determination by the people of Palau. The Compact they approved defines their relationship with the United States, as well as their international political status after the present trusteeship is terminated.

The Palauans were asked other questions on the ballot, including the political status they would prefer if free association were not approved. Slightly more than half the voters chose to answer this question, which was optional, 56 percent of them voting in favor of a relationship with the United States closer than free association, and 44 percent voting in favor of independence. The 2,250 people supporting a relationship closer than free association were 31 percent of the turnout; the 1,850 people voting in favor of independence were 25 percent of the turnout. The total voter turnout on February 10, 1983 was 7,246.[27]

The Department of State interpretation of the fate of Question (B) was to suggest that

> The ballot included an internal referendum question which asked the voters to approve a Palauan-American agreement relating to hazardous, including nuclear, substances. A majority—53 percent—voted to approve this agreement. However, because of provisions in the Palau constitution, this, or a similar specific question, requires approval by a 75 percent margin before the Compact of Free Association can come into effect. This means that the Palauan authorities must now devise an acceptable method of reconciling their constitutional provisions to comply with the mandate of the Palauan electorate for free association with the United States.

The administering authority continued to insist on the superiority of the Compact over the constitution, whilst refusing to acknowledge that part B of the ballot bound Part A in what it variously described as a plebiscite and a referendum. On April 25, 1983 President Haruo Remeliik of Palau declared that the Compact had been duly approved and that he was appointing a task force to implement it. Within days the Traditional Paramount Leader of the Republic of Palau, the Ibedul Gibbons and six senators of the *Olbiil Era Kelualu* filed suit in the Supreme Court of Palau seeking a declaratory judgement that the Compact had been disapproved in its entirety by the people of Palau on February 10 together with declaratory and personal judgements against the defendants—the President, Vice President, the Ambassador for Status Negotiations and the Minister of Administration—for misappropriation of the education campaign monies.

Despite this filing, the Vice President and the Ambassador of Palau joined the United States Ambassador in announcing that the Compact had been duly approved by the Palauan people to the Trusteeship Council in May. Then in July the United States and Palau initialled a treaty that substantially modified the Compact, in the hope of rendering moot the lawsuit. The Ibedul led a campaign in the Palauan Senate to adopt a resolution to reject the initialled treaty. His chief legal adviser Patrick M. Smith, filed for summary judgement on the issues of the suit on July 24. Two days later Smith's boat was burned to the water. The oral argument was heard on August 4, and Judge Robert Hefner of the Supreme Court of Palau rendered his second judgement for the year relating to the plebiscite and referendum.

Judge Hefner found unequivocally that "the Compact of Free Association and its integral and subsidiary parts that include the Harmful Substances Agreement, were disapproved by the people of the Republic of Palau in the February 10, 1983 referendum and plebiscite."[28] Judge Hefner rejected the 'severability' argument of the plaintiffs relating to the two parts of Proposition One as resting on "meaningless semantic differences" adduced between the words "approve" and "take effect." He also gave extensive evidence that in the earlier case the same parties that were now arguing the severability of the parts A and B had recognized "that the voting on the Compact was to be an all or nothing proposition" in the documents before the Court in its January decision, and that January decision had affirmed that understanding.

The administering authority was exceedingly frustrated by this decision of the Supreme Court of Palau. Ambassador Zeder interpreted the outcome as follows in a cable to his Palauan counterpart, Lazarus Salii:

> 3. Question A on the ballot consisted of a plebiscite on the overall political status question seeking approval or disapproval of the status of free association, and expressly indicated that a simple majority was required for approval. Question B was an internal referendum appended to the plebiscite ballot, needed, in Palau's view, for internal, domestic legal ratification and eventual implementation of the Compact. We consider that the court's decision purports to interpret the effect of the internal referendum results (Question B) upon the plebiscite results (Question A), when the two are considered together, completely without regard to the separate statement on each question concerning the majority required.

> 4. United States obligations as the administering authority under both the UN Charter and the Trusteeship Agreement require that the right of self-determination of the Palauan people be assured, for which purpose an opportunity had been provided to the Palauans to exercise that right in the plebiscite. When such a plebiscite that has been freely and fairly conducted yields a reasonably strong, unequivocal majority vote indicating a preference for the negotiated political status, the right of self-determination can be deemed satisfied in accordance with the general international practice concerning such plebiscites. Accordingly, in this international context, the strong majority

plebiscite results suffice for approval of the Compact. . . . We therefore take the position that the decision does not establish the approval criteria applicable to the plebiscite, which was set out, in accordance with generally accepted practice, in the ballot and in Compact section 412.

5. In view of the above, the United States Government maintains, as it has since the February 10 plebiscite, that the people of Palau have approved the Compact of Free Association and its related agreements. We believe that the United States as administering authority, has discharged the above-mentioned obligation to afford the people of Palau the opportunity freely to choose self-government or independence. A United Nations visiting mission has attested to the validity of the plebiscite as an act of self-determination.

The United States maintained that the 62 percent support for the first part of the proposition on the ballot constituted the act of self-determination of the Palauan people even though the Compact overrode the basic instrument of self-government, the constitution of Palau.

The United States then argued that the second part of the ballot was an internal referendum to amend the constitution to bring it into conformity with the Compact and subsidiary agreements even though Article 13, Section 6 of the constitution provided for amendment of the relevant parts concerning the use, testing, storage or disposal of harmful substances such as nuclear, chemical, gas, or biological weapons intended for use in warfare, nuclear power plants, and waste materials therefrom in "a referendum submitted on this specific question." Ambassador Zeder went on to argue that

Because Question B of Proposition One was not approved by the requisite 75 percent majority, the Governments of Palau and the United States negotiated an agreement on July 1, 1983, which would delete section 314 from the Compact and rescind the Section 314 subsidiary agreement to which Question B of Proposition One of the ballot had applied. The Parties intended by this agreement to overcome any perceived need, under Palauan law, for a separate referendum approval of those provisions.

The United States perceived this agreement, while needing ratification by the *Olbiil Era Kelulau*,

> would not require a new plebiscite for approval, so long as the principal features of the political status established under the Compact remained intact

although it did acknowledge that there might be need for a domestic referendum to ratify the changes. This is what the administering authority considered to be "Palau's next steps in completion of the compact approval process"—ratification of the July agreements.

The two groups—pro-Compact and anti-Compact—were now agreed that the February 10, 1983 plebiscite was definitive as the act of self-determination of the Palauan people. The problem was that they interpreted it in diametrically opposite ways—the pro-Compact group as Ambassador Zeder outlined, dismissing the failure of Part B to gain 75 percent as a ratification problem to be resolved within Palau if they wanted to seal the Compact of Free Association; the anti-Compact forces assuming that the Supreme Court judgement finding that the failure of Part B caused Part A to fall also meant that the Compact of Free Association had not been accepted by the Palauan people because they did not wish to amend the nuclear-free elements of their constitution.

One aspect of the February 10, 1983 plebiscite was to remain unresolved. Judge Hefner had required the defendants to produce documents relating to the allegations about financial misspending to the Court on August 15. On August 14, 1983 the senior lawyer for the Ibedul in the case, Patrick M. Smith, and his wife were victims of a firebomb attack and left the island within twenty-four hours together with their legal assistant. This left the anti-Compact forces on the island with very limited legal expertise and strength to continue to fight the issue; it also meant that the issue of misappropriation of the education campaign fund was never fully explored and so it was never clearly established if the February 10, 1983 plebiscite had indeed been the "free and fairly conducted" vote that the United Nations would require, or that the promise of the United States Ambassador to the Trusteeship Council that

> the plebiscites in Micronesia are to be organized, conducted
> and run by constitutional elected Micronesian governments,
> not by the United States[29]

had been honored in the Palauan case. The United States, it soon became apparent, did not learn from this experience that it could not tamper with the self-determination process nor place technical legal constructions on the plain language required of a ballot in a plebiscite and expect legal and political acceptance of the outcome, either in Micronesia or in the United Nations.

Despite the fact that the United States officials held that the Compact of Free Association had been approved in February and only required some internal Palauan constitutional adjustments to bring it into effect, it soon became apparent that a wholesale renegotiation would have to be conducted because of the increasing scrutiny of the international community and the anti-Compact forces who pointed out that

> What is referred to as 'an agreement related to the Compact'
> is in fact an amalgam of several sections of the Compact,
> notably sections 311, 312 and 314 and the Agreement
> Regarding Radioactive, Chemical and Biological Substances,
> which modifies those sections in significant ways. The
> sections of the Compact and the Agreement in question do
> not run afoul of 'a provision' of the Constitution, but of two
> separate provisions, Article II, Section 3 and Article XIII,
> Section 6. [30]

The United States officials appeared to be completely insensitive to the dangers of pressuring the Palauans to amend their constitution so extensively that it would no longer seem to be an instrument of self-government sufficient even to legitimate the act of self-determination, much less to constitute sufficient constitutional independence to begin to make claims on sovereignty in its future political status.

Officials of the United States Office for Micronesian Status Negotiations made clear that their security and strategic interests in the islands, not least in Palau, were non-negotiable. Richard Teare, interviewed by James Heddle for the documentary film *Strategic Trust*, released in 1983, said

We are committed to defend those islands as the United States and its people are defended. That provision of their constitution would make it impossible for us to carry out the defense responsibilities which we were otherwise prepared to undertake. Right now under the Trusteeship Agreement, of course, we have the right to establish facilities in Palau. The fact that we haven't done so in the 35 years of the Trusteeship to date doesn't mean that we will never have an interest in doing so . . . Guam is the linchpin of our next line of defence in the western Pacific. Our defense planners believe that the facilities on Guam might have to be complemented by others on Tinian, conceivably in Palau. . . . As you probably know, most of our modern ships are nuclear powered, and particularly those we use for long distances from their home ports on the West Coast or Hawaii. And that means that virtually any ship that we are apt to have operating in Palauan waters for Palau's defense will be nuclear-powered. That ship may have to put into Palauan waters, and, under the Palauan Constitution as written, it couldn't do so.

In the last quarter of 1983 the Federated States of Micronesia approved the Compact of Free Association by 79 percent and the Marshall Islands by 58 percent. But the Palauan Compact was being substantially revised on the basis of not the July agreement but a new draft prepared by the Palauan Legislature, the *Olbiil Era Kalulau*, which proposed increased United States funding and lump sums for capital improvements and investments while at the same time restricting transit of United States military forces through the territorial jurisdiction of Palau "provided they in no way violate the constitution of Palau." Furthermore, this draft made the United States right to land use for military purposes "consistent with the constitution of Palau." Some agreement seemed to be developing in meetings in Honolulu in November but they did not survive scrutiny in Washington, which now spoke increasingly of taking the Compact to the United States Congress for ratification in a piecemeal fashion if necessary in an attempt to indicate to the Palauans that they might get the smallest portion of the appropriations pie if they continued to be laggardly and recalcitrant.

Transmittal of the Incomplete Compact of Free Association to Congress, March 1984

President Reagan transmitted a Draft of a Joint Resolution to Approve the Compact of Free Association for the Federated States of Micronesia and the Republic of the Marshall Islands to the United States Congress on March 30, 1984. All references to the Republic of Palau had been excised from the documents, and the president noted that the Northern Mariana Islands would become a commonwealth of the United States upon termination of the Trusteeship Agreement. The President recommended the draft to the Congress pointing out that

> The defense and land use provisions of the Compact extend indefinitely the right of the United States to foreclose access to the area to third countries for military purposes. These provisions are of great importance to our strategic position in the Pacific and enable us to continue preserving regional security and peace.[31]

The transmittal of the document provoked a jurisdictional dispute within the Congress about the appropriate committees to consider the Joint Resolution. The Parliamentarian ruled that the committees that had been monitoring the trusteeship—Interior and Insular Affairs—had primary concern with the termination process; another school of thought saw it as necessarily a function of the Foreign Affairs and Foreign Relations committees, whilst the Defense Department maintained a close interest in the proceedings.

1984 was a presidential election year, and the Office of Micronesian Status Negotiations still hoped to negotiate a solution in Palau, which itself was scheduled for presidential elections in November, which in turn could be brought to the 98th United States Congress. While the Subcommittee on Public Lands and National Parks of the House Interior Committee began an extensive series of twenty hearings on the Joint Resolution, the Senate Committee on Energy and Natural Resources held only one day of hearings at which public witnesses were permitted to make five-minute statements.

At much the same time the United Nations Trusteeship Council held its annual meeting on the Trust Territory well aware that the process toward termination had now begun, despite the failure to reach an agreement with Palau. In its report the administering authority acknowledged that after 37 years of American trusteeship there was no public health laboratory in the territory, no maternity home, leprosarium, infectious diseases or mental hospital. Figures were not reported for the Marshalls or Palau but in the rest of Micronesia there were only 34 doctors. In 1983 nearly 2,500 cases of cholera or suspected cholera had been reported in the Federated States of Micronesia.[32]

As part of the congressional scrutiny of the proposed Compacts the Congressional Research Service reviewed the drafts. Daniel Hill Zafren, Specialist in American Public Law, reported on July 19, 1984 considerable dissatisfaction with the drafting of the Compact and confusions and ambiguities arising out of proposed agreements that the Office of Micronesian Status Negotiations acknowledged had "no precedent in United States Constitutional practice and few precedents in international law."[33]

The Congressional Research Service memorandum found that the "provision declaring that the people are self-governing appears to be legally uncertain. There is some confusion and ambiguity as to the intent and effect of this provision." (Section 111) Although "on its face" Section 121

> represents a recognition by the United States that these Governments have their own international legal personality . . . legally, at most this can be deemed to be a recognition in the declaratory sense. It is merely the unilateral political expression by the United States, and such legal existence is brought into being between the United States and the respective Governments.

When read in conjunction with Section 123 which provides that in the conduct of certain foreign affairs the governments must consult with the United States, "it can be argued that there cannot be a true exercise of any sovereign power to conduct foreign affairs, in general or in specific fields, if there has to be consultation with another nation and such conduct stymied if that nation makes a contrary unilateral determination." At the same time, Section 471 "by virtue of declaring the Compact a statute under the laws of the United States would seem to give the United States the right to unilaterally amend the compact by any subsequent statute," despite other provisions calling for mutual agreement to amend the Compact.[34]

The Second Palau Plebiscite, September 1984

On May 24, 1984 the Palauan and United States negotiators initialled another version of the Compact. It incorporated the essence of the July 1983 treaty which had been agreed in principle which deleted Section 314 and its subsidiary agreement. The Office of Micronesian Status Negotiations reversed itself in thinking that the new proposals would not require a plebiscite of the Palauan people. President Haruo Remeliik had been unable to persuade the *Olbiil Era Kelulau* to pass legislation to endorse its acceptance by executive order. Indeed, it was difficult to get the support of the *Olbiil Era Kelulau* for a plebiscite on this new version of the Compact which upon close inspection proved to be ambiguous on the central question of admission of nuclear substances into Palau. The 1984 version deleted Section 314, one of the sections empowering the United States to introduce nuclear substances. In a memorandum entitled "Summary of the New Compact" the Office of the President of Palau stated in its first paragraph that "The Compact does not allow any nuclear or other harmful substances in Palau. For military purposes Section 314 of the original Compact which was disapproved by the voters in the 1st referendum has been taken out."

But the new version of Section 312 gave the government of the United States "full authority and responsibility for security and defense matters in or relating to Palau" and entitled the United States to "conduct within the lands, water and airspace of Palau the activities and operations necessary for the exercise of its authority and responsibility under this Title." The new Section 312 also entitled the United States to "invite the armed forces of other nations to use military areas and facilities in Palau in conjunction with and under the control of United States Armed Forces." Since the United States is explicitly committed to a nuclear defense, the Senate of Palau in its Analysis of the 1984 Compact of Free Association concluded that

> The United States is likely to construe Section 312 as giving them the authority to bring nuclear and other harmful substances into Palau when it is necessary to carry out its *full authority and responsibility* for security and defense matters.

This interpretation seemed completely confirmed by the new version of Section 411 (b) which now required

> Approval by the people of Palau in accordance with the Constitution of Palau by not less than three-fourths of the votes cast in a referendum called for that purpose. . . .

As the Senate legislative counsel wrote in a memorandum on June 22, 1984

> The new Compact deletes Section 314 of the old Compact as well as other references to nuclear and other harmful substances. But the new Compact, by its very terms, requires approval of three-fourths of the people of Palau. Through this requirement the United States is still requiring authority to bring nuclear and other harmful substances into the Republic when such action is needed to fulfill its responsibilities over security and defense matters.

The House of Delegates of Palau agreed on June 12 to hold another vote on this new Compact but the Palauan Senate refused to agree. There were fewer than thirty copies of the new Compact and its subsidiary agreements in Palau and the documents were never translated into Palauan in their entirety. The Senate felt it should hold a series of public hearings before the people had to vote on the issues again and resolved to postpone another vote until May 31, 1985. The House rejected this Senate proposal. President Remeliik thereupon issued an Executive Order setting the date for the vote as September 4, 1984.

However the Office of Micronesian Status Negotiations and the United States State Department, eager as they were for another vote, realized that no plebiscite or referendum held under these conditions would ever be upheld in the Palauan courts nor in the United Nations, and did not request an official United Nations observer to monitor this exercise. Even as the vote proceeded a petition with 4,900 signatures—

more than half the electorate—called upon President Remeliik to resign.

Again more than twice as many ballots were printed as there were voters, and $50,000 of education campaign funds provided by the United States were spent on sending an education team to the numerically important group of absentee voters in Hawaii and the west coast of the United States. In the event, 66 percent of the voters supported the new Compact and 34 percent opposed it. President Remeliik failed to resolve the issue by obtaining a popular mandate that entitled him to forge ahead in resolving any outstanding issues by negotiation and executive order. A substantial majority of the Palauan people supported free association with the United States but not enough of them were prepared to sacrifice the central element of their constitution. If the United States negotiators were intensely frustrated at the end of President Reagan's first administration, so was the executive branch of the Republic of Palau which reported to the United Nations Trusteeship Council in 1983 that

> Aside from other direct and indirect assistance received from the United States through the Department of the Interior in preparing Palau for self-support, the government of Palau has continued, since the initiation of its self-governing in January, 1981, to face threats of closing its doors and declaring bankruptcy. In this situation there is much uncertainty as to whether or not the self-government will survive. The obvious problem is that the funds available to the Republic have not been sufficient to meet the basic funding requirements of the government. At the same time the economic basis is too weak and there are no hopes for the private sector to absorb some of the obligations of the government most importantly employment in the near future. . . .[35]

The IPSECO Problem

President Remeliik and other members of the government were anxious that the funds premised on passage of the Compact of Free Association should begin to flow sooner rather than later to enable them to meet their commitment in both the public and private sectors. The most pressing of these were the loan repayments due on the contract the President had signed with the British company International Power Systems Ltd. (IPSECO) to provide a 16-megawatt power station for $32,500,000 on June 8, 1983. According to Christopher Reed of *The Guardian*

> The project is being financed via an unusual loan structure in which two London banks share the 32.5 million and are underwritten by the government-backed Export Credit Guarantee Department. This is in turn guaranteed by a consortium of five international banks headed by Morgan Grenfell and insured by Lloyd of London.[36]

The President of Palau had entered into this contract even though a report of the Inspector General of the Department of the Interior pointed out that

> the efforts were not in accordance with acceptable management practices and existing law. Specifically, the Government had not performed a feasibility study to determine Palau's future power requirements prior to entering into a contract for construction of a power plant and fuel storage facility. The proposed facilities appeared to be in excess of Palau's needs. Also, the Government did not advertise the construction work to allow for full and free competition and did not negotiate with the contractor for the best possible price.
>
> The contractor arranged for loans to fund the construction project. However, documentation was unavailable to show that the Palau Government negotiated for the most desirable financial arrangements. Moreover, based on a review of revenue expectations from the power plant and fuel storage

facility, and the Government's available revenue sources, we concluded that the Government would be unable to meet payments specified under the loan agreements.[37]

Despite these reservations, all parties proceeded with the loan arrangements and Public Law 1-54 of the Republic of Palau authorizing the venture was not vetoed by the High Commissioner of the Trust Territory of the Pacific Islands. The Inspector General's report noted that

> The loan documents further provided that the Republic of Palau could not review or know the terms of the policy. Agreement to this type of loan provision ignores sound financial management practices.

The revenue projected from the sale of fuel to fishing fleets and to the domestic consumers of Palau were "arbitrary and unrealistic." It was noted that Palau expected to receive approximately $28,000,000 for energy production and $36,000,000 for capital infrastructure projects under the fifteen year economic agreements of the Compact. "However, the effective date of the Compact is unknown."

In defending the arrangements President Remeliik wrote to the Inspector General on September 2, 1983 stating *inter alia* that the two relevant senior officials, Ambassador for Micronesian Status Negotiations Fred M. Zeder and Interior Secretary Pedro Sanjuan had given the British lenders their assurance "that the Office for Micronesian Status Negotiations and the Office of the Assistant Secretary of the Interior for Territorial and International Affairs fully support the efforts of the Government of Palau to improve its present power-generating capability." However an August 16, 1983 letter to the Inspector General from Secretary Sanjuan recognized that

> Based on your audit findings, it would be virtually impossible for Palau to repay loans totalling 32.5 million for the construction of a 16 megawatt power plant and a six million gallon fuel storage facility, even under the best of circumstances.

According to Reed,

> Ipseco's Washington lawyer, Mr. John Armstrong,[38] dismisses the Inspector-General's report as almost completely erroneous, based on blatant misinformation

while the Traditional Paramount Leader of Koror, Ibedul Gibbons, told the Trusteeship Council on May 23, 1985 that the whole arrangement was

> a misguided, self-serving and totally inappropriate but cleverly conceived scheme by which the present administration came to accept an outrageously expensive public project which is financially doomed for failure.[39]

However the Ibedul lost much of the supporting evidence for his analysis when his legal counsel's home was firebombed in August 1983.

Two years after he had signed the IPSECO deal, President Haruo Remeliik was in deep political trouble. Although he insisted that

> The Compact itself is not dead. It is just sitting, waiting for senate approval.[40]

the new Senate elected in the presidential elections of December 1984 which returned Remeliik to the presidency and put Status Negotiations Ambassador Lazarus Salii in the Senate did not agree with his assertion that Palau would remain one hundred percent nuclear free under the Compact as then written. Asked his vision of the future, President Haruo Remeliik replied

> I would like to see Palau remain as Palau, and become economically self-sufficient and independent.[41]

But in fact his government was defaulting on the IPSECO loan repayments and despite his personal mandate Haruo Remeliik was not able to deliver Palauan acceptance of the Compact. On the night of June 30, 1985—the evening before he was to give a television report on the IPSECO problem to the people of Palau —the President of Palau was fatally shot four times outside his home on a well-lit street as he returned from a fishing trip.

The Kwajalein Problem

Palau was not the only part of the Trust Territory where the administering authority was meeting resistance to its proposed terms of settlement in the Compact. Landowners who had formed the Kwajalein Atoll Corporation to protect their interests from both the United States and the Republic of the Marshall Islands government filed suit in December 1984 in the District of Columbia alleging that the United States had breached the Trusteeship Agreement, specifically Article 6 concerning the promotion of political, economic and social advancement in its seizure of the Kwajalein lands and the removal of the people to Ebeye.

The plaintiffs were displeased with the compensation proposals and the fact that payments would be made to the Marshall Islands government which would not necessarily transfer them to the individual landowners. They also sought damages for the suffering of the approximately 8,500 people (one-fifth of the Marshall Islands population) living on the 66 acres of Ebeye made available to them in a population density "greater than, for example, if the entire population of the United States were moved to Connecticut. There is no space for farming or, with the exception of a basketball court and a baseball field, for recreation."[42] The available housing stock was said to consist of 630 dwellings, and the Marshall Islands government purchased 240,000 gallons of water from Kwajalein (i.e. from the administering authority) three times a week. Employment rates ran at about 12 percent for the 4,000 adults and teenagers on Ebeye; only about 150 were among the 585 Marshallese employed on Kwajalein. While there were 1,000 students enrolled in elementary school on Ebeye, the atoll had no high school.

The request that the United States District Court should issue a judgement declaring that the United States had violated the Trusteeship Agreement and for injunctions to cure the situation were potentially deeply embarrassing to the administering authority as it prepared to argue for termination of the Strategic Trusteeship. Moreover, the current lease on the Kwajalein missile base site was due to expire on October 1, 1985. The lease termination was critical for the United States as was apparent from the congressional debates on the

Compact for the Marshall Islands and the Federated States in the second half of 1985. Congressman Stephen Solarz, Chair of the Asian and Pacific Affairs Subcommittee of the House Committee on Foreign Affairs recommended the agreements to his colleagues because

> this agreement is very much in the interest of the United States. Strategically, this agreement gives us the right to strategic denial so that we are in a position for *the rest of time* to prevent any foreign power from establishing a military presence in Micronesia without our consent. That is an extraordinary concession made by the Micronesians and a very real achievement for the United States. It also gives us a 30-year lease agreement at the Kwajalein missile range, which is *the single most important missile range we have in the entire world.* . . . It is very much in our economic interest, because this compromise would provide an authorization for 2.4 billion over the next 15 years to the Micronesians, which is 300 million *less that we would otherwise be giving to the Micronesians if the present trust territory status was maintained.* . . . *we have exclusive control over their security* but they are exclusively responsible for their domestic affairs and where they consult with us on foreign policy.[43] [emphases added]

The United States Congress Adopts and Amends the Incomplete Compact of Free Association, November 1985

There were some concerns expressed over elements of the agreement such as the espousal clause 177 which the Congressional Research Service Specialist in American Public Law, Daniel Zafren had doubted was possible between the United States and a government not yet established as truly sovereign in international law.[44] In November 1985 the House adopted Joint Resolution 355 by an overwhelming vote of 360-12 and the Senate soon followed suit. However in the process the Congress had unilaterally amended the Compacts for the Federated States of Micronesia and the Marshall Islands because of the fear expressed by the Secretary of the Treasury James A. Baker III that the Compact would create tax-haven status for the Freely Associated States by granting broad exemptions from United States tax for United States citizens who establish residency in the Freely Associated States.[45]

The prospect of investment incentives for the Micronesian territories alarmed the other 'flag territories' of the United States such as American Samoa, Guam, and Puerto Rico as well as the proponents of President Reagan's tax reform proposals which were before the Congress at the same time. The other point of view was expressed by Congressman Jim Leach who argued that the trade and tax incentives in the original version

> provide the prospect of binding these island states economically as closely as possible to the United States rather than to our trade rivals or strategic adversaries.[46]

The compromise amendment and the very ability of the Congress to amend the Compact which had been in negotiation since 1969 was to a certain extent a revelation to some of the Micronesian negotiators. The Governor of the State of Ponape (which anthropologist Glenn Peterson had argued to the Trusteeship Council and Decolonization Committee was the least happy of the entities composing the Federated States of Micronesia) wrote a strongly worded letter to the President of the Federated States, Tosiwo Nakayama, protesting the amendments. Governor Moses detected now

> the true attitudes of American lawmakers and their concept of what the Compact means to the United States. . . . The multitude of amendments offered by the House of Representatives of the United States Congress represent something much different than a recognition of our inherent sovereignty and our dignity as a self-governing people. The amendments are patronizing in language, condescending in spirit, and meddlesome in fact. . . . A constant referencing to American flag territories, especially in the House, drew for us a picture which recreated the former Trust Territory entities as continuing wards of the United States, dependencies over which they exercise control and for whom they feel responsible. . . . It is most disappointing that after 40 years of administration, the chief law makers of the United States, especially in the House committee entrusted with oversight of the Trust Territory, apparently are unable to grasp the

most fundamental aspects of the United Nations Trusteeship system and the goals and aspirations of the peoples who came under the protection of this international organization.[47]

Another amendment was added to the Joint Resolution to Approve the Compact of Free Association with the Federated States of Micronesia and the Republic of the Marshall Islands on November 14, 1985: the May 23, 1984 version of the Compact of Free Association with the Republic of Palau, as yet unratified by the people of Palau in a manner conforming with their constitution, was tacked on to the other documents to express "the sense of the Congress that future action on the Palau Compact, once approved, certified and submitted, will be expeditious."[48]

The Election of President Lazarus Salii, December 1985

The assassination of the first President of Palau of course did nothing to ease domestic political tensions, and the failure to clearly identify the assassins only enhanced unrest. An American student who spent the period from 1979 to 1981 in Palau observing the move from the Congress of Micronesia to the Republic and its constitution and the early years of the negotiation of the future political status noted even then

> an ethno-historical and contemporary Palauan fear that the balanced and controlled competition of traditional Palau might be totally superseded by a new, 'winner-take-all' game.[49]

Three weeks after the assassination a son and a nephew of one of the major political opponents of the Compact, Roman Tmetchul (who had lost the election for the first presidency to Haruo Remeliik by 300 votes) together with a third man were arrested and charged with conspiracy in relation to the murder, although it was held that a fourth, unapprehended man had fired the shots. On August 17, 1985, however, the prosecution dropped all charges against these three men because a key witness had failed a polygraph test. In those three weeks, however, the presidential election had been held, resulting in the election of the former Palauan Ambassador for Status Negotiations, Lazarus Salii, to the presidency. The other major potential candidate, Roman Tmetuchl, was not a contender because of the fact that his young relatives were charged with the assassination.

Two months later, in November 1985, the same defendants were re-arrested on the same evidence and were convicted without a jury trial[50] in February 1986, two days after yet another referendum on a revised Compact of Free Association for Palau.

In one of his earliest acts President Salii had signed Executive Order No. 35-85 creating an Office of the Council of Chiefs within the Executive Office of the President in an attempt to "make the best possible use of the wisdom and counsel of the Traditional Leaders in making decisions and policies that affect the future of the Republic of Palau."[51] The uses of this office in bringing the traditional leadership into line with the new political leadership is indicated by the fact that the first Administrative Officer of the Council of Chiefs was Alan Seid, a close adviser to the Ibedul of Koror, who participated in the Council. Having isolated Tmetuchl, Salii was keen to bring the traditional leadership into the process of devising an effective compromise solution. A revised Compact was initialled by the negotiators for both sides on January 10, 1986. It was approved by both houses of the *Olbiil Era Kelulau* on January 24. The Compact with the Marshall Islands and the Federated States of Micronesia had been approved by the United States Congress and became Public Law 99-239 on January 14, 1986.

The Third Palauan Plebiscite, February 1986

A plebiscite—the third—on the new Palauan Compact was held on February 21, 1986 and 72.2 percent of the voters who participated supported the new Compact. President Salii immediately interpreted this as a sufficient majority to approve the Compact, and certified the results on February 24, despite a protest from a substantial group of traditional leaders that the Government of Palau had told the electorate that the new version required 75 percent support to pass, and the one month education campaign had been far too short especially considering that Palauan versions of the documents were available only days prior to the vote. Nevertheless the Palau Compact of Free Association was transmitted to the Congress for approval on April 10, 1986. Brief hearings were held within ten days of this transmittal. However, in late May a suit was filed in the Supreme Court of Palau seeking a declaratory judgement that the Compact had not been properly ratified. The 1986 version of the Palauan Compact was designed to permit the United States to transit nuclear substances and weapons through the territory of Palau, including its maritime territory which was very narrowly defined in contrast to the wider definition implicit in the Palauan constitution. The drafting of the new version seemed to depend on the same sort of "meaningless semantic differences" that Judge Hefner had criticized in the 1983 Supreme Court decisions. Section 324 now read:

> In the exercise in Palau of its authority and responsibility under this Title, the Government of the United States shall not use, test, store or dispose of nuclear, toxic chemical, gas or biological weapons intended for use in warfare and the Government of Palau assures the Government of the United States that in carrying out its security and defense responsibilities under this Title, the Government of the United States has the right to operate nuclear capable or nuclear propelled vessels and aircraft within the jurisdiction of Palau without either confirming or denying the presence or absence of such weapons within the jurisdiction of Palau.

The first part of this Section tracks the constitutional prohibition on nuclear substances in Palau, but the second half permits the United States to "operate" such activities in Palau. Since 'operate' is a synonym for 'use,' particularly with reference to machinery, it is difficult to see a substantive semantic difference between what is prohibited in the first half and what is permitted in the second.

The public education campaign conducted in the month prior to the vote clearly presented the new compact as requiring a 75 percent affirmation because

Although the United States agrees not to use, test or store nuclear weapons in Palau, they have ships whose engines run on nuclear fuel which fall within the definition of nuclear power plants. Article XIII Section 6 of the Palau Constitution requires 75 percent voter approval for nuclear powered ships in Palau's waters. Only a court could decide that less than 75 percent is required.[52]

In answering "What are the biggest differences between Trusteeship and the improved Compact?," the same document stated that while the Trusteeship involved "Full United States military rights including nuclear" the Compact involved "Full military rights but nuclear transit only."

As well as permitting the transit of nuclear weapons and other substances through Palau, the new Section 453 (a) now provided that

> The provisions of Section 311, even if Title Three should terminate, are binding and shall remain in effect for a period of 50 years and thereafter until terminated or otherwise amended by mutual consent;

As Professor Clark pointed out to the Trusteeship Council in May, 1986

> What in the 1980 and 1982 versions of the Compact had been a provision permitting an extension by mutual consent and thus a veto by *Palau*, now became the reverse—a provision continuing the arrangement in perpetuity unless *the United States* agrees otherwise.[53]

The combined effect of the internal cross-referencing of the restrictive and exclusive clauses of the new version meant that most of its terms could not be terminated unilaterally by Palau and therefore would survive until mutual consent, or the United States agreement to termination.

James R. Lilley, Deputy Assistant Secretary of State for East Asia and Pacific Affairs explained the United States strategy to the Subcommittee on Public Lands of the House of Representatives on April 18, 1986:

> In Section 324 of the current Compact, the United States has agreed that in the exercise of its authority under Title Three of the Compact, it will not engage in those specific actions

which, under Article II, Section 3 of the constitution, require 75 percent popular approval before the Government of Palau could certify completion of its approval process. While United States agreement to accept those specific limitations served to achieve the necessary compatibility, it was recognized by both sides that the United States could not accept restrictions which could impair the ability of the United States to carry out fully our defense role under the Compact. Thus, Palau agreed in the same Compact Section 324 to recognize our ability to operate nuclear-powered or nuclear capable vessels and aircraft in Palau without confirming or denying the presence or absence of nuclear or other types of weapons.

As Ferdinand Marcos lost control of the Philippines and New Zealand's Prime Minister David Lange was proving intransigent on the same issue of transit rights for nuclear-powered or armed vessels, the United States was under great pressure to secure access to the potential naval and land sites of Palau. The most senior staff officer of the Office of Micronesian Status Negotiations told the *Washington Post* on January 18, 1986 that

To the degree that one looks at the next forward area for naval and air installations, we have completed the arc. Palau is important but clearly third in importance. [after Clark Air Force Base and Subic Bay Naval Base.][54]

Indeed, the Assistant Secretary of State for East Asia and Pacific Affairs appeared to close off any prospect of the outcome of the 1986 vote being challenged in any Palauan court. According to Mr. Lilley,

Because of the agreement reached in Compact Section 324, we also agreed to revise the provisions of Section 411 relating to the approval process for the Compact. Since the February 10, 1983, plebiscite still has international legal standing as an act of self-determination, and Compact Section 324 removed the procedural requirement under Article II, Section 3 of Palau's constitution for a 75 percent approval, it was agreed that the approval process called for in Section 411 would be described simply as a referendum. The principle underlying this approach is that interpretation of Palau's constitution— particularly as to its internal process for approving the Compact—is exclusively a matter for Palau to determine. In its February 24, 1986 certification of the plebiscite results, the

> Government of Palau informed the United States formally
> that the Compact approval process was complete and was
> accomplished in full compliance with the requirements of the
> Palau Constitution. Thus, as a matter of international law and
> practice, Palau cannot invoke any subsequently stated
> reasons based upon internal Palauan law to avoid its
> compliance with the provisions of the Compact.

That is, the United States was viewing the February 1986 vote as a referendum made necessary by the fact that the February 1983 plebiscite mandated accommodation of the constitution to the Compact, although the form in which the issue was presented in February 1986 was a substantively renegotiated Compact which other observers held would require a plebiscite to determine if the people of Palau accepted it inasmuch as it differed in major respects from the 1983 Compact. Moreover, the Assistant Secretary of State was suggesting that the presidential certification of the results of the 1986 vote constituted the binding of Palau to the agreement even if the president was ultimately found to have been acting *ultra vires* by a Palauan court, since the Assistant Secretary was relying on a rule of international law which applied to sovereign states, even though Palau was on February 24, 1986—the date of certification—not a sovereign entity but in some limbo area of self-government prior to termination of the trusteeship.

Ambassador Patricia M. Byrne presented an even simpler formulation of the implications of the February 1986 vote to the Trusteeship Council a month later. On May 12, 1986 she reported that

> The terms of the Compact were essentially the same as the
> Compact approved in 1983, except for revisions to make it
> conform to changes made by the United States Congress in
> the Compact for the FSM and Marshall Islands and a change
> in the defense section of the Compact to make it conform to
> Palau's Constitution.

She further informed the Trusteeship Council on May 15—in disregard of the published materials of the government-funded political education campaign—that

> The Administering Authority would like to point out that the
> position of the Government of Palau and of the Government
> of the United States that a simple majority was required to

approve the Compact was a matter of public record and was widely reported in the press before the plebiscite .

According to the official record President Lazarus Salii told the Trusteeship Council that

> on 25 April, 1986, in his capacity as President of Palau, he had certified the Compact to the President of the United States, officially advising him that it had been approved by the people of Palau in the manner prescribed by Palau's national congress and in conformity with its national Constitution. At the current session, he was bringing the same message to the members of the Trusteeship Council.[55]

In what was thought at the time to be probably the last session of the Trusteeship Council, representatives of Vanuatu, Australia, Fiji, New Zealand, Papua New Guinea, Samoa and the Solomon Islands all spoke firmly in support of termination of the trusteeship for all four territories, making no criticisms of the process in Palau. The United States, that is, had lined up the South Pacific Forum countries behind the termination of the trusteeship. Britain and France made predictable speeches in favor of termination and the Soviet Union an equally predictable one against.

At the May 28, 1986 meeting of the Trusteeship Council resolution 2183 (LIII) was proposed and adopted by the inevitable 3:1 vote. The resolution noted

> that the peoples of the Northern Mariana Islands, the Marshall Islands, the Federated States of Micronesia and Palau have freely exercised their right to self-determination in plebiscites observed by the visiting missions of the Trusteeship Council and have chosen free association with the United States of America in the case of the Marshall Islands, the Federated States of Micronesia and Palau and Commonwealth status in the case of the Northern Mariana islands.

The Trusteeship Council therefore requested

> the Government of the United States, in consultation with the Governments of the Federated States of Micronesia, the Marshall Islands, Palau and the Northern Mariana Islands, to agree on a date not later than 30 September 1986 for the

full entry into force of the Compact of Free Association and Commonwealth Covenant and to inform the Secretary-General of the United Nations of that date.

The Trusteeship Council considered

> that the Government of the United States, as the Administering Authority, has satisfactorily discharged its obligations under the terms of the Trusteeship Agreement and it is appropriate for that Agreement to be terminated with effect from the date referred to. . . .[56]

The same resolution requested the Secretary-General of the United Nations to circulate resolution 2183 (LIII) as an official document of the Security Council, thus transmitting the decision of the Trusteeship Council to consider the Trust Agreement of the Pacific Islands to be terminated as of September 30, 1986 if all five parties entered into bilateral agreement thereto.

The only problem with this strategy was that President Salii had acted *ultra vires* in certifying to the President of the United States and the Trusteeship Council that the Compact of Free Association for Palau had been approved by the people of Palau in a manner prescribed by Palau's constitution. Traditional High Chief Ibedul Yutaka M. Gibbons and three other Palauans filed suit in Palau's Supreme Court charging that the president had implemented the Compact prematurely and therefore acted *ultra vires.*

This is what Judge Robert Gibson indeed found when he issued his summary judgement in July 1986.

> I have diligently sought to find some reasonable basis upon which to ground an escape from the conclusion that Section 324 of the Compact unconstitutionally impinges Article II, Section 3 and Article XIII, Section 6 of the Constitution of the Republic of Palau. I deeply regret that I have been unable to find support to sustain my search. It is patent that the intent of the Constitutional Convention delegates was to make it well-nigh impossible to, as plaintiffs say, override the constitution. Each and every source to which I turned for help in endeavoring to find validity for the Compact, confirmed a contrary intent and the further unarguable conclusion that it was the intention of the delegates to make, within the limits of their power, Palau forever nuclear-free. It is somewhat surprising to the Court that even the 75 percent majority vote

to admit nuclear weapons and substances mustered sufficiently [sic] votes in the Constitutional Convention to be adopted. This being the Court's findings, it follows of natural consequence that all things sounding of nuclear warfare, including nuclear propelled and nuclear capable vessels are forbidden to transit, enter or port in the Palauan waters.[57]

The judge was very unhappy about this decision, chastising the minority of voters who brought the case even as he found the evidence of the constitutional conventions' intentions overwhelming. He feared that the decision would have a "devastating effect on Palau" at a time when "the prevailing attitude of the United States in terms of foreign and fiscal policy (does not) bode well for Palau in the ongoing excruciating path towards security and economic reality."

But few observers thought that the United States would consider this checkmate. As the chairman of the United Nations Special Visiting Mission who had observed the February 1986 vote in Palau, Mr. David Gore-Booth of the United Kingdom, had observed at the time: "If the Soviet Union exercises its veto, termination of the Trusteeship will be blocked. The question of implementation of the Compact is quite separate and is a matter for the Government of Palau and the United States administration."

Here stood the stalemate in mid-1986.

Notes

[1] Arthur John Armstrong, "Strategic Underpinnings of the Legal Regime of Free Association: The Negotiations for the Future Political Status of Micronesia," *Brooklyn Journal of International Law* VII/2 (Summer 1981): 197; hereafter cited as "Strategic Underpinnings."

[2] "Strategic Underpinnings, " 197.

[3] See *Decolonization*, 23 for the elements of the federal system adopted by the Republic of Palau.

[4] *Decolonization*, 24.

[5] *Decolonization*, 24.

[6] Arthur John Armstrong, "The Negotiations for the Future Political Status of Micronesia," *American Journal of International Law* 74 (1980): 690.

[7] See Armstrong, "Negotiations."

[8] "Strategic Underpinnings," 202.

[9] "Strategic Underpinnings," 202.

[10] "Strategic Underpinnings," 225.

[11] Clark, "Self-Determination," 28, footnotes 155 and 67.

[12] Clark, "Self-Determination," 28

[13] *Center Magazine* (September/October1980): 22.

[14] *Center Magazine*, 23.

[15] *Center Magazine*, 24.

[16] *Center Magazine*, 25.

[17] *Center Magazine,"* 25.

[18] *Center Magazine,* 31.

[19] *Center Magazine,* 27. Hills relies on the reports of a Trust Territory government economist, Elizabeth Udui.

[20] Roger S. Clark, "The Current State of the Trust Territory Negotiations: Who has Tentatively Agreed to What?" A working paper prepared for the Micronesia Support Committee, typescript, August 1981, 5-6.

[21] Clark, "Current State," 32.

[22] The people of Bikini and Rongelap were in the middle of litigating for settlement of the damages resulting from the nuclear tests of the 1950s and 1960s and this provision would have 'estopped' any future claims. Their lawyer, Jonathan Weisgall, has written the history of these litigations, see *inter alia* "The Nuclear Nomads of Bikini," *Foreign Policy* 39 (1980): 74-98 and "Micronesia and the Nuclear Pacific Since Hiroshima," *SAIS* 5/22 (1985).

[23] B. David Williams, "The Marshall Islands: From Self-Reliance to Compact of Free Association" in *Marshall Islands: 37 Years After* [Background Information of the Commission of the Churches on International Affairs of the World Council of Churches] (Geneva and N.Y., 1983) no. 5, 24-25.

[24] For the details of their anxieties, see the testimonies of Glenn Alcalay of the Committee for Nuclear Victims before the Trusteeship Council and Special Committee on Decolonization 1982-1986.

[25] Patrick M. Smith, "Memorandum on Interference with the Legal Processes of the Republic of Palau," Typescript, 1983, 1-2.

[26] Smith, "Memorandum," 2.

[27] Palau Plebiscite Results as certified by the President of the Republic of Palau reprinted in Roger S. Clark and Sue Rabbitt Roff, *Micronesia: The Problem of Palau* (London and New York: Minority Rights Group, 1984), 17.

[28] *Gibbons et. al. v. Remeliik*, Civil Action No. 67-83 of the Supreme Court of the Republic of Palau, Order Granting Partial Summary Judgement, August 6, 1983.

[29] United Nations Document T/PV. 1543 at 37.

[30] Roger S. Clark, "Petition Concerning the Trust Territory of the Pacific Islands Presented to the United Nations Trusteeship Council on Behalf of the International League for Human Rights," May 20, 1983, 7.

[31] Message from the President of the United States Transmitting a Draft of A Joint Resolution to Approve the Compact of Free Associaton, House Document 98-192, March 30, 1984.

[32] Department of State, *Trust Territory of the Pacific Islands, 36th Annual Report to the United Nations* (1984).

[33] Office of Micronesian Status Negotiations, "The Political Status Negotiations for the Trust Territory of the Pacific Islands and the Compact of Free Association." (April 1984): 2.

[34] Daniel Hill Zafren, "The Compact of Free Association—Foreign Policy Provisions: A Section by Section Legal Analysis." Congressional Research Service, July 19, 1984.

[35] Department of State, *Trust Territory of the Pacific Islands, 36th Annual Report to the United Nations* (1984).

[36] Christopher Reed, "Stormy Waters Surround Pacific Islands' Power Problems," *The Guardian* (June 4, 1984): 16-17.

[37] Letter of Inspector General of United States Department of the Interior [November 17, 1983] transmitting report to President of the Republic of Palau.

[38] An OMSN official during the Carter Administration.

[39] Petition to Trusteeship Council, May 23, 1985.

[40] Interview with E. Rampell, "Palau Edges Closer to Compact," *Pacific Islands Monthly* (April 1985): 19.

[41] "Palau Edges Closer to Compact," 21.

[42] *Laji Taft, Aini Betwel, Kwajalein Atoll Corporation v. U.S.A.*, Civil Action 84-3708, United States District Court, District of Columbia, 21.

[43] *Congressional Record—House*, July 25, 1985, H6341.

[44] Daniel Zafren, "Espousal of Claims under the Compact for Free Association," Congressional Research Service (April 2, 1985). Reprinted in *Congressional Record—House*, H6345-6. The same issue was raised in the U.S. Senate on November 14, 1985, see *Congressional Record—Senate*, S15607-10. Glenn Alcalay discussed Section 177 extensively in his submissions to the Trusteeship Council and Decolonization Committee in 1983, 1984, 1985 and 1986.

[45] Letter [August 8, 1985] to Secretary of State George P. Schultz. Reprinted in *Congressional Record—Senate*, November 14, 1985, S15572.

[46] Reprinted in *Congressional Record—Senate*, November 14, 1985, S15571.

[47] Letter [August 9, 1985] from Governor of Ponape State to President of the Federated States of Micronesia.

[48] *Congressional Record—Senate*, November 14, 1985, S15581.

[49] Joshua L. Epstein, "Dependency and Affluence as Challenges to National Development in Palau," Ph.D. diss. (Honolulu: University of Hawaii, 1986), 18.

[50] One of the major grounds for their subsequent appeal was the denial of right to a jury trial in a territory that the defense argued had to be treated for legal purposes as a United States flag territory despite the evolution of a judicial system in the development of self-government.

[51] *Palau Gazette* 17 (January 10, 1986): 8 [Weekly publication of the Executive Branch, Government of Palau]

[52] Republic of Palau, 'Common Questions,' February 8, 1986.

[53] Roger S. Clark, Petition Concerning the Trust Territory of the Pacific Islands presented to the United Nations Trusteeship Council on Behalf of the International League for Human Rights, May 13, 1986.

[54] Michael Weisskopf, "U.S. Wins Pact for Bases," *Washington Post* (January 18, 1986).

[55] *Security Council Official Records*, 41st Year, Special Supplement no.1, Report of the Trusteeship Council to the Security Council on the Trust Territory of the Pacific Islands 12 July 1985-30 June 1986, 7.

[56] See note 55.

[57] *Gibbons et. al. vs. Salii*, Appellate Division of the Supreme Court of Palau.

Chapter Four

The Next Four Plebiscites

The Fourth Palauan Plebiscite

Two-thirds through the Reagan Administration, the Palauan voters had thrice refused to permit the Compact of Free Association to override their constitution—and had been upheld every time by their Supreme Court. The Kwajalein landowners and the radiation victims were actively suing the United States and seeking a denial of the right of the self-governing executives to espouse their claims as if they were fully sovereign.

The IPSECO scandal indicated the uses to which the Compact funding was being put even before it became available to the Palauan government. President Remiliik had been assassinated probably because he was about to expose the corruption involved in the IPSECO deal; his successor Lazarus Salii entered on a period of deficit financing of his government (even though this was unconstitutional) predicated on effective garnisheeing of the future Compact funding.

The American negotiators were in danger of overreaching their duties as administering power in their efforts to retain *de facto* control over the territories in order to be able to use them on short notice for military installations. Their need became only more urgent with the crisis in the Philippines. The United States insistence that the constitution had to be reconciled with the Compact in Palau rather than *vice versa* violated the requirement of allowing the process of self-determination to proceed unfettered in the territories. Every time the Compact met with rejection by the Palauan people it was renegotiated in such a way as to relocate the problematic areas back into the subsidiary agreements. Soon the international community would begin to scrutinize the whole process and begin to wonder if effective transfer of the essentials of sovereignty had taken place in Palau—or the Federated States of Micronesia and the Republic of the Marshall Islands.

Time was running out on the Reagan Administration and before the end of 1986 the American negotiators tried one more time to seal the deal. They apparently were not privy to the findings of Larry N. Gerston, chairman of the Department of Political Science at San Jose State University who surveyed 120 of Palau's 238 schoolteachers in June and July 1986. Professor Gerston found that 96 percent of the teaching community voted in the February 21, 1986 plebiscite, in contrast to about 70 percent of the registered voters as a whole. But the reported votes of the teachers exactly mirrored that of the outcome—72.5 percent supported the Compact proposals while 27.5 percent opposed them. The survey consisted of 51 men and 69 women, but there were no major gender-determined differences in the voting pattern.

One significant finding was that support for the Compact was age-linked—it was strongest among the youngest teachers, the 18-20 year-olds and declined with every successive age group up to 50 years (Gerston's sample was not statistically significant after 50.) A second significant finding was that as teachers acquired more education, they were less likely to approve the Compact. More than half the opponents of the Compact did so because of the nuclear substances issue. Only one-fifth opposed it because not enough money was being offered by the United States to Palau. As Professor Gerston concluded

> Prior to the vote, conventional wisdom among the negotiators on both sides of the Pacific believed that increased financial support from the United States would dissipate the 'no' vote. Yet, most of those against the Compact argued another reason entirely, namely the possibility of nuclear materials in their country. Inasmuch as no amount of money could offset such concern, it would seem that the initial strategy was flawed, if not misconceived.[1]

Professor Gerston's predictions would be vindicated in the fourth Palauan plebiscite, held on December 2, 1986.

On September 17, 1986 the Supreme Court of Palau's Appellate Division ruled definitively that even transit of nuclear substances, including the operating of nuclear vessels in Palau, was banned by the constitution and would require a 75 percent vote of the electors in a referendum, devoted specifically to the question in order to be overridden.[2] This effectively set aside President Salii's ratification of the February 21, 1986 referendum, which had achieved only 72 percent of the 71 percent voter turnout for the Compact of Free Association.

Nevertheless, on October 16, 1986 legislation entitled the "Palau Compact of Free Association Act" (H.J. Res. 626, as amended) was passed by both houses of the United States Congress. This legislation included the body of the Compact of Free Association as voted on by the people of Palau on February 21 but also included provisions not yet seen by the people of Palau under the headings "Approval of Compact; Interpretation of, and United States Policies Regarding, Compact; Supplemental Provisions."

On October 24, 1986 the United States Ambassador to the United Nations, Vernon A. Walters. wrote the following letter to the Secretary-General of the United Nations

> I have the honor to refer to resolution 2183 (LIII) of the Trusteeship Council, adopted 28 May 1986 (S/18124, annex), in which the Trusteeship Council noted that the peoples of the Northern Mariana Islands, the Marshall Islands, the Federated States of Micronesia, and Palau have freely exercised their right to self-determination in choosing their future status, and considered that the United States Government has satisfactorily discharged its obligations under their terms of the Trusteeship Agreement of 17 July 1947. The Council emphasized the clearly expressed wish of the entities to enter their new status and urged the United States to come to an early agreement with them on the entry into force of these new relationships.
>
> I therefore have the honor to inform you that, as a consequence of consultations held between the United States Government and the Government of the Marshall Islands, agreement has been reached that 21 October 1986 is the date upon which the Compact of Free Association with the Marshall Islands enters fully into force. Furthermore, I am pleased to inform you that the Compact of Free Association with the Federated States of Micronesia and the Commonwealth Covenant with the Northern Mariana Islands will enter into force on 3 November 1986.
>
> I shall inform you of arrangements for entry into force of the Compact of Free Association with Palau once accord has been reached on the effective date of that agreement.

Chapter Four: Next Four Plebiscites | 145

> I would be grateful if you would circulate this letter as a document of the Security Council and of the Trusteeship Council.[3]

The United States was thus indicating that it considered the Trusteeship Council to have disposed of the question of termination of the Strategic Trusteeship of the Pacific Islands. It was declaring that the future political status indicated by the Compact of Free Association was now operative in two of the parts of the Strategic Trusteeship and Commonwealth status in the fourth. The United States promised to inform the Secretary-General when the same situation had been achieved in Palau. In asking for the circulation of this letter of information to both the Security Council and the Trusteeship Council, the United States was attempting to "sign off" on the issue of termination of the trusteeship. The onus would now be on its critics to mount a resolution denying the validity of the United States' view of the situation. Three parts of the territory at least were no longer administered under the terms of the Trusteeship Agreement of 1947 according to the United States; there were now bilateral treaties in force.

In lieu of a definitive United Nations resolution approving these arrangements and the one to be entered into with Palau, it could be argued that the United States had engaged in unilateral termination of the trusteeship in violation of forty years of United Nations principle and practice. But the implicit United States view was that the absence of substantive criticism, reflected in a resolution that achieved majority support, would mean international acceptance of the termination of the trusteeship. It would be in effect "termination by default."

Certainly the Trusteeship Council was not going to be the forum of criticism since Britain and France had held firm against Soviet criticisms for more than a decade of debate. There was a move in the Fourth Committee to monitor the situation more closely, but the United States had effectively prevented it from ripening at this critical time and the issue of New Caledonia provided a fortuitous diversion which is probably why the United States permitted its proxy Australia to spearhead the campaign for reinscription of that territory in the fortieth General Assembly. The only arena in which the United States was taking a calculated risk was the Security Council. Here the Soviet

Union had a veto in substantive matters, just as the United States did. If the issue entered the agenda of the Security Council there could be a stalemate: the Soviet Union would veto any United States-sponsored resolution accepting termination while the United States would apply the same tactic against any Soviet resolution denying termination. The result would be the technical continuation of the Trusteeship Agreement (and of the Trusteeship Council, though possibly with the refusal of the United States to cooperate even as it had refused to acknowledge the jurisdiction of the Fourth Committee) but the *de facto* implementation of the Compacts of Free Association just as the Commonwealth agreement was in force in the Northern Marianas.

But would the Soviet Union exercise its veto in the Security Council or would it prefer to acquiesce in that it might be ready to accept as inevitable United States hegemony in Micronesia for the present at least? The Soviet Union might well be willing to trade that acquiescence for concessions elsewhere in superpower negotiations. The great weakness of the Soviet position was that it was widely perceived as being purely self-interested and part of the broader strategic struggle. Many members of the United Nations did not look closely enough at the real problems in Micronesia because they thought that the Soviets were simply trying to achieve an advantage in this region

The United States however was under perhaps the greatest pressure it had been in the long history of the Micronesian negotiations to bring the issue to its culmination before the end of 1986. In the November 1986 election President Reagan lost control of the United States Senate; on January 1, 1987 he faced a whole new committee lineup that might well undertake yet another review of the Compacts of Free Association, and be more sensitive to the complaints of the various Micronesian communities. At the same time, the United States held the presidency of the Security Council in December 1986. As with most institutions, the presidency of the Security Council brings with it considerable control over procedure and agenda. The five permanent members of the Security Council have the power of veto on substantive matters only; they do not have that power over procedural matters. A skillful president can construe some issues as merely procedural if he wishes to avoid them risking the veto. The Secretary-General of the United Nations had been asked to 'circulate' Ambassador Walters' letter of October 24, 1986 to the Security Council; simple procedural acceptance of that information could be held to constitute termination of the trusteeship by observers sympathetic to the United States position. The Soviet Union would have an uphill battle to mount a substantive resolution denying a procedural motion.

There was one major obstacle to this strategy of "termination by default"[4]—the "hold out" position of Palau, now reaffirmed by the Appellate Division of the Supreme Court of Palau. The United States determined to force Palau to a decision by the end of 1986; in this tactic it had the full support of the Salii administration since Lazarus Salii had been the chief negotiator for the Compact from the Palauan side throughout and was dependent for the funds he needed to support major development projects in Palau on the Compact funds that were inaccessible to him until the Compact was passed. The United States needed to get the right decision in Palau—75 percent of the voter turnout to support the override provisions—and transmit that to the United Nations in a letter of information such that it could say that all the terms prefigured in the October 24 letter to the Secretary-General had been fulfilled by a simple procedural motion (ruled upon as such by the United States-controlled presidency) by the end of the year.

The first step in achieving this outcome was the passage on October 28, 1986 by the Second *Olbiil Era Kelulau* of Law No. 2-22, an Act to reapprove the Compact of Free Association, to provide for a referendum on the Compact of Free Association and its Subsidiary Agreements, as signed on January 10, 1986 by the President of the Republic of Palau and the representative of the Government of the United States, including the amendment subsequently made by the United States Congress, and to provide for the administration of necessary referendum.

In order to make possible this enabling legislation for the referendum, two-thirds of each of the houses of the Palau Legislature approved the Compact so that it could proceed to the popular ratification process. As was soon evident, this approval was *pro forma* since nearly twenty members of the *Olbiil Era Kelulau* came out against the Compact. The enabling legislation was itself passed into law although it contained the following phrase

> (5) The Appellate Division of the Supreme Court of Palau has recognized the right of innocent passage of nuclear powered and nuclear armed vessels and aircraft without further approval by the voters of Palau;

which was a highly contentious reading of some parts of the Appellate Division decision. The legislature also approved the following formulation of the question to be put to the people, although many felt that it did not constitute the single specific question on the override provision as required by the constitution and the Appellate Division decision:

> DO YOU APPROVE FREE ASSOCIATION WITH THE UNITED STATES AS SET FORTH IN THE COMPACT OF FREE ASSOCIATION SIGNED ON JANUARY 10, 1986 INCLUSIVE OF ITS SUBSIDIARY AGREEMENTS AND AS SUBSEQUENTLY ENACTED BY THE UNITED STATES CONGRESS EXPRESSLY APPROVING THE PROVISIONS OF THE COMPACT, INCLUDING ITS SECTION 324, WHEREBY THE GOVERNMENT OF THE UNITED STATES, IN CARRYING OUT ITS SECURITY AND DEFENSE RESPONSIBILITIES UNDER THE COMPACT OF FREE ASSOCIATION, HAS THE RIGHT TO OPERATE NUCLEAR CAPABLE OR NUCLEAR PROPELLED VESSELS WITHIN THE JURISDICTION OF PALAU?

Critics of the Compact and of the drafting of this question argued that it placed undue emphasis on Section 324 which was not the only section referring to nuclear substances. Many wanted a very specific question addressed to the single issue of nuclear substances in Palau. But others saw that there were certain advantages in the question as formulated by the administration, since on one reading at least it put the full Compact on the line at this referendum in a way that it hadn't been since the February 1983 vote. The Compact was clearly joined to the nuclear provisions; it was clearly acknowledged that the latter required 75 percent approval of the voter turnout. It could be held that if the administration failed to get the 75 percent, the whole Compact as presently drafted failed. In the event, the 'constitutionalists,' those who favoured the 1979 Palau constitution over subsequent versions of the Compact of Free Association, specifically in the nuclear substances issue, decided to fight the referendum, 'on the issues' rather than seeking to prevent the referendum on technical grounds. They felt that they had the chance of getting a definitive decision from the people, if only they could protect the integrity of the referendum process. To this end, they invited a group of international observers to be present in Palau to monitor the election process; they were also successful in urging the presence of an observer mission from the United Nations Trusteeship Council.

Opponents of the Compact wanted to be in good shape to mount a legal challenge to the referendum if it proved to be intolerably unfair. Three lawyers, a New Zealander, a Canadian and an American—joined by a Danish Member of the European Parliament and the present writer, United Nations delegate of an international non-governmental organization, Minority Rights Group, prepared to be in Palau for five days to observe the last days of the campaign, the vote, and the beginning of the counting.

Although Public Law 2-22 provided that "The President shall choose one day for the referendum," the Rules and Regulations for the Conduct of the Referendum on the Compact of Free Association issued by the Referendum Commissioner (the Minister of State, John O. Ngiraked) on November 20 provided for a referendum to be held in various stages. While the vote in Palau would take place on December 2, Palauan voters in Saipan, Guam, Colonia (Yap), Moen (Truk), Kolonia (Ponhpei) and Majuro (Marshalls) would vote on November 29 and those in Honolulu, Los Angeles, San Francisco and Portland would vote on December 7. Absentee voters had to make their request in writing for a ballot to the Referendum Commissioner by December 1, have it postmarked for return no later than December 2 and received by the Referendum Commissioner by December 4. These 'hurdles' faced by the absentee voters, those scattered throughout the United States in colleges and occupations far from the west coast clusters of Palauan communities, contrasted with the great efforts the Salii government made to get out the vote in Palau itself.

The Cost of the Vote

Public Law 2-22 appropriated "the sum of $275,000 from the National Treasury, as granted to the Republic by the United States Department of the Interior pursuant to the request of the President of the Republic, to fund the Special Election and Political Education." One hundred thousand dollars was to be administered by the Election Commissioner for the Special Election; $175,000 was to be administered by the chairman of the Political Education Committee "and shall be used exclusively to fund political education of the voters."

The Political Education Committee was charged with organizing a political education program on the Compact of Free Association and its Subsidiary Agreements that "shall be conducted in a manner aimed at informing and educating the people of the Republic of Palau in an impartial manner."

The United States representative to the Trusteeship Council, Patricia M. Byrne, informed the Council on November 20, 1986 that "$275,000 had been allocated to the education campaign. Of that sum, $250,000 had been provided by the United States." At best, this was loose speaking since $100,000 of the appropriation was intended for the mechanics of the election. Moreover, in a letter dated November 6, 1986 from Assistant Secretary of State Richard T. Montoya to President Salii in response to the latter's request for $400,000 to conduct the referendum, the $250,000 was clearly taken from the territory's annual budget. [5] Montoya wrote

> The Department of the Interior does not have available discretionary funding to pay for political education and other election costs associated with the plebiscite The best and most expeditious help that we can offer is to advance operations funding through the Trust Territory Government. We are willing to advance up to $250,000 in addition to the normal November allotment for government operations.
>
> If the plebiscite is successful, there would be no significant adverse impact on Palau since I believe we could safely assume that the Compact would be implemented during fiscal year 1987. If for some reason the plebiscite is not successful and the Compact cannot be implemented, Palau would still have nearly ten months remaining in the fiscal year to reduce government expenditures or obtain additional revenues to cover any operational shortfall.

The Political Education Committee was formed less than a month before the December 2 voting date. In an interview on the morning prior to the vote, its chairman noted that there were only five members of the Committee and about as many support staff. According to their budget, provided by the chairman, they spent nearly $160,000 in a month on travel and educational materials and television advertising.

In the estimation of some observers, the only budget item that remotely resembled the real cost of services bought by the Political Education Committee in the month was television time at $25,000. As well as the administration of the referendum and the needs of the Political Education Committee, $68,335 were apparently also appropriated for the Task Force for Compact. This Task Force worked explicitly and energetically for the acceptance of the Compact, and seems to have done so with government funds. Appendix B contain documents reporting payments made by the Political Education Committee prior to the fourth vote.

The Campaign

On November 14 President Reagan had signed Public Law No. 99-685 approving the Compact of Free Association between the United States and the Republic of Palau—eventhough it had not yet been ratified by the voters of Palau, indeed had been rejected three times. As President of the Republic of Palau, Lazarus Salii was unequivocally committed to passage of the Compact as indicated from the advertisement taken from the weekly *Palau Gazette* of November 28, published by the Executive Branch of the Government of the Republic of Palau (see Appendix C.) Both the United States—the administering authority of the Trust Territory of the Pacific Islands—and the Salii administration then began to actively campaign for a particular future political status for Palau, the Compact of Free Association with its nuclear provisions. Both governments used extensive governments resources and funds in these campaigns.

On November 17 the Minister for Social Services issued a memorandum stating that approval of the Compact was a "priority program" and that government personnel who did not campaign for the Compact were to be reported at once. Four days later the Assistant Director of Education closed the schools for the duration of the campaign and required all school teachers to campaign for the Compact during civil service hours (see Appendix D.)

President Salii explained his view of the situation in a statement to the Seventh Island Conference of Public Administration meeting in

Guam on November 21. According to the *Pacific Daily News* report of November 21, 1986

> Under the terms of the compact, according to Salii, the United States cannot place or store nuclear arms in the jurisdiction of Palau. All that is allowed is to have nuclear arms enter the jurisdiction in transit, although that presence will never be revealed, Salii said.

President Salii also pointed out that

> Fortunately, we will still be a trusteeship of the United States until we decide if we want commonwealth status or independence

in the event that the compact was not approved.

Thanksgiving Day, November 27, 1986 was momentous for Palau. While the Guam *Tribune* was giving editorial thanks that it didn't have Micronesia's problems, it also noted that " if war comes this way, God help Guam whose people are sitting in a nest of nuclear armaments—the biggest such nest in the Asia-Pacific region." The *New York Times* was featuring a major two-page story beginning on page one on the doubts clinging to the Palau assassination verdict, retracing the events leading to the assassination of President Remeliik on June 30, 1985 and suggesting that rough justice was being done to the three men accused of conspiring to murder him.

But of most significance to Palauans—because it was quickly distributed in photocopy form by both pro- and anti-compact campaigners—was a statement by Howard Hills of the Office for Micronesian Status Negotiations that if the Palauans failed to approve the compact

> in theory we could negotiate independence, commonwealth or keep negotiating for another 10-20 years on free association

but

> There is no support in the administration and the United States Congress for increasing funding levels.[6]

Hills' remarks were in response to an advertisement (see Appendix E) in the regional newspapers during the week signed by seventeen members of the Palau Legislature, including the Speaker and Vice Speaker of the House of Delegates, and six Senators including the recently-replaced Senate President.

Ambassador Fred M. Zeder of the Office of Micronesian Status Negotiations responded immediately to these points in a letter dated November 28 which was also widely circulated in Palau by the Political Education Committee in both English and Belauan. Ambassador Zeder emphasized the 'front-end loading' of the Compact funds which would make $141,000,000 available in the first year—a great windfall for any incumbent administration—and $420,000,000 in total in the first fifteen years in contrast to a projected $500,000,000 over fifty years. Zeder reaffirmed that

> there are significant economic, political and foreign policy reasons why the United States will not agree to increase or further front-end load Compact funding. Thus, it must be understood that—particularly from an economic point of view—the Compact as approved by the United States Congress represents what free association with Palau means with the United States.

The administering authority was thus indicating clearly on the eve of the referendum on the future political status that it wished to regard the Compact as non-renegotiable. Ambassador Zeder stated that federal programs would not end under the Compact, for three years at earliest. He was most nearly disingenuous in asserting that "the political relationship can still be terminated unilaterally by Palau at any time" and in suggesting that the fifty year term on the Palau 'political relationship' is significantly different from the terms of the relationship with the other two Compact territories only in that it has a $70,000,000 trust fund established.

Ambassador Zeder did provide a clarifying statement of what he viewed as the the point of the present process

> Last year the United States agreed for the first time not to store nuclear weapons in Palau. Contrary to some reports, Palau's agreement in Section 324 to join with the United States in observing a neither confirm nor deny policy as to equipment on ships and aircraft operating in Palau would not

enable my Government to secretly store weapons in Palau. While we thought the promise was sufficient to allow approval of the Compact by 50 percent vote, the recent court ruling made it clear that the Compact needs 75 percent approval.

On the same day, November 28, a memorandum on "The Right to Vote" was circulated to all government employees (approximately 1,500 of the 10,000 electorate) signed by John O. Ngiraked as Election Commissioner/Minister of State. It sought to clarify the memoranda of ten days earlier requiring civil servants to campaign for the Compact and closing the schools to permit the teachers to do so. The election commissioner explained that the President had worked for many years to negotiate a future political status with the United States that would be in the best interests of "you, your children, and your grandchildren." Support of the Compact was the official position of the government. Thus the government—and no distinction was made between the legislative, executive or administrative branches—could and should require its employees to work actively for 'its' policy during working hours "if the management official approves of the campaigning" since "it is not a candidate for public office who is being elected. In this case Palau's future, and the future of you and your children, is being put to the test." Moreover, "since the Government wholeheartedly supports the Compact, the Government can allow use of government properties in support of the government's own position. Conversely, should anyone campaign against the Compact and against the Government's position, it is surely within the power of the government to request that no government property be used for such a campaign."

There was no pretense of neutrality for the civil service. The election commissioner and minister of state thought it sufficient to guarantee that "All of you have the right to vote as you wish. We support the Compact, and exercise our rights to campaign and urge you to vote for the Compact. However, we do not intend to in any manner infringe or disrupt your right to vote as you wish." However, he did require civil servants to campaign for the Compact during their office hours no matter what their consciences dictated.

Four senior members of the opposition group—Ibedul, Yutaka M. Gibbons; Rebes, Alfonso Oiterong; Senator, Isiforo Rudimch and Speaker, Santos Olikong—issued a statement from the People's

Headquarters for Belau Constitution and Compact Improvements to all government employees

> We know that many of you are afraid to voice your opinion or question regarding the upcoming referendum on the Compact of Free Association. We are also aware that there are many reasons for your fear and reluctance to publicly express your concerns. We are in complete sympathy with all of you and offer our sympathy and assistance in the struggle to rid our government of this unethical and unhealthy atmosphere.

The independent observer mission wrote to the President of Palau criticizing the directives to civil servants and pointing out that they infringed parts 11 and 14 of the Rules and Regulations of the National Civil Service Board of Palau affirming the right to free expression of civil servants and prohibiting political campaigning by civil servants in their official capacity.

The United Nations Trusteeship Council Mission to Observe the Plebiscite—consisting of representatives of France, Britain, Fiji and Papua New Guinea together with several secretariat staff—arrived in Palau on November 30. They stayed at the Palau Pacific Resort, a tourist hotel standing in a well-guarded complex well away from the center of Koror and frequented mainly by American and Japanese businessmen and tourists. They entered on a series of formal meetings in the resort with the legislature, the election commissioner, the president and other officials.

By December 1 both camps were pessimistic. President Salii told the *Pacific Daily News* that

> opponents who believe the compact with the United States can be renegotiated and improved are unrealistic. There can be no new negotiations . . . the Reagan administration said late last week that the pact will not be renegotiated.
>
> We [Palau and the U.S.] went our separate ways through our own processes. . . . The United States completed its process before we completed ours.

The opposition group was not optimistic that their supporters would be able to resist the cumulative pressure of the government to vote for the Compact. The legislative leadership of the anti-compact group declined an invitation to attend a "Special Meeting on Compact" scheduled for December 1 at Asahi Baseball Stadium because

> they thought it was more like a dare to come and they didn't want to go there and they figured if they went it would cause more confusion because they had already asked for a debate at one point. They wanted a debate set up with rules and regulations of debate, and a moderator, and set it up right, and be done as debate instead of a yelling and screaming match. The other thing they were saying was the President of the Senate, if he calls a meeting of the Senators it should be in the Senate chamber. He doesn't use his chair as the President of the Senate to call them to a ballfield for a rally.[7]

The same senators had not been informed of a meeting with the Trusteeship Council mission scheduled for the morning of December 1.

The rally took place at the ballfield, attended by several hundred people who listened attentively to several speeches from ministers, senators, delegates and other officials in support of the Compact. One speaker told them that voting in the referendum was like taking an exam, but it was a simple exam. They only needed to know two words— 'Yes' and 'Ni'—Belauan for 'Yes.' The hamlet chief of the vicinity of the ballfield came to offer his blessing so that when they entered the polling booths they would vote 'Yes.' The Minister for Social Services told them that if they wanted medicines in the hospital dispensary and schools for their children they should vote 'Yes.' Most remarkably, the chairman of the Political Education Committee—who had spent an hour earlier in the day assuring the independent observer mission of the neutrality of his committee's work—gave a rousing political speech culminating in an exhortation to vote 'Yes' as he himself would.

An interview with a middle-aged schoolteacher after the rally was typical of discussions with supporters of the Compact.

> [If they don't get 75 percent tomorrow, when do you think you should have the next try?]

> It will be depending. Maybe if you talk about free association, maybe like this one, then maybe we talk about ten, twenty years from now. I think, by reading, I think I read it in the *Journal*, the *Congress Journal*, the last Congress, 99th congress, I think I read something about this in the *Journal* that while the Congressman Seiberling try to sell this to the

Congressmen that the United States has reached the bottom line in this negotiation; if we disapprove it, I don't know because if you really think back to the time when they start to frame this Compact of Free Association, I don't know whether you remember this, the Hilo 9—it was a very controversial issue in that we didn't want any military, it was actually the Compact of Free Association was based on that Hilo 9, so if we build it up to here and if we come here and change it, the it is different from the foundations so I think Belau cannot escape from that.

[So your impression is that there won't be any military here if the Compact is approved?]

I'm not saying that.

[Or would that not be a change from the base though?]

I'm not saying that there would be no military here because it says in the Compact that United States may come. I only base my observation or my idea on the experience because we had been under the Trusteeship Agreement for forty years and the United States, if they did want to bring military to Belau they did have a full authority and power to do that in the forty years. They have a right under the Trusteeship Agreement and they didn't do so. I think we in Balau we cannot run away from reality because the world is quite a small world and we cannot always stay and be out from and be away from all this development. . . . We have to negotiate with somebody, at least I think this the best alternative at this time is the United States and to accept this Compact and go into it whatever adjustment to it or amendment to Compact can be done while we are inside it. I see this like this: we contract a carpenter to build our house and the house is finished and the door is open and tomorrow we'll be standing right outside of the house and some will say that the house have a problem with the sink, it's leaking; the house have not painted roof, something like that. I think it best to go inside and we have done that three times; we stand out from the outside of the house and raining and sun and everything and we criticize inside that something is not right. So we tear the whole building down three times. Tomorrow another building will standing outside, and this has been going on—some people say the Compact money is not enough; other people say the Compact money is enough; what we receive from the Compact is different and what we receive from the

Trusteeship right now is status quo. . . . I don't say we cannot renegotiate the Compact. It probably will be taking a long time. I don't know by looking at Congress if the United States, the Congress, you know it change a lot in this election. You don't know if they decide to shelve things and say we study about it. We started with the administration of Carter and Carter was studying for quite some times and then Reagan and Reagan has DECIDED [his emphasis] to work on it and we have the opportunity right now whatever minor problems in the Compact it can be ironed out while we are IN [his emphasis] the Compact. We be emphasizing that we want those 10,000 people to go to the polls tomorrow to share their decision, to confirm the decision that they really want. And we cannot stop that there are people who are never satisfied. But the only thing I didn't agree with this, this democracy that people go by majority.

[What do you think will happen if you get a decision 62%? How will the community react? Will they get angry, or sad, or will they say 'Oh, to hell,' you know, 'enough of politics!'?]

I'll be sad too and feel insecure. I will be feeling insecure. To tell you the truth I will be insecure because if these people have a definite say that we vote no and go along with the negotiation and have something to offer, then I know, but they just say that we need to negotiate because there is something wrong with this Compact but they don't have an alternative to offer what are we going to become, independent or what, remain on this status quo? Fortunately, we are briefed about the financial situation of our government. I am worried because at the end of second quarter we have no money left. How would we run our government, how would we run our schools?

[So you feel the 75 percent in your Constitution. . .?]

Is FAIR [his emphasis]. It's good because it protect our Constitution but those who are opponents of the Compact should know that majority of Palau is pro-Compact, they should join the majority, not work against it.

[Does the Compact not make some overrides to the Constitution and changes?]

My understanding of reading Compact and Constitution, it goes side by side.

[There's no problem even with the nuclear passages?]

I think it reconciled in Compact because Constitution and Compact has been reconciled, the only thing we want to get permission, why it is 75%, it that transit article, because nuclear and all this is banned from Palau in our Constitution.

The concerns of those who opposed ratification of the Compact of Free Association as drafted were summed up by a major leader of the opposition forces in an interview at the office of the People's Headquarters for Belau Constitution and Compact Improvement on November 29, 1986.

If there is no Compact of Free Association, Palau will continue to have a simple life. There is no poverty here; it is not poverty like India. It is the simplicity of life, but once that simplicity of life is turned into a poverty we will be dependent on the cash from the United States, on the food stamps from the United States. It will turn us from what we are today into developments that in the long run will be bad for us. We are not really against development but what we are saying is that development should be for us. We are not against technology but we want appropriate technology. I think what the Ipseco power plant has done to us is a lesson to everyone. If we lose? if we lose, it will . . . well, No. 1 Palau will not be the same as what we see here. Within the next five years the population will triple because the immigration law is open, open for anyone with United States passport or for us to go to the United States. The door is supposedly open, but how many of us can go there and make a life in the United States? I think I see Palau will be more or less ruled as a . . . the government in Palau will be more or less a company. The President will be like the chairman of the board. The senators and the members of Congress will be like the other members of the board and the Constitution of Palau will be a thing of the past, no-one will take any notice of it. No one here is really against the concept of being friendly with the US or against the concept of Free Association. Let's be friends, we establish this treaty of friendship. But fifty years is too long, we be depriving the future generation of their land and we be accepting the military when we do not know if it is the wishes of the future generation.

The Vote

The air was not festive on December 2, 1986 in Palau as voters went to the polls for the fourth referendum on the Compact of Free Association, and the seventh on the nuclear-free clause of their constitution. The apprehensions voiced by the schoolteacher after the 'Yes' rally were shared by most Palauans, but in fact there was no violence. There was also a strong element of curiosity, of waiting to see the results.

The polling was very well conducted. Civil servants had volunteered (on a paid basis) to staff the polls as they had in the previous votes. Even in polling stations reachable only by boat, there was a uniformity of good organization. At each booth there was at least one police officer responsible for enforcing the rule against campaigning and carrying the polling boxes to the central counting station in Koror. The only shortcoming in the management of the actual vote was the fact that the ballots were not numbered. By contrast, all polling officers observed had copies of very well-prepared computer printouts of the 10,760 registered voters. No one could explain why the same technological sophistication that produced that list could not have produced numbered ballots, especially since there had been charges in earlier referenda of forged ballots.

The count began late in the evening in the legislative building under the watchful eye of both the United Nations Observer Mission and the independent observers. The trend was clear from the first counts. 8,824 of the registered 10,760 voters, or 82 percent, had voted. Over half these votes were cast in Koror; barely one-fifth of the voters had voted in the polling booths in the fifteen states outside Koror. Another one-fifth had voted off-island, in Guam, Saipan, Yap, Truk, Ponape, the Marshalls, Hawaii, Portland, San Francisco and Los Angeles.

While 5,789 of the voters, 65.97 percent, supported the Compact, enough voters—2,986 or 34.03 percent—disapproved the override of the nuclear provisions of the constitution to prevent the Compact going into effect. Half of the 'No' votes were cast in Koror; one-fifth in the other states; one-sixth off-islands and the remaining by people voting at polling places other than their state polling booths at home or in Koror.[8]

Collapse of the Rule of Law in Palau

In 1987 the farce degenerated into tragedy. The United States government and the Salii administration combined to put even more pressure on the Palauans to accept the Compact. In March, James Berg of the newly created Office of Freely Associated State Affairs (which in the Department of State's view had succeeded the Office of Micronesian Status Negotiations) restated the Thanksgiving message that there was no prospect for renegotiation of the terms of the compact. Two senior ranking members of the House Interior Committee, Delegate Ron de Lugo (D-Virgin Islands) and Representative Robert Lagomarsino (R-California) visited Palau over the Easter recess and told them firmly that not only was it President Reagan's position that the Compact should not be renegotiated but

> Even if the administration were to change its position and ask Congress for more money for Palau, they couldn't get it. There are too many other countries in the world that have been our friends that are being cut back. It's just not in the cards. [9]

President Salii announced that there would be a shortfall of at least two million dollars in the last quarter of fiscal year 1987 (which ends September 30.) He therefore reduced the weekly work hours of government employees from 40 to 32; reduced grants to the Palauan States; placed limitations on power usage, travel, government hirings and other expenses. He threatened to furlough the majority of the Palauan workforce.

In this atmosphere of tension that affected every family in Palau, no less than seven lawsuits were filed against Salii and his administration in March and April for fraud and misappropriation of public funds. The lawyers for the three young men charged with assassinating President Remelik filed their appeal.

In May the Salii government announced that a fifth plebiscite would be held in June—the third on precisely the same Compact as was presented to the people in February and December 1986. In a statement from Koror at the time of the Trusteeship Council meetings in May 1987 the Ibedul said

> The U.N. Trusteeship Agreement with respect to the Republic of Palau has not been terminated. This is due to the fact that the Compact of Free Association for Palau has been defeated in the last four (4) plebiscites and that in no plebiscite has the Compact been approved by more than 75% of the votes cast as required by our constitution. The highest court in the Republic of Palau has also ruled that the Compact of Free Association was not approved by the people of the Republic of Palau.

> The source of the conflict between the Compact and our constitution lies in the nuclear-free provisions of our constitution. Our constitution contains the expression of my people that Palau, and hopefully the Pacific, will be nuclear free. Our constitution was originally adopted in 1979 by 92% of the Palauan electorate. That provision in our constitution may only be waived by 75% of the votes cast. The Compact of Free Association with the United States contains a provision allowing the United States to neither confirm nor deny the presence of nuclear substances on their aircraft and ships transiting, overflying or making port visits to Palau. I believe that for the U. S. to continue to seek to override our constitutional ban on nuclear weapons and technology in Palau undermines the integrity of our constitution.

> Additionally, the Compact of Free Association violates our constitution by providing that the United States may establish and use defense sites in Palau and may designate for this purpose land and water areas for its use. These defense sites are undefined as to location and area. The Compact of Free Association and related agreements grant the United States the right to request that the Republic of Palau make such defense sites available for its use within 60 days. If the Government of the Republic of Palau is unable to make such defense sites available, then the United States may take possession of such defense sites anyway. Yet our constitution forbids our government from using its powers of eminent domain to provide land for the benefit of a foreign entity. And, of course, the people of Palau want their rights to their own land respected.

Despite the clear results of the 4 plebiscites so far, the U. S., through their representatives who have come to Palau in recent months, both from the executive and legislative branches of the United States Government, has advised the Palauan leaders that the Compact cannot be renegotiated. This position of the U. S. has created an impasse, the only solution being for Palau to continue to have referenda indefinitely until the necessary 75% vote is achieved. Alternatively, my people could amend their constitution, rendering our constitution compatible with the Compact of Free Association.

In view of the position taken by the U. S., the Government of the Republic of Palau has been forced to call for a fifth referendum to be held in June, despite the fact that this identical document was disapproved in the last referendum held on December 2, 1986. There is no reason to believe that the 75% requirement can be achieved in this next referendum. Further, the Government of the Republic of Palau has declared that in the event that the Compact of Free Association fails to receive 75% of the votes in the June referendum, a new referendum to amend our constitution will be called for immediately thereafter. [10]

Despite the absurdity of the repeated plebiscites, the Trusteeship Council sent another Visiting Mission to Palau in June 1987. The plebiscite was called for June 23 but at the last moment the Supreme Court of Palau ruled that the procedures for collecting the ballots in Hawaii and the mainland United States were illegal so the plebiscite was postponed to June 30. The outcome was virtually the same as in December—67% of the voters supported the Compact—despite the pressures brought to bear on the community.

The tension immediately escalated into violence. On June 27 legislation was prepared ordering an emergency furlough of 900 of Palau's 1,300 civil servants until the start of the new fiscal year in October. The order was signed on June 30, the day of the fifth referendum. It was followed on July 3 by another emergency order which cut off money from various government branches including the *Olbiil Era Kelulau*, the judiciary, the state governments, the non-public schools, and scholarships. Many of the furloughed workers set up a camp outside the *Olbiil Era Kelulau* and formed a "Furlough Committee" which began to harass members of the Palauan legislature during its Eleventh Regular Session. Their goal was the adoption of RPPL-2-30 which enabled two more referenda—one to amend the constitution to allow adoption of the Compact by simple majority of those voting and the second to submit the Compact for the sixth time to the people of Palau under the amended constitution which would require only fifty percent for adoption. Death threats were made against several legislators, including Speaker of the House, Santos Olikong.

The referendum on the amendment of the constitution to permit fifty percent adoption of the Compact took place on August 4 amidst what the International Commission of Jurists mission of inquiry described subsequently as a breakdown of the rule of law—a breakdown permitted by the United States which sent no reinforcements to the Salii administration (which probably did not request them.) The amendment to the constitution was adopted by a majority in three-quarters of the Palauan states with a total 'yes' vote of 73.33 percent (5,645) and 'no' vote of 26.67 percent (2,053). On August 21, 1987 the Palauan electorate voted for the sixth time directly on the Compact of Free Association. Despite the intimidation, the 'no' vote held at 26.96 percent (2,201) and the 'yes' vote did not make the required 75 percent, being 73.04 percent (5,964).

The frustration of the Furlough Committee, the Salii administration and the erstwhile Office of Micronesian Status Negotiations was intense. Furthermore, the level of violence that had been permitted in Koror over the past few months had alarmed the United States Congress. The Subcommittee on Insular and International Affairs of the House Interior Committee held emergency meetings on Palau on July 23 with unprecedented full attendance, including that of Morris Udall, chairman of the Interior Committee. On July 29 pro-constitutionalists in Palau filed *Merep et al. vs. Salii et. al* (Civil Action 139-87) in the Supreme Court of Palau seeking a declaratory judgement that RPPL-2-30 authorizing the amendment referendum was null and void and unconstitutional and a preliminary and permanent injunction enjoining the government from carrying out the proposed two August plebiscites. On August 18 Chief Justice Nakamura refused to enjoin the plebiscite itself but did enjoin the tabulation of the voting until the full court could consider the constitutional issues. The Chief Justice immediately became the target of intimidation; as a direct result he reversed himself and denied motion for a preliminary injunction in full and recused himself from the case, appointing Judge Hefner, an Associate Judge of the Supreme Court of Palau who lived on Saipan, in his place. The plaintiffs meanwhile withdrew their case under pressure from the Ibedul who said he had come to an agreement with President Salii that the Council of Chiefs of Palau would be charged with the responsibility of considering all requests by the United States government for land use rights pursuant to the Compact.

However, on August 31, 1987 a group of women elders filed *Ngirmang et al. vs. Salii* (Civil Action 161-87) which as the International Commission of Jurists observers noted " . . . essentially repeated, almost word for word, the allegations of *Merep*." [11] The women could not get a fully qualified counsel to represent them and had to act *pro se*, on their own behalf. The government filed a Motion to Dismiss the suit alleging that the issues had already been heard in *Merep* and a hearing was set for September 8 before Judge Hefner. However, on the eve of the hearing the father of one of the plaintiffs and the assistant counsel for the women was killed in his son's law office after a week of threats that included shots into women's homes and the firebombing of supporters' homes.

On September 8, 1987 only one of the women plaintiffs, Rafaela Sumang, appeared in court to file a petition for an adjournment to obtain counsel. She was offered a Stipulation of Dismissal but Judge Hefner required that it be signed by all the plaintiffs; the signatures were rounded up under pressure. Although Judge Hefner was then presented with twenty-two signatures he refused to simply sign the stipulation, instead offering an extended opinion that the plaintiffs had been intimidated. The International Commission of Jurists mission team noted

> When Judge Hefner left for the airport to return to Saipan on September 9, 1987, he was accompanied by a cadre of twelve policemen apparently because of the government's concern for his personal safety in light of what he had felt obliged to do and say. [12]

The breakdown of law and order in Palau culminated in the murder of Bedor Bins. Roman Bedor, son of the murdered man, described the events surrounding his father's death in a subsequent deposition:

September 7th: While working in the office in the morning Rafaela and Gabriela Ngirmang came and they were really scared about their security. We talked about the security for them and decided that we should ask the Minister of Justice to provide security. Gabriela and Rafaela left to see the Minister of Justice at his house [Thomas Remengesau]. Security was not provided. In the evening, at 7:00 p.m., I met with Gabriela and Rafaela at her daughter's house which is close to my parents' house. Gabriela was worried about the security; she advised me that she feared for her life and the life of all women in the case. She told me that she will be spending a night at her daughter's house. I went to the office to work after my discussion with Gabriela. About 7:30 p.m., I received a telephone call. I answered the phone but no one responded. I could only hear noise and background music. At about 8:30 and 9:30 a car stopped in front of the office and it appears that the driver of the car was stepping on the gas/accelerator. It left. I did not see the make of the car. About 10:00 p.m. my cousin called me over to my parents' home. I went and was there for some time, for about half an hour. About 10:30 or 10:45, while all the relatives were in the house, and I was outside with some of them barbecuing fish all the power was cut off all over the islands. Immediately thereafter, a bomb exploded at Gabriela's house and Abai Ra Metal Night Club was firebombed. My father went to the office to pick up his flashlight and while in the office he was shot twice by a man with a white mask covering his head. I ran outside toward my father and met my father walking toward me from the office and he told me he was shot. I saw the red car leaving the premises and the people were still shooting, more than two people according to my father. My father was bleeding and I thought he was not really badly injured because he told me secure the kids and ladies in the house because he thought the people who were shooting were still around, and to never mind about him. I went to secure the kids and the women in the house, Bernie and Bill [her husband] came out. We couldn't call the ambulance because the telephone was out of order. We couldn't call the police either. The whole island was in total darkness, but we must get my father to the hospital. Bill and Bernie and my cousins took my father to the hospital as I stayed behind watching the house. They took my father to the hospital and while there the doctors or the hospital staff couldn't operate or do anything to him. [the hospital has an emergency support generator] We do not know why the staff did not act right away. My brother-in-law, Peter, went out to look for a private doctor. He was able to locate Dr. Yano to take him to the hospital to see my father. When they arrived, it was about an hour later. By then my father had lost a lot of blood and he was already unconscious. Dr. Yano immediately began an operation on him.

Curiously, President Salii came to the hospital a few minutes after Bernie and Bill arrived with my father, and asked who has been injured.

September 8th: The operation on my father continued from last night until this morning. Dr. Yano advised us that the chance of survival is 50/50 as my father is really seriously injured. My father died at 10:30 a.m. And at 12:00 relatives and friends came to the house to ask me to ask Bernie to dismiss the case and they told me that 'they' will be coming to attack the house tonight if the suit is not dismissed. I did not approach Bernie, but some of the relatives approached her and she refused.

The murder of Bedor Bins was intolerable to four congressional leaders who jointly wrote to Secretary of the Interior Donald Hodel on September 18 in a rare bipartisan letter. Representatives Morris Udall (D-Arizona), Don Young (R-Alaska), Ron de Lugo (D-Virgin Islands) and Robert Lagomarsino (R-California) warned

We need to be assured that the Compact of Free Association has been constitutionally approved in the islands with individual rights and constitutional processes secure before we will be able to support legislation to implement the compact. [13]

They urged that the Interior Secretary send a personal representative to the islands to deal with the serious problems now apparent there.

This marked a new level of critical examination of the Compact approval process by Congress. In October the Congressional Research Service, which was asked for an opinion on whether or not Palau's constitution could be amended only in a general election, agreed with Roman Bedor and other constitutionalists that the attempt to amend the constitution on August 4, 1987 was invalid. [14] November saw the revelation that Lazarus Salii, his brother Carlos and Ibedul Y. M. Gibbons had received $450,000 in July 1983 from the International

Power Systems Company Ltd. (IPSECO) to facilitate approval of the power plant deal. [15] At the end of the month it was announced that the General Accounting Office (the investigative arm of the United States Congress) would send a three-person team to Palau "to look into everything you can think of." [15]

Congressional Scrutiny At The End Of The Reagan Administration

In January 1988 the three member International Commission of Jurists inquiry mission was in Palau while three women elders were in Washington testifying before congressional committees. Appendix F contains the findings, conclusions and recommendations of the inquiry mission. Gabriela Ngirmang explained to the Senate Energy and Natural Resources Committee on January 26, 1988

> In Palau women play an important role in issues of policy, as I suspect is the case in Washington as well. Women traditionally own and devise land. We control the clan money. We traditionally select our chiefs; women place and remove them. Having observed their upbringing closely, we are able to decide which men have the talent to represent our interests. From birth, Palauan women are responsible for the men. When the men marry, the women arrange for the settlement and when the men die, the women bury them.

> I came here because the women feel that our interests are not being satisfactorily protected, and out of concern for the Palauan citizens. We feel that those who voted for the Compact do not understand the content of the document. Those who voted in favor of the Compact did not and do not understand its meaning or effect. The Compact is hundreds of pages long, it is written by lawyers, and the political education on the document is biased to support the political needs of the president of Palau. Despite much public relations and efforts to sell the Compact, we clearly understand that the implementation of the Compact gives the United States the right to conduct military operations on as much as one-third of our land—forever. We see that the Compact says military rights may end in fifty years if

mutually agreed. This means, we understand, that if the United States wishes to continue its control of our land, it need only say and this will go on forever. This is unacceptable.

She also pointed out

I have been assured repeatedly that the United States has no present intention of exercising its rights to use our land for military purposes. I am not reassured. We do not seek options on U. S. land. We assume that if you seek options on Palauan land, you at some point will use them. If they are not important to you, then please remove them from the discussions in the future. In any event, the Trusteeship Agreement involved the promise that our country would be given roads, docks, hospitals, power—the things we need to live in a dignified way. And, forty years later, we do not have them. So promises with regard to future actions are not as important to us as keeping our land.

Despite hearing these concerns, the Senate Energy and Natural Resources Committee approved Senate Joint Resolution 231 on March 23 that would put the Compact into effect. However, House Joint Resolution 497 approved by the Foreign Affairs Subcommittee on Asian and Pacific Affairs was stalled by the reservations of the House Interior and Insular Affairs Committee which still had serious questions regarding the constitutionality of the process hereto.

The twenty-two women plaintiffs in *Ngirmang v. Salii* refiled their challenge to the August 4, 1987 constitutional amendment referendum and 141 new plaintiffs signed-on to the case, which now became *Fritz v. Salii* (Civil Appeal 8-88). On April 22, 1988 Associate Justice Robert Hefner ruled that the August 4 referendum was null and void because it was a legal process intended to apply only to amendments to eliminate inconsistencies between the constitution and the Compact of Free Association. In fact, there was no inconsistency as such, since the constitution clearly provided the 75 percent amendment requirement in order to change the constitution to permit nuclear substances, and the 75 percent had not been reached. Judge Hefner commented

Palau is still under the trusteeship umbrella of the United States. Under all the circumstances surrounding this case

> (presumably within the knowledge of the United States government) and the political background and intimate connection of the United States and Palau (certainly within the the the knowledge of the United States), the unquestioned reliance upon the certification of the President of Palau [that the Compact was ratified] does not comport with the reputation of the United States for fostering and supporting democracies for emerging countries under its political wing.

Nevertheless, the United States government filed an appeal. In May the report of the International Commission of Jurists inquiry team was published which confirmed the congressional critics of the process in their determination to demand stronger security and accounting practices in Palau.

The tide had turned against President Salii. With presidential elections looming in both the United States and Palau, a new coalition formed to oppose Salii. Called the 'Coalition for Open, Honest and Just Government,' it included Roman Tmetchul, Moses Uludong, Vice President Thomas Remengesau, Speaker Santos Olikong and Ibedul Yukata Gibbons. [17] The following week United States District Court Judge Robert Sweet in New York ruled that Palau must pay $44,300,000 in loan repayments to the consortium of interests that had financed the IPSECO power generation facility. [18] The Palau Supreme Court was hearing oral arguments on the appeal against the ruling on the August 4 referendum. Congressmen were pressing President Salii to accept more investigations from the General Accounting Office and permanent auditing requirements of government spending. On August 20, 1988 after spending several days destroying documents, President Lazarus Salii committed suicide at his home. On August 29, 1988 the three judge appellate panel of the Supreme Court of Palau affirmed Judge Hefner's ruling that the attempt at constitutional amendment a year earlier had been unconstitutional.

Time was running out for the Reagan administration. Delegate Ron de Lugo introduced in June an enabling bill, House Joint Resolution 597; by September it had 40 co-sponsors from both parties. It would increase Compact funding by about $24,000,000 for hospitals, substance abuse prevention and capital improvements and increased access to federal educational programs during the Compacts' first fifteen years. It also required an independent office of public auditor to be established in Palau for the fifteen years and for a strengthened public prosecution office. Most importantly, the congressional sponsors were fully educated about the pressures to avoid the 75 percent requirement of the Palauan constitution that had to be met to implement the Compact. As Delegate de Lugo told Speaker Santos Olikong in July hearings,

> When you first came to me with your concerns, I was not easily persuaded. Far from it. At first, I thought this was local politics, that many of the things you were saying were exaggerated. Unfortunately, and to my sorrow, the investigations of this committee have borne out all that you said. [19]

De Lugo rejected the interpretation of James Berg of the State Department's Office of Freely Associated States that the objections to the Compact in Palau were caused by outsiders. De Lugo said

> Mr. Berg, several times, talked about these 'outside forces.' And I bought that at first, that the whole focus of whether the people of Palau want this compact or not is being impeded by outside 'do-gooders' and others. When we went and took a real look, we found that the real concern about the Compact, about Palau's future under the Contract, is held by the Palauans themselves, not all these so-called 'do-gooders' with their banners and their little emblems and their almost-mimeograph letters that they send to this committee. It's the Palauans themselves. And when you have a community of that size, and you have outside forces with lots of money, and outside forces that are corrupt, hit men, people involved in the most outrageous adventures who have washed up on the shores of Palau, and huge sums of money—IPSECO, Mathews and Wright [an indicted bond firm which tried to sell Palau a $400,000,000 bond issue in 1986-87]—the impact on the people of Palau and their government is incredible. [20]

Delegate de Lugo noted in the *Congressional Record* on October 6, 1988

> A federal court . . . ruled that Palau owes a now estimated $46,000,000 for facilities probably worth half that much. The debt is more than twice Palau's annual budget and the General Accounting Office tells us that other deals—many of them questionable—push the total debt to nearly $100,000,000. [21]

Towards a New Consensus in Palau?

Elections were held in both Palau and the United States in November 1988. Ngiratkel Etpison was declared the new President of Palau by 31 votes over the objections of the Coalition for Open, Honest and Just Government and a challenge to the integrity of the counting process by the loser, Roman Tmetchul. One of President Bush's earliest appointments was of former Ambassador for Micronesian Status Negotiations, Fred M. Zeder, to head the Overseas Private Investment Corporation despite his role in the debacle of the IPSECO scandal.

One of President Etpison's first steps was to permit the creation of a bipartisan Commission on Future Palau/United States Relations in the *Olbiil Era Kelulau*. By mid-January it had produced a unified position paper which read

> The leaders of Palau are unified and have agreed to place a high priority on the ultimate resolution of the future political status for Palau. The Palau leaders find that the six unsuccessful attempts by the Palau electorate to ratify the Compact of Free Association in the past demonstrated clearly the need to address and resolve the political status issues which impact on the sovereignty and lives of the Palauan people.

> Despite repeated failures by the Palau electorate to muster the 75 percent constitutionally-mandated majority approval of the Compact of Free Association, Palau leaders continue to believe that an overwhelming majority of the Palau electorate still favors and supports the concept of a fully constituted and self-governing Palau freely associated with the United States. This concept is based on the recognition of two inescapable realities. On the one hand, there is the expressed desire of Palau to control its land and other resources and on the other, the obvious need for outside technical and financial assistance. The longstanding American interest in this area for defense and for the promotion of international peace and security in this part of the world is recognized.

> What is more, the international trusteeship obligations of the U.S. towards Palau to prepare Palau to achieve self-government or independence as may be appropriate to circumstances of the people of Palau fell far short of

expectations and will now have to be accommodated under the terms of reference of Compact of Free Association. In that regard, it is the Palau consensus that any reconciliation of any possible conflict or inconsistency between the Palau Constitution and the Compact with the U. S. will ultimately result in the changes to be sought within the four corners of the Compact with the U. S. and any proposal to accommodate changes by effecting amendments to the Palau constitution will not be considered.

On another plane, Palau wants to establish a political status of free association with the United States because its present status as the last Trust Territory smacks of a quasi-colonial status which is degrading to Palauan people and unworthy of America. A Compact of Free Association with all of its subsidiary agreements, if it properly addresses identified needs in and without the Compact, could forge a unique partnership between Palau and the United States, not as between guardian and ward, but more as between equal partners.

A Compact of Free Association, in order to obtain the unqualified approval of the overwhelming majority of the Palauan electorate, must take into account minimum political, economic, and social requirements of the Palauan people to enable them to make smooth transition from their present state to a new one. To this end, a political status entity will be organized at the earliest possible time representing all segments of Palau leadership and reflecting various points of view on the future political status issues for Palau. This entity should be given mandates to address Palau's basic concerns with the United States toward resolving the future political status of Palau and to seek broad agreements on a Compact of Free Association which in its opinion will be best suited to the needs, interests, and aspirations of the Palauan people.

The next month a high ranking delegation from the United States Congress visited Palau with the new Secretary of the Interior, Manuel Lujan, Jr., a former member of Congress with long service on the House Committee on Interior and Insular Affairs. This delegation sought to revive House Joint Resolution 597 as a compromise solution. However, this attempt to once again force the pace from Washington failed due to congressional concerns about the need for stricter accounting and public prosecution measures. Despite having requested another United

Nations Visiting Mission to Palau in early 1989, the United States was not able to present a ratified Compact to the Trusteeship Council in May. It was able to report to the closing session that a new subsidiary agreement had been negotiated that would provide an additional $9,300,000 to address deficiencies in Palau's hospitals, prisons, substance abuse programs, and offices of public prosecution and auditing. However, the new monies meant problems in the progress of the revised agreements through Congress which was now more cautious than it had ever been of signing-off on a deal before it was ratified by the Palauan electorate. The new agreements did provide President Etpison with an excuse to call a seventh plebiscite on the Compact of Free Association, which was scheduled for February 1990. But despite the fifteen months of consensus building since the end of the Reagan administration, the Palauan people once again refused to override the nuclear-free clauses of their constitution on February 6, 1990. In fact, they "defeated the Compact by the largest margin ever in the seven plebiscites of the past seven years." [22]

Notes

[1] Larry Gerston, "Political Leadership in Palau," *New Zealand International Review* IX/6 (November/December 1986).

[2] For a very useful analysis of the Appellate Division decision, see Annex A, Study Paper Prepared by the Micronesia Coalition of *Gibbons et. al. vs. Salii*, A Summary of the Appellate Division of the Supreme Court of the Republic of Palau, November 6, 1986.

[3] Document S/18424, October 24, 1986.

[4] Which as we have noted in an earlier chapter was anticipated more than a decade ago by such observers as Donald McHenry.

[5] Document provided under the Freedom of Information Act to Roger S. Clark, December 23, 1986.

[6] *Sunday News* (November 30, 1986): 1.

[7] Interview with Bill Keldermans, December 1, 1986.

[8] *Report of the United Nations Visiting Mission to Observe the Plebiscite in Palau, Trust Territory of the Pacific Islands December, 1986* [Document T/1906 of the Trusteeship Council, May-June 1987]; *Report of the International Observer Mission Palau Referendum December 1986* [communicated to the United Nations at T/COM.10/L, 374, May 13, 1987 Trusteeship Council]; see also discussion at T/PV 1635, May 22, 1987, Trusteeship Council, 22-68.

[9] *Pacific Daily News* (April 17, 1987).

[10] Press release, Center for Constitutional Rights [New York] (May 15, 1987).

[11] William J. Butler and others. *Palau, A Challenge to the Rule of Law in Micronesia: Report of a Mission.* (New York: American Association for the International Commission of Jurists, 1988), 32.

[12] Palau, *A Challenge to the Rule of Law*, 38

[13] *Washington Pacific Report* 6: 1 (October 1, 1987): 3.

[14] Esther Iverem, "Vote to End Pacific Islands' Atom-Arms Ban is Challenged," *New York Times* (October 13, 1987).

[15] *San Jose Mercury News* (November 29, 1987).

[16] *Pacific Daily News* (November 28, 1987).

[17] *Washington Pacific Report* 6: 21 (August 1, 1988): 6.

[18] *Washington Pacific Report* 6: 22 (August 15, 1988): 2.

[19] *Belau Update* 15 (September 10, 1988): 5.

[20] *Belau Update*: 6.

[21] *Asian Pacific Issues News* (January 1989): 3 [Portland, American Friends Service Committee].

[22] Petition to the United Nations Trusteeship Council, Charles Scheiner, May 22, 1990.

Chapter Five

Prospects for Popular Ratification of the Compact of Free Association in Palau

While Palauans are weary of the issue and the repeated referenda there is something in the process that speaks to their traditional view of government. Many Palauans explained to the international observers that the traditional notion of consensus meant that an issue had to be debated until eighty or ninety percent of the community accepted the decision. This could often take a long time. They did not think it inappropriate for 25 percent of the voters to have a veto on 75 percent; the provision for a "mere" 75 percent "consensus" was considered very modern by many Palauans. What was not appreciated was intransigence—either on the part of the 75 percent or the 25 percent. A solution was not emerging despite the protracted process in the effort to reconcile the constitution and the Compact; and the failure of President Salii to engineer that consensus drew at least as much criticism as the failure of the opponents of the Compact to devise a compromise. However, Palauan political culture is not fragile and may be able to continue absorbing tensions and pressures in a time-honored way.

In the immediate postwar period, American ethnographers noted the strongly diadic, factionalized nature of Palauan politics. Arthur J. Vidich tended to assume that this factionalism was dysfunctional: that it was

> characterized as one in which the groups competing for power because of differing value premises, hold in question the central tenets of the society, and thus turn the factionalism against the going system. Such a situation usually develops when alternative choices confront a society as a result of certain internal or external forces impinging on the society. . . [and/or] the unorthodox abuse of power by those elements defined as the legitimate focus of authority, thus causing social, cultural or material depreciation to certain groups.[1]

In their fieldwork two decades later, Roland and Maryann Force noted that

> At the time of contact with the Western world, Palau was conceived of by Palauans as being divided into two regions of roughly equal size—one comprising the northeastern portion of the island group, the other the southwestern portion. Membership in these confederations varied somewhat over time as a consequence of warfare and general rivalry in the course of which a village or district comprising a number of villages would change its affiliation ties. . . . The two principal divisions of the island chain formed political confederations. The northern was under the control of the ranking chief of Melekeok and the southern under the ranking chief of Koror. These two chiefs bore hereditary titles—Aibedul for the chief of Koror, and Reklai for the chief of Melekeok—and competed with each other for island supremacy.[2]

The Forces saw this Manichean perspective as being pervasive of Palauan culture both ontologically and epistemologically

> The concept of duality was one of the most important cultural patterns in Palau, pervading concepts of the physical social and psychological worlds. The Palauan's island home, his villages, the important social institutions of his culture, and the activities of the society in which he participated, all were bisected. Indeed, this dichotomous pattern is apparent in Palauan conceptualization generally. Something either is or it is not.[3]

But they point out that this pervasive opposition is not confrontationist but dualist.

> Implicit in the usage is a two-part balance. Although two sections may be in competition with each other, the word *bital* [other] does not connote dominance of one section over the other. By warfare and intrigue, however, some village halves, some villages, and even some individuals became dominant over others. It is of interest that while a pattern of cultural duality existed without doubt, the dynamics of the interaction of the two parts produced a cultural unity.[4]

This unity was reflected in the arrangements for leadership

The major political figures in a village were the first- and second-ranking chiefs. The highest-ranking male member of the highest-ranking kin group was the first-ranking chief (*rubak*) and the highest ranking male from the second-ranking kin group was the second-ranking chief of a village.[5]

Clearly traditional Palauan culture worked hard to prevent the polity bifurcating into the "ins" v. the "outs." The Forces remarked that "the route to power in the old days was via kinship." [6]

Moreover, there was a safety valve to the restrictions and constrictions of kinship for the politically ambitious. Vidich explained that

> In Palau, perhaps one of the most significant configurations which motivates socially acceptable and deviant behavior, is the prestige orientation of the culture. This takes a varied form in behavior including the performance of distinctive feats, possession of exceptional knowledge (such as specializing in the knowledge of Palau currency) or controlling political power. Prestige is an implicit normative goal for which all Palauans strive, and explains in part their excessive interest in status rights, obligations and functions. In addition, the indigenous institutional structure, because of its fluidity, fostered this prestige striving. As a corollary to this prestige orientation, there is the extreme emphasis on competition between individuals, clans or districts.[7]

H.G. Barnett also noted (in the forties and fifties) that

> Being Palauan is being interested in money, in the same sense that being American is being interested in money. It is not the whole of existence, but it strikes the outsider as commanding or coloring a great part of it.[8]

Palauan money, like so much else in Palau, came in two forms. Men's money was made of one of three materials—hard, glassy pottery; variegated porcelain; old imperfect glass—the origins of which are still obscure. Women's money is turtle shell, cut and moulded to form small trays. While men's money is finite, because the number of pieces in circulation is broadly known and no new pieces can be generated, women's money can be minted from the turtles. The circulation of these two forms of money is very complex and continues today as a form of exchange for a whole category of services from housebuilding to bride prices. Much of the traditional attitude to raising money—by communal collections among kin groups or others under obligation—has extended to the United States dollar earned in modern commercial transactions or more frequently as weekly labor. Prestige is dependent on wealth and its visible circulation for the benefit of one's kin and village and political affiliates.

Vidich discerned that

> A man who is clever or shrewd in the manipulation of Palau money and who is able to accumulate wealth is able to achieve prestige and respect and thus enjoys a certain amount of political power and the deference of others who may be in his own rank or even ranks above him. . . . Thus this status may be viewed as an institutionalized outlet for avoiding certain strains in the social system which arise when a particularly clever and ambitious person views with dissatisfaction his hereditarily determined rank position.[9]

In fact, while the traditional social structure keeps individuals ranked in a hierarchical order, Palauan money has long performed a "catalytic function" in the society.

> It has functioned as a means of settling war disputes, as a support to the status system, as a basic element in the major events such as birth, marriage, and death, and finally, as a factor in mediating personal differences and in adjusting criminal offenses. Palau money, the tangible object, has served to order and regulate the whole area of human relations and to provide an objective basis through which actual or potential strains in the social system could be either assuaged or averted.[10]

The postwar ethnographers, then, found a society in which the principle of "opposing forces" permeated virtually all the social and political structures. Vidich likened it to the American system of checks and balances in the federal government—the chiefs v. the shamans; men's clubs v. the two major political confederations each of which comprised approximately half the population in order to "check each other, through their respective authorities, in actions which are potentially disruptive of a balanced power situation."[11]

And then came the Americans with apparently infinite amounts of the new dollar currency and a wish to democratize or open up the old system of rank and prestige.

Until then, Palau's five or six thousand people were living in fourteen main village clusters throughout the islands. Donald Shuster[12] has traced the evolution of sixteen states from these fourteen sub-polities. The United States was very keen to introduce Western-style political institutions, and began with the village communities. Norman Meller notes that

> At last count there were 115 recognized units of local government in the Trust Territory of which two-fifths were formally charted.[13]

The result in Palau was the proliferation of government in Lilliputian proportions as indicated by the map on page 46 showing the populations of the sixteen states in 1982. At the same time, the concentration of resources in Palau—which had been the headquarters of the Japanese administration of Micronesia—together with the tripling of the population in forty years resulted in rapid "urbanization." Koror has the only high school and only hospital in Palau; it is the site of the Micronesian Occupational College. It has several major hotels catering primarily to the Japanese tourist trade, a few service industries and is the seat of government administration which employs 1,500 Palauans. So Koror state—governed by the relatively young (late 30s) Ibedul, Yutaka M. Gibbons—had a population in 1982 of 7,685 while Arai, the most proximate and second most-populous state had a population of 672. Airai is the seat of Roman Tmetchul, a man in his late fifties who was one of the three main contenders of political power in postwar Palau in the 1980s—the others being Haruo Remeliik and Lazarus Salii. Political anthropologists—many of them under contract to the United States administration—have detailed the evolution of a modern secular leadership throughout Micronesia in the past four decades.

Although the ethnographic details differ widely, all the observers remark on the same general process—the gradual emergence of a modern secular leadership from the age-group of young men in 1945 which challenged the political leadership of the traditional chiefs. These young men took advantage of United States-sponsored education to become technocrats in the postwar administration of their islands; some went into business and took advantage of the new opportunities, several becoming rich in the process. At the same time they accepted and employed electoral politics as a way of relating to the United States administration. These younger men (and a handful of women) were willing to staff municipal and state level governments; they participated in the six district legislatures created by the United States, in the Council of Micronesia and its successor the Congress of Micronesia. By the time the Congress came to grips with the issue of the future political status for the Trust Territory, these leaders—now middle aged and confident of their own abilities—found it more attractive to opt for separate polities rather than submerge their differences and pool their resources into the proposed Federated States of Micronesia.

Norman Meller, a senior advisor to several Micronesian legislatures and staff member of the Constitutional Convention of the Congress of Micronesia during its fraught 90-day life in 1975, has given his account of how and why the proposed Federation failed (*Constitutionalism in Micronesia*, 1985.) He places the primary blame on what he calls "The Palauan Ploy" in which the Palauan delegation engaged in confrontationist politics epitomized by their presentation early in the meeting of seven non-negotiable demands. While Roman Tmetchul was a member of the Palauan delegation, Meller blames Lazarus Salii for his 'firebrand' political style which in effect ensured that the several parts of Micronesia would go their separate ways. In 1975 Meller saw Salii as interested in free association with the United States while Tmetchul was talking independence. Yet Salii presented the demand that Koror be the capital of the new Federated States and that all the districts receive equal shares of the combined revenue despite their disparities. Meller gives a succinct but unsympathetic account of what happened in Palau after the collapse of the Federated States proposal

> Palau's parturition proved to be exceedingly prolonged, touching on the comedy of the absurd. A Palauan constitutional convention held in the spring of 1979 produced a document which Ambassador Rosenblatt told the district legislature violated the negotiated terms of the status compact. He objected to its provisions on eminent domain, nuclear prohibitions, marine boundaries, and return of public

lands. Senator Tmetchul's group within the district convention had favored a parliamentary system of government, but had been defeated by a rival bloc headed by Senator Salii, which adopted a more conventional—that is, American—system of government and a harder line on matters crucial to the future relations with the United States. A court decision in effect nullified the popular referendum accepting this document. Next, the district legislature, in which the Tmetchul faction dominated, attempted to have the constitution rewritten so as to bring it in line with the compact to which the Tmetchul-led Palau Status Commission subscribed. The revised constitution then met a decisive popular defeat. The following year, in mid-1980, a new legislature now controlled by anti-Tmetchul forces resubmitted the original constitution to the voters, and it was overwhelmingly reaffirmed at the polls, the third constitutional referendum in less than twelve months.[14]

This view of recent Palauan history is extended by another United States government participant, Howard Hills in a letter dated December 5, 1986 giving the Office of Micronesian Status Negotiations' official objections to a proposed feature on Palau being prepared by the "20/20" ABC television program. In claiming to correct distortions apparent in some documents, Hills, the legal advisor to OMSN in the Reagan Administration and a Peace Corps worker in Micronesia before that, states that,

> it should be noted that the *Summary Journal* of the Forty-Ninth Day of the Palau Constitutional Convention records that Delegate Lazarus Salii was one of the framers of the nuclear provision of Palau's constitution which requires 75 percent approval of the treaty we have negotiated with Palau. His brother Carlos proposed the final amendment which clarified the applicability of the provision to United States military activities.

> It should also be noted that Governor Tmetchul was Palau's Chief political status negotiator and deserves credit as one of the principal architects of free association as defined in the Compact. When the 1979 constitutional convention produced a draft constitution requiring 75 percent approval of the Compact he had negotiated, Tmetchul led the movement to nullify the draft constitution, and served as chairman of a constitutional drafting committee which

produced a revised constitution which was intended to accommodate United States military operational requirements.

That revised constitution was rejected by the people, and the original constitution was later adopted. Tmetchul ran against Remeliik and lost in the first two national elections under the new constitution which he had opposed . . . the major difference between the Compact negotiated by Tmetchul and the final version negotiated by Salii is that the original Compact for which Tmetchul was responsible authorized the United States to store nuclear weapons in Palau, while the Compact negotiated by Salii does not allow the United States to store nuclear weapons anywhere in Palau under any circumstances.

Roman Tmetchul was neutralized as an explicit political force in Palau in the 1980s by the conviction of his son and nephew in the conspiracy to murder Haruo Remeliik. Although considerable doubts remain about the role of the young men associated with Tmetchul in the actual murder (doubts summarized in the Defense Brief of the American Civil Liberties Union in the case and reported in the *New York Times* in a major full-length article on November 27, 1986 which secured their acquittal in July 1987) the implication of Tmetchul in the affair was sufficient to prevent him running for the presidency against Lazarus Salii. Barnett noted that "Palauans are not interested in kinship as such. Their primary concern is with wealth, and kinship for them is a vehicle for its manipulation."[15]

The Forces noted that "Even the murder of a close relative, in order to obtain his chiefly title and power, could be atoned for by paying the proper monetary fine."[16] It is sadly tempting to view the machinations of the Palauan political leadership of this group—the Salii, Remeliik, Tmetchul triumvirate—as a modern version of a more traditional division of the spoils. But there are major differences—the spoils are much more substantial than forty years ago (corruption surrounding the IPESCO power plant has been calculated in millions of dollars) and the "dualist" nature of traditional politics—which would have given the loser a place in the government as leader of the second-ranking group—has given way to a "winner take all" mentality.

But most significantly, the subsequent generation of leaders—men and women now in their late twenties and thirties—are challenging the wealth and prestige priorities of their fathers and grandfathers because they are concerned with the more fundamental issue of preventing the introduction of nuclear substances. Educated enough to know the perils of nuclear substances and to know that other communities have successfully resisted having them sited among them, these young people are also at variance with the "middle generation" in their view of Palau's future. Ironically, they are often more traditionalist than their fathers. Having studied in the United States, they have chosen against settling on the mainland. They want to make a life and a living on Palau. They know they need land to to do that. They are not persuaded that massive industrial and commercial development of a tourist economy such as Guam's is what they want or what could absorb their labor and that of their children. Casting about for more balanced forms of economic development, they do not want to see Palau's only main road become a Ginza Strip. They are joined in this view by enough members of the older generations who remember Hiroshima and Nagasaki, who have met people from Bikini and Uterik, who want to keep their land too. In refusing to accomodate their concerns, Salii polarized Palauan politics just as he polarized the Constitutional Convention of the Congress of Micronesia in 1974 until federation became impossible.

Consensus is a tradition within the American polity too. Why did the United States lock itself into a series of nonnegotiable demands on Palau that would not stand scrutiny outside the Trusteeship Council where by the 1980s the United States could count on French and British collaboration in outvoting the only other active member, the Soviet Union? From the outset, it was clear that the United States perceived itself as having vital strategic interests in the Trust Territory of the Pacific Islands—denial of the territory to potential invaders and use of the remoter atolls for atomic testing and then weapons development. The goals of the United States were delineated during the Kennedy Administration in the Solomon Report.

During the 1960s and 1970s every administration attempted to implement the goals of the Solomon Report. The failure of the Constitutional Convention of the Congress of Micronesia represented a failure of the Solomon gameplan but at the time there were many analysts within the government who did not regret the fragmentation of Micronesia. Negotiations moved ahead relatively smoothly within the Commonwealth of the Northern Marianas, the Republic of the

Marshall Islands and the Federated States of Micronesia. It was on Palau that trouble began at the end of the Carter administration with the drafting of the nuclear free clauses in the constitution for the nascent Republic of Palau.

There are some who have come to believe that in playing a game as old as human polities, the Palauans were at least as skilled as the Americans. And future analysts might be able to detect a symbiosis between two visions of Palau's good, between those who were negotiating for increased funding for Palau in the Compact and those who were defending the nuclear free clauses of the constitution. But whatever the final analysis, the Palauans at least appreciate the wisdom of a comment made by Representative Ron de Lugo, chairman of the Subcommittee on Insular and International Affairs in May 1988 when recriminations were flying about who was "stalling" the Compact:

> If anything has stalled the compact it is the negative approach of the junior officers guiding the Reagan Administration on the issue.

> They misled the president and Congress in 1986 by saying that Palau had approved the Compact. If the appeals court sustains the recent Palau Supreme Court ruling, these junior officers will have misled us once again.

> They have been unwilling to admit Palau's problems and actually helped to create some of them. They have failed to give accurate information and have spread fantasies of political motivations.

> If the administration does not stop pursuing the shortsighted policy these junior officers have led it into, their fears of non-approval of the compact this year could become a self-fulfilling prophecy.

> If the administration really wants to get a compact bill passed, as we do, then it should cooperate in solving Palau's very real problems. The sooner we face these problems, the better we can resolve them and protect our long-term interests in the region. [17]

As it is, the United States has surely overreached its rights as administering authority in the Trust Territory of the Pacific Islands in insisting on seven plebiscites—more than the South African government staged in the Transkei—in its determination to have the nuclear-free clauses of the constitution of the Republic of Palau overridden.[18] And the United States stands even more exposed as unwilling to permit the unfettered evolution of a future political status for Palau as Namibia attained its independence even as Palauans were once again voting on a Compact which does not meet their needs and which they have rejected many times.

Notes

[1] Arthur J. Vidich, *Political Factionalism in Palau, Its Rise and Development* (Pacific Science Board, National Research Council, 1949), 2; hereafter cited as *Political Factionalism*.

[2] Roland Force and Maryann Force, *Just One House A Description and Analysis of Kinship in the Palau Islands* (Honolulu: Bernice P. Bishop Museum *Bulletin* 235, 1972), 10; hereafter cited as *Just One House*.

[3] *Just One House*, 12.

[4] *Just One House.*, 12

[5] *Just One House*, 12.

[6] *Just One House*, 15.

[7] *Political Factionalism*, 17.

[8] H.G. Barnett, *Being a Palauan* (Holt, Rinehart and Winston, 1960), 37.

[9] *Political Factionalism*, 36.

[10] *Political Factionalism*, 49.

[11] *Political Factionalism*, 18.

[12] Donald Shuster, "More Constitutions for Palau," in *The Politics of Evolving Cultures of the Pacific Islands* (Brigham Young University, 1982).

[13] Norman Meller, *Constitutionalism in Micronesia* (Honolulu: University of Hawaii Press, 1985), 31.

[14] *Constitutionalism in Micronesia*, 332.

[15] *Being a Palauan*, 51.

[16] *Just One House*, 10.

[17] Letter to the editor, *Washington Post* (May 17, 1988).

[18] See referenda chart in Appendix G.

Appendices

Appendix A

United Nations Trusteeship Agreement United States Trust Territory of the Pacific Islands

---

PREAMBLE

WHEREAS Article 75 of the Charter of the United Nations provides for the establishment of an international trusteeship system for the administration and supervision of such territories as may be placed thereunder by subsequent agreements; and

WHEREAS under Article 77 of the said Charter the trusteeship system may be applied to territories now held under mandate; and

WHEREAS on 17 December 1920 the Council of the League of Nations confirmed a mandate for the former German islands north of the equator to Japan, to be administered in accordance with Article 22 of the Covenant of the League of Nations; and

WHEREAS Japan, as a result of the Second World War, has ceased to exercise any authority in these islands;

NOW, THEREFORE, the Security Council of the United Nations, having satisfied itself that the relevant articles of the Charter have been complied with, hereby resolves to approve the following terms of trusteeship for the Pacific Islands formerly under mandate to Japan.

ARTICLE 1

The Territory of the Pacific Islands, consisting of the islands formerly held by Japan under mandate in accordance with Article 22 of the Covenant of the League of Nations, is hereby designated as a strategic area and placed under the trusteeship system established in the Charter of the United Nations. The Territory of the Pacific Islands is hereinafter referred to as the trust territory.

ARTICLE 2

The United States of America is designated as the administering authority of the trust territory.

ARTICLE 3

The administering authority shall have full powers of administration, legislation, and jurisdiction over the territory subject to the provisions of this agreements, and may apply to the trust territory, subject to any modifications which the administering authority may consider desirable, such of the laws of the United States as it may deem appropriate to local conditions and requirements.

ARTICLE 4

The administering authority, in discharging the obligations of trusteeship in the trust territory, shall act in accordance with the Charter of the United Nations, and the provisions of this agreement, and shall, as specified in Article 83 (2) of the Charter, apply the objectives of the international trusteeship system, as set forth in Article 76 of the Charter, to the people of the trust territory.

ARTICLE 5

In discharging its obligations under Article 76(a) and Article 84, of the Charter, the administering authority shall ensure that the trust territory shall play its part, in accordance with the Charter of the United Nations, in the maintenance of international peace and security. To this end the administering authority shall be entitled:

1. to establish naval, military and air bases and to erect fortifications in the trust territory;

2. to station and employ armed forces in the territory; and

3. to make use of volunteer forces, facilities and assistance from the trust territory in carrying out the obligations toward the Security Council undertaken in this regard by the administering authority, as well as for the local defense and maintenance of law and order within the trust territory.

ARTICLE 6

In discharging its obligations under Article 76(b) of the Charter, the administering authority shall:

1. foster the development of such political institutions as are suited to the trust territory and shall promote the development of the inhabitants of the trust territory toward self-government or independence as may be appropriate to the particular circumstances of the trust territory and its peoples and the freely expressed wishes of the peoples concerned; and to this end shall give to the inhabitants of the trust territory a progressively increasing share in the administrative services in the territory; shall develop their participation in government; shall give due recognition to the customs of the inhabitants in providing a system of law for the territory; and shall take other appropriate measures toward these ends;

2. promote the economic advancement and self-sufficiency of the inhabitants, and to this end shall regulate the use of natural resources; encourage the development of fisheries, agriculture, and industries; protect the inhabitants against the loss of their lands and resources; and improve the means of transportation and communications;

3. promote the social advancement of the inhabitants, and to this end shall protect the rights and fundamental freedoms of all elements of the population without discrimination; protect the health of the inhabitants; control the traffic in arms and ammunition, opium and other dangerous drugs; and institute such other regulations as may be necessary to protect the inhabitants against social abuses; and

4. promote the educational advancement of the inhabitants, and to this end shall take steps toward the establishment of a general system of elementary education; facilitate the vocational and cultural advancement of the population; and shall encourage qualified students to pursue higher education, including training on the professional level.

ARTICLE 7

In discharging its obligations under Article 76(c), of the Charter, the administering authority shall guarantee to the inhabitants of the trust territory freedom of conscience, and, subject only to the requirements of public order and security, freedom of speech, of the press, and of assembly; freedom of worship, and of religious teaching; and freedom of migration and movement.

ARTICLE 8

1. In discharging its obligations under Article 76(d) of the Charter, as defined by Article 83 (2) of the Charter, the administering authority, subject to the requirements of security, and the obligation to promote the advancement of the inhabitants, shall accord to nationals of each Member of the United Nations and to companies and associations organized in conformity with the laws of such Member, treatment in the trust territory no less favorable than that accorded there to nationals, companies and associations of any other United Nations except the administering authority.

2. The administering authority shall ensure equal treatment to the Members of the United Nations and their nationals in the administration of justice.

3. Nothing in this Article shall be so construed as to accord traffic rights to aircraft flying into and out of the trust territory. Such rights shall be subject to agreement between the administering authority and the state whose nationality such aircraft possesses.

4. The administering authority may negotiate and conclude commercial and other treaties and agreements with Members of the United Nations and other states, designed to attain for the inhabitants of the trust territory treatment by the Members of the United Nations and other states no less favourable than that guaranteed by them to the nationals of other states. The Security Council may recommend, or invite other organs of the United Nations to consider and recommend, what rights the inhabitants of the trust territory should acquire in consideration of the rights obtained by Members of the United Nations in the trust territory.

ARTICLE 9

The administering authority shall be entitled to constitute the trust territory into a customs, fiscal, or administrative union or federation with other territories under United States jurisdiction and to establish common services between such territories and the trust territory where such measures are not inconsistent with the basic objectives of the International Trusteeship System and with the terms of this agreement.

ARTICLE 10

The administering authority, acting under the provisions of Article 3 of this agreement, may accept membership in any regional advisory commission, regional authority, or technical organization, or other voluntary association of states, may co-operate with specialized international bodies, public or private, and may engage in other forms of international co-operation.

ARTICLE 11

1. The administering authority shall take the necessary steps to provide the status of citizenship of the trust territory for the inhabitants of the trust territory.

2. The administering authority shall afford diplomatic and consular protection to inhabitants of the trust territory when outside the territorial limits of the trust territory or of the territory of the administering authority.

ARTICLE 12

The administering authority shall enact such legislation as may be necessary to place the provisions of this agreement in effect in the trust territory.

Appendices | 193

ARTICLE 13

The provisions of Articles 87 and 88 of the Charter shall be applicable to the trust territory, provided that the administering authority may determine the extent of their applicability to any areas which may from time to time be specified by it as closed for security reasons.

ARTICLE 14

The administering authority undertakes to apply in the trust territory the provisions of any international conventions and recommendations which may be appropriate to the particular circumstances of the trust territory and which would be conducive to the achievement of the basic objectives of Article 6 of this agreement.

ARTICLE 15

The terms of the present agreement shall not be altered, amended or terminated without the consent of the administering authority.

ARTICLE 16

The present agreement shall come into force when approved by the Security Council of the United Nations and by the Government of the United States after due constitutional process.

Appendix B

Miscellaneous Budget Documents
November 1986 Compact Ratification

MINISTRY OF NATIONAL RESOURCES
P.O. Box 100, Koror, Republic of Palau 96940

November 17, 1986

STATE BUDGET REQUESTS
FOR COMPACT

	STATE	INDIVIDUAL	TOTAL AMOUNT
1.	AIMELIIK....Senator Lucius Malsol.........	$	4,000.00
2.	KOROR.......Floor Leader Joseph Adachi....		26,000.00
3.	MELEKEOK....CTF Comm Chair Daniel Miner....		4,915.00
4.	NGARAARD....Speaker Martin Sokau..........		5,720.00
5.	NGARDMAU.......Senator Lucius Malsol......		3,500.00
6.	NGAREMLENGUI...Senator Lucius Malsol......		4,000.00
7.	NGCHESAR.......Senator Seit Andres........		3,795.00
8.	NGIWAL.......Speaker Anthonio Takada......		4,580.00
9.	PELELIU......Planner Koichi Wong..........		4,000.00
10.	NGARCHELONG....Koichi West................		7,825.00
		TOTAL	$ 68,335.00

Memorandum

To   : Minister Administration

From   : Chairman, Task Force for Compact

Subject : State Budget Requests for Compact

Please issue checks in the amount of fifty percent (50%) of
each state requested budget, in the name of the individuals
indicated along names of each state, accordingly as we
discussed and agreed this morning.

Thank you.

Wilhelm K. Rengiil

REPUBLIC OF PALAU

BUDGET WORK SHEET

DATE: _____

STATE/DEPARTMENT: __POLITICAL EDUCATION COMMITTEE__

ACTIVITY: _____

ACCOUNT: _____

CLASS CODE	OBJECT CLASSIFICATION	FY 19 ___	FY 19 ___	FY 19 ___	INC (+) or DEC (-)	REMARKS
111	Expatriates Personnel Services	- 0 -				
112	Local Personnel Services	$ 5,500.00				
115	Personnel Benefits/Expatriates	- 0 -				
116	Personnel Benefits/Local -	1,000.00				
212	Committee Members Comp (5)	9,000.00				
	Subtotal	$ 15,500.00				
211	Travel & Transportation of Person	$ 55,000.00				
221	Freight					
231	Rental (Vehicles - 2)	3,500.00				
241	Printing & Reproduction	10,000.00				
251	Contractual Services (TV)	25,000.00				
260	Supplies & Materials	15,000.00				
261	Petrolium Oil Lubricants	3,000.00				
262	Food Stuff	3,000.00				
263	Books & Library Materials	- 0 -				
264	State Politcal Education	40,000.00				
311	Equipment--(Copier, typewriter, friz	5,000.00				
400	Grants, Subsidies & Contributions	- 0 -				
	Subtotal					
	TOTAL	$175,000.00				

Appendix C

President Salii's Advertisement in Support
of the Compact

VOTE "YES"

ON THE COMPACT I ASK ALL PALAUAN VOTERS TO

VOTE YES

ON DECEMBER 2, 1986

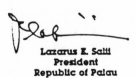

Lazarus E. Salii
President
Republic of Palau

Appendix D

Miscellaneous Documents
Civil Service and Compact Ratification

OFFICE OF THE MINISTER
Ministry of Social Services
P. O. Box 100
Koror, Republic of Palau 96940

November 17, 1986

MEMORANDUM

TO   : Director of Bureau of ...
           Director of Bureau of Health Services
           Director of Bureau of ... ...
           Acting Director of Area Agency on Aging
           Acting Ex. Director of Belau National Museum

FROM   : Minister of Social Services

SUBJECT: APPROVAL OF COMPACT AS PRIORITY PROGRAM

Since the approval of the Compact of Free Association with United States of America is the top priority program of the Executive Branch of our National Government, it is expected of all personnel to vigorously campaign for the Compact in order that a 75% approval on December 2 referendum be obtained.

Any personnel under your supervision who chooses to campaign otherwise shall be reported to me at once. Also if any such personnel uses materials, equipments, or the likes that are properties of the National Government to campaign against the Compact, I request that the matter be brought to my attention immediately. It is no longer tolerable for civil service employees to appose the system while remaining in it and enjoying all benefits due dedicated employees.

I request that you treat this matter very important to the well being of us all.

Nobuo S. ...

REPUBLIC of PALAU

Department of Social Services
Bureau of Education
P. O. Box 189
Koror, Palau 96940

November 21, 1986

MEMORANDUM

TO   : All Public School Principals

FROM   : Assistant, Director of Education

SUBJECT : Temporary Suspension of School Instruction

Public elementary school principals are hereby informed that begining Monday, November 24, 1986, all school instructional activities shall be suspended until December 2, 1986. Normal instructional program or activities will resume on December 3, Wednesday 1986.

Palau High School shall suspend instructional activities, beginign November 25, 1986. However, students are requested to wear their school uniform and join the Government Rally on Friday, November 28, 1986 at 1:00 p.m. at the Palau Baseball Stadium. Instruction at the Palau High School shall also resume on December 3, 1986.

All public school teachers shall go on administration leave to campaign for the Compact of Free Association with the United States. All other education personnel are aslo requested to join the Government Rally on Friday, November 28, 1986 at 1:00 p.m. at the Palau Baseball Stadium.

This memo is based on the direction and instruction by the Minister of Social Services.

Steve Umetaro

cc: Minister of Social Services
     All Education Division and activities

Appendix E

Message to the People of Palau

MESSAGE TO THE PEOPLE OF PALAU

Constituents, Voters, People of Palau

As Legislators, one of our duties and obligations is to review and examine contracts and treaties between our Republic and other foreign nations. If our review reveals that any such agreements are in the best interest of our people, then it is our duty to so advise you. Likewise, if for any reason these agreements do not benefit Palau or could be improved, it is equally our duty to advise you of this.

After considerable review and deliberation, we hereby setforth our findings on the Compact of Free Association that will be presented to the People of Palau in the proposed December referendum.

Before setting forth our six major findings, we would like to share with you our mutual belief that, the Compact being presented to the voters is not a take it or leave it proposition. We firmly believe that, if the People of Palau choose to, the Compact of Free Association could be renegotiated and improved. Our conviction in saying this not only comes from our experience as legislators, but also from looking at the historical development of the Compact and the current political changes taking place in the Pacific. Therefore, if you choose to vote for this compact please do so because you are satisfied with it, not because of a mistaken belief that it is our only alternative.

Our review of the Compact has revealed the following:

1. The Compact as written, if approved will work a severe hardship on our students, elderly and people needing medical attention. Once the Compact is approved, the much needed and depended upon federal programs for education, old age and health will be drastically cut. Such important programs as M.O.C., P.C.A.A., F.H.A., Palau Housing Authority, Food service and Old Age programs will no longer be funded. Although, we will be able to provide some funding for some of these programs, it will not be at a pre-compact level.

2. The Compact fails to provide a workable fall back mechanism for renegotiations of Title III problems if political conditions in the Pacific should change. For instance, the Philippines receive approximately 900 million dollars a year for the military bases located there. If the Philippines were to decide to have the U.S. pull out these bases and they were subsequently moved to Palau there is no workable provision for renegotiating additional funding absent use obtaining mutual consent from the United States.

3. The level of funding Palau will receive under the Compact is less than what it received as a Trust Territory. According to the testimony of Ambassador Zeder the United States will save 80 million dollars by getting Palau to accept the Compact.

4. The duration of the Compact and its related agreements are too long for the benefits that have been offered. Unlike the 15 year Federated States of Micronesia and Marshalls Compact, Palau's Compact is for 50 years. Moreover, this 50 year period may continue further for certain provisions if the United States does not mutually agree to terminate the Compact.

5. There are numerous ambiguities and unclear provisions in the Compact. These in the past have resulted in the long history associated with trying to find a Compact consistent with the needs of Palau and its Constitution. For this reason alone it may be time to re-evaluate our needs and other alternatives; and

6. The Supreme Court of Palau, in Gibbons vs Salii raised serious concerns about the constitutionality of the eminent domain provisions of the Compact. The constitutional questions about the eminent domain provisions in the Compact were left unchanged in the Compact. This could result in another law suit being filed on the Compact and our possibly losing our funding. This problem is further compounded when one considers that the land issues in Palau have still not been resolved.

The findings mentioned above along with other concerns has brought us to a conclusion which we all agree upon, but regrettably must state, and that is that this Compact, as written will not serve the best interest of our People now, nor in the future. For this reason we can not in good conscience endorse the Compact of Free Association to be presented to the voters at the December referendum. We therefore recommend that you cast a NO vote on the Compact.

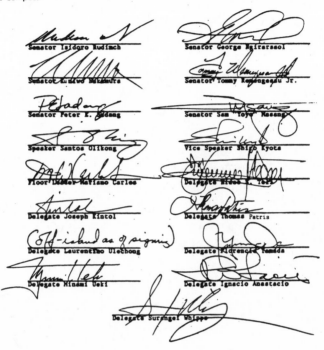

Senator Isidoro Rudimch

Senator Andres Matsutaru

Senator Peter K. Sugang

Speaker Santos Olikong

Floor Leader Mariano Carlos

Delegate Joseph Kintol

Delegate Laurentino Ulechong

Delegate Minami Ueki

Senator George Ngirarsaol

Senator Tommy Remengesau Jr.

Senator Sam "Yoyo" Masang

Vice Speaker Shiro Kyota

Delegate Bruce L. Yano

Delegate Thomas Patris

Delegate Aldrence Yamada

Delegate Ignacio Anastacio

Delegate Surangel Whipps

Reprinted from the *Pacific Daily News* November 28, 1986

Appendix F

Findings, Conclusions and Recommendations of the International Commission of Jurists

FINDINGS AND CONCLUSIONS

1. Faced with conditions tantamount to economic bankruptcy, the resultant loss of jobs in the public sector, which employs 60% of its workforce, Palauan Executive, Political and Judicial Institutions, for the period beginning in July 1987 to September 1987, were under such severe strain as to cause us to conclude that there existed a virtual breakdown of the Rule of Law during that period.

2. Even six months later, when the Mission visited Palau, we felt that there was ample evidence that the right of Palauan citizens to seek redress of their constitutional rights in the courts of Palau was, at the very least, inhibited and in some instances prohibited by a climate of fear and intimidation originating from certain segments of Palauan society.

3. In the last eight years the Palauan people have had four referenda relating to their constitution which in 1979 they ratified by a 92% vote and six referenda on the Compact of Free Association with the U.S. All of the referenda of the Compact and two of the amendment referenda on the Constitution were apparently a result of sustained pressure on Palau by the Administering Power designed to persuade it to alter its constitution either to allow the United States to "store" nuclear weapons or, at a later stage, to "operate" ships and aircraft with nuclear devices within the territorial jurisdiction of Palau.

4. The August 1987 referendum purporting to authorize, by an amendment to the constitution, a 50% vote on the Compact of Free Association, raises serious, substantial and arguable questions of constitutionality which can only finally be passed upon by the Supreme Court of Palau.

5. Attempts by Palauan citizens to raise these questions have been thwarted in the first instance by a behind-the-scenes arrangement between top government officials and the litigants and in the second instance by threats of violence and intimidation against the plaintiffs. These acts, many of which were plainly criminal in nature, included fire bombing, shooting at the homes of some of the plaintiffs, direct threats of violence to many of the plaintiffs, and the murder of the father of one of the main plaintiffs.

6. There has been an illegal and improper interference with and pressure upon the independence of the judiciary in that:

A. Members of the Legislature engaged in express threats to the Chief Justice;

B. Members of the Furlough Committee have filed a petition for the removal of the Chief Justice from a case;

C. A series of oral threats were made directly and indirectly to the members of the Judiciary of Palau and their families; and

D. An organized attempt to threaten the Judiciary by surrounding the Supreme Court building with campers who wore "red bands" and who camouflaged a government truck to appear to be a coffin with words inscribed on it "red September".

7. Specifically we conclude that the withdrawal of this case entitled *Ngirmang, et al. vs. Salii, et al.* was involuntary. Such withdrawal was brought about by "intimidation

through the use of violence". Accordingly we conclude that because substantial constitutional issues cannot be challenged and determined in Palauan courts because of threats to litigants, lawyers and the Judiciary, there has been a breakdown of the Rule of Law in Palau.

8. It is our duty to report our conclusion that there is evidence of government complicity in many of the matters raised in this report, such as:

- Constant and repeated public statements by government officials on the government-controlled radio attacking or denigrating the Judiciary or referring to the "tyranny of the courts".
- Police participation or acquiescence in these events by failing to maintain law and order, and by the failure of police and the Attorney General to pursue claims.
- Constant pressure on legitimate opposition, such as threatened loss of jobs and assignment of opponents to uncomfortable shifts.
- Threats by police officials concerning the withdrawal of legal actions.
- Threats of the denial of scholarships to members of the families of those opposing the Compact.
- Sadly there are also serious allegations of corruption against prominent Palauans, which we consider it proper to mention but not elaborate. There were also many allegations of incompetence and waste, the use of government property for private purposes and alleged bribes regarding the building of a power plant.

9. We conclude that the Eleventh Legislative Session of the National Congress of Palau of July 1987 was held in a climate of near hysteria; that Legislators were coerced into voting in favor of the bill authorizing the Amendment to

the Constitution and approval of the Compact referenda of August 1987 and that such legislation did not freely reflect the considered political will of the Palauan National Congress, as the Constitution of Palau envisaged that it would be expressed.

10. We conclude that the Palauan Bar Association failed in its duty to maintain the Rule of Law when it knew, or should have known, that judges, lawyers and litigants were being threatened in their professional capacity. It should be pointed out that the brother of the President, Carlos Salii, is the President of the Palauan Bar Association.

Independence of the Judiciary and the Legal Profession

11. The constitution of the Republic of Palau established an independent judiciary. There is much evidence that the Supreme Court of Palau has exercised its independence and in numerous suits reversed the acts of legislative and executive branches of government when the constitution or law of Palau was held so to require.

12. The justices of the Supreme Court are sufficiently alert to the challenges to their independence and to the operation of the Rule of Law in Palau whilst at the same time sensitive to the lack of understanding, in governmental and other quarters of the vital importance, for the long term welfare of Palau, of adherence to constitutional processes and compliance with legal forms.

13. Proof positive of the independence of the justices of the Supreme Court can be found not only in the history of governmental litigation generally. It can be found in many decisions associated with the constitutional evolution of Palau. Most notable of these have been the judgments in *Gibbons vs. Remeliik* and *Gibbons vs. Salii* and the very ob-

servations of Judge Hefner in *Ngirmang vs. Salii* which contributed to the reason for this Mission.

14. The current circumstances in Palau make it more important than ever that the judicial branch of government be supported by the citizens and by all those having it in their power to lend support. The reasons include not only the fine principle of the Rule of Law as the best guarantee of freedom and the defense of human rights. They extend beyond the vital importance of constitutionality at this critical stage of transition in the evolution of Palau to full independence in the community of nations. They concern the very practical problems of everyday importance to Palau and its people: the growth of higher levels of violence, the evidence of social disruption, new problems involving narcotic drugs and the breakdown of the effectiveness of traditional authority. These problems, and the need for a strong judicial branch of government to deal with them, are appreciated by many in responsible positions in Palau. They are certainly appreciated by the judiciary. But they are not appreciated by all.

15. Unprecedented and unacceptable pressure—and the public appearance of pressure—was placed upon the Supreme Court of Palau during the third quarter of 1987. It took the form of petitions to the Chief Justice threatening his removal if he did not decide a constitutional case before him in a designated way; letters to him by members of the legislature expressed in intimidating language designed to influence his performance of his judicial duties; and the gathering of large and violent crowds in the vicinity of his courthouse. Peaceful demonstration of a point of view is a mark of a free society. Mob rule around the courts, with threats to the judiciary, and to litigants is the very negation of freedom under law. It is vital that the government

and citizens of Palau—and all others watching these events—should realize this. What is at stake is not just the wish of the people, democratically elected. It is nothing less than the right of litigants to test the compliance of that democratic expression against the requirements of the people's constitution and the entitlement of the judiciary to determine that question. If legal processes break down once, a dangerous precedent is set—and the rule of violence, intimidation and oppression replaces the Rule of Law.

16. In the sequence of events disclosed in this report there is a possible appearance that Chief Justice Nakamura yielded to that pressure. He made an order which was unpopular. Yet within a very short time of doing so he vacated that order and revoked it and soon after disqualified himself. He did so, as is publicly known, after the receipt of intimidating letters and a petition threatening his removal. In these circumstances, the appearance of the independence of the judiciary was damaged. The blame for this fact must be placed principally at the door of those persons responsible who publicly or otherwise threatened the Chief Justice. We do not say that the Chief Justice was actually intimidated. But damage can be done by the appearances of intimidation and the appearance of yielding to pressure. The question is what reasonable observers of these events would infer from them and the conclusions they might draw concerning the independence of the Supreme Court of Palau.

17. The Mission was greatly impressed by the insight of the Justices of the Supreme Court of Palau into the important principles at stake here, vital for the well being of the people of Palau. The assignment of the litigation to Judge Hefner and his memorandum referring to possible intimidation is proof, if it be needed, of the independence and

courage of the Justices. It would be a misfortune if it were considered necessary or even desirable in such sensitive situations, always to resort to off-island judges of non-Palauan origin. For the survival of the Rule of Law in Palau in the long term, it is essential that such independence be demonstrated, repeatedly, by indigenous judges in Palau. The rule of Law is most important when it is most severely tested.

18. Statements were made to the Mission, which it also accepts and finds believable, that the litigants before the Supreme Court in the cases designed to test the constitutionality of the amendment for the purpose of adopting the compact, were intimidated and discontinued those proceedings out of fear. The Ibedul, who was believed by many to be supporting the litigation in the *Merep* case, was afraid of the breakdown of law and order and had himself been the subject of thinly veiled threats. The Palauan women, who then brought a case in virtually identical terms, were then subjected to unprecedented coercion in order to dissuade them from exercising their constitutional rights before the Supreme Court of Palau. The coercion is fully set out above. But in summary it included:

- Fire bombing of houses.
- The interruption to the power supply.
- The gathering of violent demonstrations in the vicinity of the courthouse and legislature.
- The actions of the demonstrators in assuming the wearing of red headbands and in painting a van used by them with threatening slogans.
- Murder of the father of one of the plaintiffs, serious escalation of violence and the outcome of a period of mob rule.
- The executive branch of government including the police were either unable or unwilling to provide security to

the litigants to defend their right to litigate a serious constitutional question in the Supreme Court.

- Individual threats were addressed to the Palauan women who brought a case in the Supreme Court as well as to their families as recounted to the Mission and set forth in this report.

19. It is not necessary for the Mission to judge—nor would it be appropriate—whether the Palauan women have a valid claim under the constitution of Palau to challenge the purported constitutional amendment preliminary to the execution of the Compact. Nor is the Mission concerned with the validity of those amendments, the application of customary law to the conduct of the women, the application of the principles of *res judicata* or the availability of defenses of accord and settlement. These are entirely matters for the Palauan courts. Nothing in this report should be read as expressing a view or any of these questions. It is sufficient for the purposes of the Mission to say that a serious constitutional question, which was arguable, was raised by the suit of the Palauan women. They should have been allowed to bring it and have it peacefully resolved in a court room. Instead they were coerced into seeking an adjournment or a discontinuance of it. That coercion undermines the Rule of Law in Palau and the appearance of the independence of the Palauan courts to resolve serious questions according to law.

20. In addition to the pressure applied to the judiciary, legislators and litigants, improper pressure was also applied to some members of the legal profession known to be concerned in the prosecution of the constitutional litigators. One of them, Roman Bedor, was the son of the man murdered and it was in his office that the murder occurred. Cars

were damaged by the smashing of the front windows. The response of the Bar Association to these shocking events was, it must be said, inadequate. Instead of rallying in a single voice to denounce these assaults on the Rule of Law and the intimidation of the Judiciary and colleagues it was decided instead to seek advice from the American Bar Association on what should have been obvious to any lawyer. Unless lawyers rally around and together defend the Rule of Law, the judiciary and constitutional institutions, they abandon their historical role. This includes, ultimately, putting individual interests aside and even the interests of particular clients aside when the very institutions by which those interests are safeguarded are under siege. In the unhappy event of a repetition challenge it is hoped that the Bar Association will show more resolve.

21. Individual lawyers have done things which appear to the Mission incompatible with respect for the judiciary and the Rule of Law. For example, it would seem quite wrong for the lawyer for the Furlough Committee to have participated in the writing of the August 19th Petition threatening the Chief Justice. Whatever the motives—which the Mission has no prerogative to judge—it would seem inconsistent with a lawyer's cardinal duty to be involved in such an act or thereafter to participate in steps intermeddling in private litigation, involving the women plaintiffs, designed to effect the discontinuance or adjournment of their proceedings which were lawfully before the court, and to secure their termination out of fear.

RECOMMENDATIONS

1. The Administering Power (the United States) should use its power and lend the efforts of its institutions (in every constitutional and proper way) to ensure that the Rule of Law is observed in Palau so long as the Administering Power has duties as a Trustee. In the long run, leaving the people of Palau independent but without respect for their constitutional institutions will not only be a rejection of the United States' own concern about a government of laws and not of men, but it will be an abdication of the trust accepted by the United States from the United Nations after the sacrifices of the Second World War.

2. The trusteeship should not be terminated by the United States and the United Nations until the constitutional processes of Palau to review a challenge to the Compact of Free Association have been fully exhausted. This will not be shown by a certificate by the Executive Government of Palau, which is not conclusive. Nor will it be shown by a certificate of the President of the United States, no doubt based on reliance upon the former. It will only be demonstrated conclusively by an authoritative decision of the only body able to give such a decision—the Supreme Court of Palau. The United States is on notice by this report and otherwise that a serious constitutional question remains to be tested *and* that by force, intimidation, vio-

lence and even murder, litigation designed to raise and determine that question have been forestalled. In discharge of its remaining duties as trustee—and in the strong tradition of constitutionality which has marked its own history—the United States of America should ensure that a test case is peacefully determined in the Court of Palau before terminating the trusteeship.

3. If the women plaintiffs—despite fears which the Mission accepts to be both sincere and well founded—decide to bring a suit or to continue their adjourned proceedings the Government of Palau should likewise provide effective protection to them to ensure that they can secure a decision in their case according to law. The Government of Palau should ensure that the judiciary, lawyers and litigants are protected fully in the discharge of their respective functions.

4. The appropriate Palauan authorities should, without delay, investigate and prosecute those responsible for the murder, acts of violence, illegal possession of firearms, and other criminal violations set forth in this report.

5. Because the successful implementation of the Rule of Law and the Constitutional Process requires an informed citizenry, we urge Palauan political leaders to take all steps necessary to educate and inform the Palauan society on the need for an independent Judiciary and on the rights of citizens guaranteed them by their constitition.

Reprinted from William J. Butler and others, *Palau: A Challenge to the Rule of Law in Micronesia. Report of a Mission on Behalf of the International Commission of Jurists*. New York: American Association for the International Commission of Jurists, 1988

Appendix G

Referenda on the Palau Compact

Votes For and Against

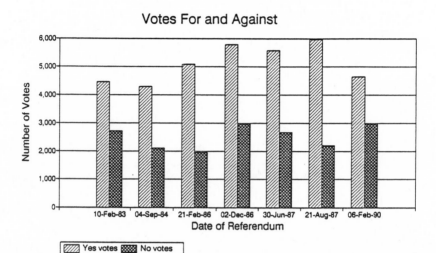

Turnout and Percent Yes Votes

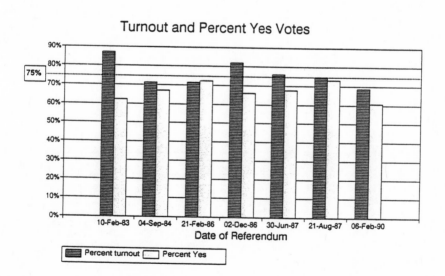

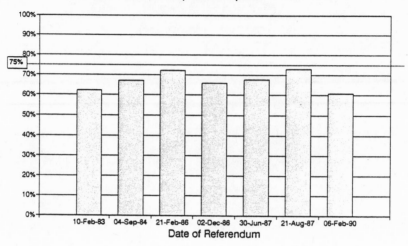

Percent Votes For the Belau Compact
75% required to pass

These three graphs provided by Charles Scheiner, *Belau Update*, Box 1182, White Plains, NY 10602

Belau Referenda Results   (courtesy Belau Update)

Date	Yes votes	No votes	Spoil votes	Tot.Reg voters	Total cast	Turnout	Yes / all	Yes / valid	Yes - No	Needed for 75%
04-Aug-87	5,645	2,053	35	10,841	7,733	71.33%	73.00%	73.33%	3592	
10-Feb-83	4,452	2,715	79	8,338	7,246	86.90%	61.44%	62.12%	1737	924
04-Sep-84	4,290	2,103	65	9,063	6,458	71.26%	66.43%	67.10%	2187	506
21-Feb-86	5,079	1,957	31	9,905	7,067	71.35%	71.87%	72.19%	3122	199
02-Dec-86	5,789	2,986	49	10,760	8,824	82.01%	65.61%	65.97%	2803	793
30-Jun-87	5,574	2,673	16	10,851	8,263	76.15%	67.46%	67.59%	2901	612
21-Aug-87	5,964	2,201	17	10,955	8,182	74.69%	72.89%	73.04%	3763	161
06-Feb-90	4,633	2,988	126	11,272	7,747	68.73%	59.80%	60.79%	1645	1084

Appendix H

Constitution of the Republic of Palau
[Excerpts]

Preamble

In exercising our inherent sovereignty, we the people of Palau proclaim and reaffirm our immemorial right to be supreme in these islands, our homeland. We renew our dedication to preserve and enhance our traditional heritage, our national identity and our respect for peace, freedom and justice for all mankind. In establishing this Constitution of the sovereign Republic of Palau, we venture into the future with full reliance on our own efforts and the divine guidance of Almighty God.

Article I: Territory

Section 1. Palau shall have jurisdiction and sovereignty over its territory which shall consist of all the islands of the Palauan archipelago, the internal waters, the territorial waters, extending to two hundred (200) nautical miles from a straight archipelagic baseline, the seabed, the subsoil, water column, insular shelves, and airspace over land and water unless otherwise limited by international treaty obligations assumed by Palau ....
Section 4. Nothing in this Article shall be interpreted to violate the right of innocent passage and the internationally recognized freedom of the high seas.

Article II: Sovereignty and Supremacy

Section 1. This Constitution is the supreme law of the land.

Section 2. Any law, act of government or agreement to which a government of Palau is not a party, shall not conflict with this Constitution and shall be invalid to the extent of such a conflict.

Section 3. Major governmental powers including but not limited to defense, security, or foreign affairs may be delegated by treaty, compact, or other agreement between the sovereign Republic of Palau and another sovereign nation or international organization, provided such a treaty, compact of agreement shall be approved by not less than two-thirds (2/3) of the members of each house of the Olbiil Era Kelulau and by a majority of the votes cast in a nationwide referendum conducted for such purpose, provided, that any such agreement which authorizes use, testing, storage or disposal of nuclear, toxic, chemical, gas or biological weapons intended for use in warfare shall require approval of not less than three-fourths (3/4) of the votes cast in such referendum.

Article IV: Fundamental Rights

Section 3. The government shall take no action to deny or impair the right of any person to peacefully assemble and petition the government for redress of grievances or to associate with others for any lawful purpose....

Section 5. Every person shall be equal under the law and shall be entitled to equal protection. The government shall take no action to discriminate against any person on the basis of sex, race, place of origin, language, religion or belief, social status or clan affiliation, except for the preferential treatment of citizens, for the protection of minors, elderly, indigent, physically and mentally handicapped, and other similar groups, and in matters concerning interstate succession and domestic relations. No person shall be treated unfairly in legislative or executive investigations.

Section 12. A citizen has the right to examine any government document and to observe the official deliberations of any agency of the government.

Article VI: Responsibilities of the National Government

The national government shall take positive action to obtain these national objectives and implement these national policies: conservation of a beautiful, healthful and resourceful natural environment; promotion of the national economy; protection of the safety and security of persons and property; promotion of the health and social welfare of the citizens through the provision of free or subsidized health care; and provision of public education for citizens which shall be free and compulsory as prescribed by law.

Article XIII: General Provisions

Section 6. Harmful substances such as nuclear, chemical, gas or biological weapons intended for use in warfare, nuclear power plants, and waste materials therefrom, shall not be used, tested, stored, or disposed of within the territorial jurisdiction of Palau without the express approval of not less than three-fourths (3/4) of the votes cast in a referendum submitted on this specific question.

Section 7. The national government shall have the power to take property for public use upon payment of just compensation. The state government shall have the power to take private property for public use upon payment of just compensation. No property shall be taken for the national government without prior consultation with the government of the state in which the property is located. The power shall not be used for the benefit of a foreign entity. This power shall be used sparingly and only as a final resort after all means of good faith negotiation with the land owner have been exhausted.

Section 8. Only citizens of Palau and corporation wholly owned by citizens of Palau may acquire title to land or waters in Palau.

Section 10. The national government shall, within five (5) years of the effective date of this Constitution, provide for the return of the original owners or their heirs any land which became part of public lands as a result of the acquisition by previous occupying powers or their nationals through force, coercion, fraud, or without just compensation or adequate consideration.

Article XIV: Amendments

Section 1. An amendment to this Constitution may be proposed by a Constitutional Convention, popular initiative, or by the Olbiil Era Kelulau, as provided herein....

Section 2. A proposed amendment to this Constitution shall become effective when approved in the next regular general election by a majority of the votes cast on that amendment and in not less than three-fourths (3/4) of the states.

Article XV: Transition

Section 5. Nothing is Section 3 or 4 of this Article [they outline the transfer of power and authority from the TTPI Administering Authority to ROP] shall be deemed to constitute a waiver or release of the Administering Authority, the Trust territory of the Pacific Islands, or any other government entity or person from any continuing or unsatisfied obligation or duty owing to the citizens of Palau, or the national government or state governments of Palau....

Section 10. Any provision of this Constitution or a law enacted pursuant to it which is in conflict with the Trusteeship Agreement between the United States of America and the United Nations Security Council shall not become effective until the date of termination of such Trusteeship Agreement.

Section 11. Any amendment of this Constitution proposed for the purpose of avoiding inconsistency with the Compact of Free Association shall require approval by a majority of the votes cast on that amendment and in not less than three-fourths (3/4) of the states. Such amendment shall remain in effect only as long as the inconsistency continues.

[Signed on April 2, 1979, by 35 convention delegates and attested to by the Convention Secretary. Approved on July 9, 1979, by 92% of the vote. TTPI High Commissioner failed to certify the results of the plebiscite. Second vote on revised Constitution on October 23, 1979, resulted in rejection by 65%. Third vote on the original draft occured on July 9, 1980, when 78% of the voters approved.]

Bibliography

Aldridge, Robert. "Palau and the Tridents." *The New Zealand International Review* VII (July-August 1982): 4.

Alkire, William H. "The Carolinians of Saipan and the Commonwealth of the Northern Mariana Islands." *Pacific Affairs* LVII : 2 (Summer 1984): 270- .

Anderson, Jon A. "Trusteeship Turmoil: The Agreement." *Micronesian Reporter* XIX : 2 (1971): 24-48.

_____. "The Special Session." *Micronesian Reporter* XIX : 2 (1971): 11-14.

Antilla, Elizabeth. *A History of the Trust Territory of the Pacific Islands and Their Education.*

"The Applicability of the Principle of Self-Determination to Unintegrated Territories of the United States: the Cases of Puerto Rico and the Trust Territory of the Pacific Islands," *Proceedings of the American Society of International Law* 67 (1973).

Armstrong, Arthur John. "The Emergence of the Micronesians into the International Community: A Study of the Creation of a New International Entity." *Brooklyn Journal of International Law* 5 (1979): 207.

_____. "The Negotiations for the Future Political Status of Micronesia." *American Journal of International Law* 74 (1980): 689.

_____. "The Negotiations for the Future Political Status of Micronesia, 1980-1984." *American Journal of International Law* 78 : 2 (April 1984): 484-97.

_____. "Strategic Underpinnings of the Legal Regime of Free Association: The Negotiations for the Future Political Status of Micronesia." *Brooklyn Journal of International Law* V : 2 (Summer 1981): 178-233.

Baker, Byron and Robert Werkheim, *Micronesia: The Breadfruit Revolution.* Honolulu, East-West Center, 1971.

Ballendorf, Dirk Anthony. "American Administration in the Trust Territories of the Pacific Islands, 1944 to 1948." *Asian Culture Quarterly* XII : 1 (Spring 1984).

_____. "An Assessment of Political Attitudes Among Elderly Palauans Toward the Compact of Free Association with the United States." Unpublished paper. 1986.

_____. "The Community College of Micronesia". *Pacific Studies* II : 2.

_____. "Post Colonial Micronesia: A Future for Japan and America." *New Zealand International Review* VII : 4 (July/August 1982): 2-5.

_____. "Secrets Without Substance: U. S. Intelligence in the Japanese Mandates 1915-1935." *Journal of Pacific History* XIX : 2 (April 1984): 87-99.

Barnett, H.G. *Being a Palauan*. New York, Holt, Rinehart and Winston, 1960.

Baron, Dona Gene. "Policy for 'Paradise': A Study of United States Decision Making Processes Respecting the Trust Territory of the Pacific Islands and the Impact Thereon of United Nations Oversight." Ph.D. diss., Columbia University.

Bascom, William. "Ponape: The Tradition of Rebellion." *Far Eastern Quarterly* 10 (1950): 56-62.

_____. *Ponape: A Pacific Economy in Transition*. [*Anthropological Records* 22] Berkeley, University of California Press, 1965.

Basilius, Bonifacio. "Congress '71." *Micronesian Reporter* XIX : 2 (1971): 6-10.

Bergsman, Peter. "The Marianas, the United States and the United Nations: the Uncertain Status of the New American Commonwealth." *California Western International Law Journal* 6 (1976).

Bernart, Luelen. *The Book of Luelen*. [*Pacific History Series*, 8] Honolulu, University of Hawaii Press, 1977.

Bikini Atoll Rehabilitation Committee. *Report No. I. Resettlement of Bikini Atoll: Feasibility and Estimated Cost of Meeting the Federal Radiation Protection Standards*. Berkeley, 1984.

Black, Peter W. "The In-Charge Complex and Tobian Political Culture," in *The Politics of Evolving Cultures in the Pacific Islands*. Honolulu, Brigham Young University, 1982.

Blaustein, Albert and Eric Blaustein. *Constitutions of Dependencies and Special Sovereignties, Trust Territory of the Pacific Islands*. Oceana, 1978.

Blaz and Lee. "The Cross of Micronesia." *Naval War College Review* 59 (1976): 69-76.

Blum, Y.Z. "The Composition of the Trusteeship Council." *American Journal of International Law* 63 (1969): 747-68.

Boss, A., R. and others. *Report of the International Observer Mission — Palau Referendum. December 1986*. New York, International League for Human Rights and the Minority Rights Group, 1987.

Branch, James A. "The Constitution of the Northern Mariana Islands: Does a Different Cultural Setting Justify Different Constitutional Standards?" *Denver Journal of International Law and Policy* 9 (1980): 35.

Bunge, Frederica A. and Melinda Cooke, eds. *Oceana: A Regional Study*. Washington, D.C., American University [Foreign Area Studies], 1984.

Butler, William J. and others. *Palau: A Challenge to the Rule of Law in Micronesia*. [Report of a Mission on Behalf of the International Commission of Jurists] New York, American Association for the International Commission of Jurists, 1988.

Chamberlain, P. "Micro Planning." *Micronesia Reporter* XX : 2 (1972): 33-43.

Chapman, Peter S. "Micronesia 1965-1974: A Bibliography." *Asian Perspectives* XVII : 2 (1974): 160-89

Chowdhuri, R. *International Mandates and Trusteeship Systems*. The Hague, M. Nijhoff, 1955.

Clark, Roger S. "The Current State of the Trust Territory Negotiations: Who Has Tentatively Agreed to What?" [Working Paper for the Micronesia Support Committee] Typescript, August 1981.

_____. "Free Association: A Critical View." [Paper presented at Conference on the Future Political Status of the U.S. Virgin Islands, February 26-27, 1988]

_____. Letter to the Editor. *American Journal of International Law* 81 (1987): 927.

_____. "Self-Determination and Free Association — Should the United Nations Terminate the Pacific Islands Trust?" *Harvard International Law Journal* XXI : 1 (Winter 1980): 2-85.

_____. "Statement Submitted by Roger S. Clark to the Subcommittee on Petitions, Information and Assistance of the United Nations Special Committee on the Implementation of the Declaration with Regard to the Granting of Independence to Colonial Countries and Peoples." Typescript, April 26, 1984.

Clyde, Paul Hibbert. *Japan's Pacific Mandate*. New York, Macmillan, 1935. [reissued by Kennikat Press, 1967]

Compact of Free Association, October 31, 1980, United States—Federated States of Micronesia—Marshall Islands (initialled by Palau, November 17, 1980) in *Brooklyn Journal of International Law* 7 (1981): 238.

Coulter, John Wesley. *The Pacific Dependencies of the United States*. New York: Macmillan, 1957.

Crocombe, Ron G. *Land Tenure in the Atolls: Cook Islands, Kiribati, Marshall Islands, Tokelau, Tuvalu*. Suva, University of the South Pacific, Institute of Pacific Studies, 1987.

_____ ed. *Land Tenure in the Pacific*. Melbourne, Oxford University Press, 1971.

_____. "Overview: the Pattern of Change in Pacific Land Tenures," in *Land Tenure in the Pacific*. Melbourne, Oxford University Press, 1971.

Cultural Considerations for Planning in Micronesia. Honolulu, Hawaii Architects and Engineers, 1968.

Dahlquist, Paul A. "Political Development at the Municipal Level: Kiti, Ponape," in Hughes and Lingenfelter (eds.), *Political Development in Micronesia*.

Dator, J. A. "Alternative Future for the Commonwealth of the Northern Marianas." *Political Science* XXXIV: 1 (July 1982): 26-65.

Dempsey, Guy. [Note] "Self Determination and Security in the Pacific: Study of the Covenant Between the United States and the Northern Mariana Islands." *New York University Journal of International Law and Politics* 9 (1976): 277.

De Smith, S. Comment on "The Participation of Microstates in International Affairs." *American Society of International Law* (1968).

_____. *Microstates and Micronesia: Problems of America's Pacific Islands and Other Minute Territories.* 1970.

Diblin, Jane. *Day of Two Suns: U.S. Nuclear Testing and the Pacific Islands.* London, Virago, 1988.

Dobbs. "A Macrostudy of Micronesia: The Ending of a Trusteeship." *New York Forum* 18 (1972): 139.

Edmonds, I. *Micronesia.*

Epstein, Joshua L. "Dependency and Affluence as Challenges to National Development in Palau." Ph.D. diss., University of Hawaii, 1986.

Esfandiary, Moshen S. [Comment on] "The Participation of Microstates in International Affairs." *American Society of International Law* 1968.

Federated States of Micronesia. Office of the Governor, Ponape State Government. Letter to President of the FSM. Typescript, August 9, 1985.

Federated States of Micronesia. Washington D.C., Federated States of Micronesia, December 1, 1983.

Firth, Stewart. *Nuclear Playground.* Honolulu and Sydney, South Sea Books and Allen and Unwin, 1987.

Fischer, John L. "The Role of the Traditional Chiefs on Ponape in the American Period." In Hughes and Lingenfelter (eds.) *Political Development in Micronesia*.

_____ and Ann M. Fischer. *The Eastern Carolines* New Haven, Human Relations Area Files, 1957.

Fisher, Roger. "The Participation of Microstates in International Affairs." *American Society of International Law*, 1968.

Five Year Indicative Development Plan (1976-81). Saipan, Congress of Micronesia, 1976.

Force, Roland W. ed. *Induced Political Change in the Pacific*. London, British Museum Press, 1965.

_____ and Maryanne Force. *Just One House: A Description and Analysis of Kinship in the Palau Islands*. Honolulu, Bernice P. Bishop Museum *Bulletin* 235 (1972).

_____ and Maryanne Force. "Political Change in Micronesia," in R. W. Force (ed.), *Induced Political Change in the Pacific*.

Gale, Roger W. *The Americanization of Micronesia*. Washington, University Press of America, 1979.

_____. "A New Political Status for Micronesia." *Pacific Affairs* 51 (Fall 1978): 427-47.

Gerston, Larry. "Political Leadership in Palau." *New Zealand International Review* XI: 6 (November/December 1986).

_____. "A Tale of Two Cultures: The Conflict Between Traditional and Modern Institutions in Palau." Paper presented to Conference of the Pacific Islands Political Studies Association, University of Guam, December 16-19, 1989. Typescript.

Ghai, Yash. *Law, Government and Politics in the Pacific Island States*. Suva, University of the South Pacific, Institute of Pacific Studies, 1988.

Goodman, Grant and Felix Moos (eds.), *The United States and Japan in the Western Pacific: Micronesia and Papua New Guinea*. Boulder, Westview Press, 1981.

Gray, K. "Modernization in Micronesia: Acculturation, Colonialism and Culture Change." Master's thesis, Western Michigan University, 1974.

Green, D. Michael. "America's Strategic Trust Dilemma: Its Humanitarian Obligations." *Texas International Law Journal* XIX: 9 (1974): 26-42.

_____. "Termination of the U.S. Pacific Islands Trusteeship." *Texas International Law Journal* XIX: 9 (1974): 175.

Gutman, James. "Micronesia: Politics and Education; Living in the Past and Future of the Trust Territory of the Pacific." *Virginia Quarterly Review* 49 (Winter 1973): 29-37.

Haas, E. B. "The Attempt to Teminate Colonization, Acceptance of the United Nations Trusteeship." In D. A. Kay (ed.) *The United Nations Political System*. New York, John Wiley, 1967.

Hanlon, David. "God Versus Gods: The First Years of the Micronesian Mission on Ponape 1852-1859." *Journal of Pacific History* XIX: 1 (January 1984): 41-59.

_____. *Upon a Stone Altar: A History of the Island of Ponhnpei to 1890. Pacific Islands Monography Series*, no. 5. Honolulu, Center for Pacific Island Studies, University of Hawaii Press, 1988.

Harris, G. T. "Food Imports and Macroeconomic Policy in the South Pacific." *The Developing Economies* XXII: 1 (March 1984). Tokyo, Institute of Developing Economies.

Hawkins, J. "Factors Affecting Micronesian Political Development." In *Political Modernization of Micronesia*. Santa Cruz, University of California, 1969.

Heath, Laurel. "Education for Confusion: A Study of Education in the Mariana Islands, 1668-1941." *Journal of Pacific History* 10 (1975).

Heddle, James. "Strategic Trust: The Making of Nuclear Free Palau." Transcript of interviews for documentary film. Typescript, 1983.

Heine, Carl. *Micronesia at the Crossroads: A Reappraisal of the Micronesian Political Dilemma.* Honolulu, University of Hawaii, 1974.

_____ "Micronesia's Unification and the Coming of Self-Government," in Marion W. Ward (ed.), *The Politics of Melanesia.* Fourth Waigani Seminar, University of Papua New Guinea, May 9-15, 1970.

Hempenstall, P. *Pacific Islanders Under German Rule: a Study in the Meaning of Colonial Resistance.* Canberra, Australian National University, 1978.

_____. "Resistance in the German Pacific Empire: Towards a Theory of Early Colonial Response." *Journal of the Polynesian Society* 84 (1975): 5-24.

Hempenstall, P. and N. Rutherford. *Protest and Dissent in the Colonial Pacific.* Suva, University of the South Pacific, 1984.

Hezel, Francis X. "The Education Explosion in Truk." *Pacific Studies* II: 2.

_____. "Looking Ahead to the End of Trusteeship. Trust Territory of the Pacific Islands." *Journal of Pacific History* XIII: 4 (1978): 204-10.

_____. "A Yankee Trader in Yap: Crayton Philo Holcomb." *Journal of Pacific History* 10 (1975).

_____ and M. L. Berg, eds. *Winds of Change.* Saipan, Omnibus Program for Social Studies—Cultural Heritage, Trust Territory of the Pacific Islands, 1979.

_____ and S. J. Hezel. "Schools in Micronesia Prior to American Administration." *Pacific Studies* VIII: 1: 95-111.

Hezel, S. J., and others, eds. *Culture Youth and Suicide in the Pacific: Papers From an East-West Center Conference.* Honolulu, University of Hawaii at Manoa, Pacific Islands Study Program, 1985.

Hills, Howard Loomis. "Compact of Free Association for Micronesia: Constitutional and International Law Issues." *International Lawyer* XVII: 3 (Summer 1984): 583-608.

_____. "Micronesia—Our Sacred Trust What Went Wrong?" *Center Magazine* (September/October 1980): 21-34.

[Hilo Principles] "Statement of Agreed Principles for Free Association." *Brooklyn Journal of International Law* 5 (1971): 260-61; and *American Journal of International Law* 72 (1978): 882-83.

Hines, Neal O. *Proving Ground: An Account of the Radiobiological Studies in the Pacific 1946-61.* Seattle, University of Washington Press, 1962.

Hirayasu. "The Process of Self-Determination and Micronesia's Future Political Status Under International Law." *University of Hawaii Law Review* 487 (1987).

Hughes, Daniel T. "Conflict and Harmony: Roles of Councilman and Section Chief on Ponape." *Oceania* XL: 1 (1969): 32-41.

_____. "Democracy in a Traditional Society: An Analysis of Sociopolitical Development in Ponape, Eastern Caroline Islands." Washington, Public Health Service Fellowship 1-F-MH-25, National Institute of Mental Health, 1968.

_____. "Democracy in a Traditional Society: Two Hypotheses on Role." *American Anthropologist* LXXI: 1 (1969): 36-45.

_____. "Democracy in the Philippines and on Ponape: A Comparison of Two Political Systems Structured on the U.S. Model." *Micronesia* IX: 1 (1973): 1-10.

_____. "Integration of the Roles of Territorial Congressman into Ponapean Society." *Oceania* XL: 2 (1973): 140-52.

_____. "Obstacles to the Integration of the District Legislature into Ponapean Society," in Hughes and Lingenfelter (eds.) *Political Development in Micronesia.*

_____. *Political Conflict and Harmony in Ponape.* New Haven, Human Relations Area Files, 1970.

_____. "Reciprocal Influence of Traditional and Democratic Leadership Roles on Ponape." *Ethnology* VIII: 3 (1969): 278-91.

_____. "The Responsibilities of Anthropologists to Pacific Islanders." *Pacific Studies* III: 2.

_____ and Stanley K. Laughlin, Jr. "Key Elements in the Evolving Political Culture of the Federated States of Micronesia," in *The Politics of Evolving Cultures in the Pacific Islands*. Honolulu, Brigham Young University, 1982.

_____ and Stanley K. Laughlin, Jr. "Key Elements in the Evolving Political Culture of the Federated States of Micronesia." *Pacific Studies* VI: 1.

_____ and Sherwood G. Lingenfelter, eds. *Political Development in Micronesia*. Columbus, Ohio State University, 1974.

"International Law and Dependent Territories: The Case of Micronesia." *Temple Law Quarterly* 50 (1976): 58.

"Interview: Fred M. Zeder." *Micronesian Reporter* (Fourth Quarter 1975): 2-8.

Isenberg, David. "Reconciling Independence and Security: the Long Term Status of the Trust Territory of the Pacific Islands." *UCLA Pacific Basin Law Journal* IV: 1, 2 (Spring/Fall, 1985): 210-43.

Jackson, Miles M., ed. *Pacific Island Studies; A Survey of the Literature*. Westport, Greenwood Press, 1986.

Jacobson, Harold. "Our 'Colonial' Problem in the Pacific." *Foreign Affairs* 39: 1(1960): 56-65.

Johnson, Donald D. "American Impact on the Pacific Islands Since World War II," in F. P. King (ed.) *Oceana and Beyond: Essays in the Pacific Since 1945*. Westport, Greenwood Press, 1976.

_____. "Trust Territory of the Pacific Islands." *Current History* 58: 344 (April 1970): 233-39.

Johnson, Giff. *Collision Course at Kwajalein: Marshall Islanders in the Shadow of the Bomb*. Honolulu, Pacific Concerns Resource Center, 1984.

Joralemon, Victoria. "Review of James People's *Islands in Trust*," in *American Anthropologist* LXXXIX: 1 (March 1987): 175.

Kahn, Ely. *A Reporter in Micronesia*. New York, Norton, 1966.

Kanost, R. F. "Localisation in the Trust Territory of the Pacific Islands," in Marion W. Ward (ed.), *The Politics of Melanesia*. Waignai Seminar, University of Papua New Guinea, 1970.

Kent, G. "Development and Planning for Micronesia." *Political Science* XXXIV: 1 (July 1982): 1-25.

_____. *The Politics of the Pacific Islands Fisheries*. Boulder, Westview Press, 1980.

Keju, Darlene and Giff Johnson. "Kwajalein: Home on the Range." *Pacific Magazine* (November/December 1982).

King, F. P., ed. *Oceana and Beyond: Essays on the Pacific Since 1945*. Westport, Greenwood Press, 1976.

Kiste, Robert Carl. *The Bikinians: a Study in Forced Migration*. Menlo Park, Cummings Publishing Co., 1974.

_____. "Changing Patterns of Land Tenure and Social Organization Among the Ex-Bikini Marshallese." Ph.D. diss., University of Oregon, 1967.

_____. *Kili Island: A Study of the Relocation of the Ex-Bikini Marshallese*. Eugene, University of Oregon, 1968.

_____. "Micronesia." in Miles Jackson (ed.), *Pacific Island Studies; a Survey of the Literature*.

_____. "The People of Enewetak Atoll vs. the U.S. Department of Defense," in Michael A. Rynkiewich and James P. Spradley (eds.), *Ethics and Anthropology: Dilemmas in Fieldwork*. New York, Wiley, 1976.

_____. "The Relocation of the Bikini Marshallese," in Michael Lieber (ed.), *Exiles and Migrants in Oceania. ASAO Monograph*, no. 5. Honolulu, University Press of Hawaii, 1977.

_____. "The Termination of the U.S. Trusteeship in Micronesia." *The Journal of Pacific History* XXI: 3, 4 (July/October 1986): 127-38.

Klee, Gary A. "Traditional Time Reckoning and Resource Utilization." *Micronesia* XXII: 2 (December 1976): 211-46.

"Law and Politics in the American Pacific." *Political Science* XXXIV: 1 (July 1982): 1-136.

Lawrock, Lawrence. "Luckier than Ben Franklin: Guam's Schoolboys in 1727." *Guam Recorder* 7 (1977): 12-18.

Leary, Paul M. "American Policy in Micronesia." *The Journal of the College of the Virgin Islands* CXXV: 5 (1979): 137.

Leibowitz, Arnold H. *Colonial Emancipation in the Pacific and Caribbean: A Legal and Political Analysis.* New York, Praeger, 1976.

_____. "The Marianas Covenant Negotiations." *Fordham International Law Journal* 4 (1981).

Levine, Stephen. "The United States and Micronesia: Towards Political Change." *New Zealand International Review* 16 (November-December 1976): 15-20.

Lingenfelter, Sherwood Galen "Administrative Officials, Peace Corps Lawyers and Directed Change on Yap," in Hughes and Lingenfelter (eds.) *Political Development in Micronesia.*

_____. *Yap: Political Leadership and Culture Change in an Island Society.* Honolulu, University Press of Hawaii, 1975.

Louis, William Roger. *National Security and International Trusteeship in the Pacific.* Annapolis, Naval Institute Press, 1972.

Lutz, Catherine. *Micronesia as Strategic Colony.* Cambridge, Mass., Cultural Survival, 1984.

MacDonald, J. Ross. "Termination of the Strategic Trusteeship: Free Association, the United Nations and International Law." *Brooklyn Journal of International Law* VII: 2 (Summer 1981): 235-81.

McDonald, A. *Trusteeship in the Pacific.* Sydney, Angus and Robertson, 1949.

McGrath, William A. "The Marshall, Caroline and Mariana Islands: Too Many Foreign Precedents," in R. Crocombe (ed.), *Land Tenure in the Pacific.*

_____. "Resolving the Land Dilemma: an Historical Outline of Land Tenure Development in Micronesia." *Micronesiaan Reporter* XIX: 1 (1971): 9-16.

McHenry, Donald. *Micronesia: Trust Betrayed.* New York, Carnegie Foundation, 1975.

McKinney, Robert. "Micronesia Under German Rule, 1885-1914." Master's thesis, Stanford University, 1947.

McKnight, Robert. "Competition in Palau." Ph.D. diss., Ohio State University, 1960.

_____. "Rigid Models and Ridiculous Boundaries: Political Development and Practice in Palau ca. 1955-1964," in Hughes and Lingenfelter (eds.), *Political Development in Micronesia.*

McNeill, John Henderson. *The Strategic Trust Territory in International Law.* London, University Faculty of Laws, 1976. [Ann Arbor, University Microfilms]

McPhetres, S. "Elections in the Northern Mariana Islands." *Political Science* XXXV: 1 (July 1983): 103-16.

McShane, R. "Is the Jury System Suitable For the Commonwealth of the Northern Mariana Islands?" *Political Science* XXXIV: 1 (1982): 66-91.

Maratita, David Q. "Trusteeship in Turmoil: The Marianas." *Micronesian Reporter* XIX: 2 (1971): 16-23.

Marshall Islands: a Chronology 1944-1983. Honolulu, Micronesia Support Committee, 1984.

Marshall Islands: 37 Years Later. [Report of a World Council of Churches Delegation to the Marshall Islands, 20 May - 4 June, 1983]

Marston, Geoffrey. "Termination of Trusteeship." *International and Comparative Law Quarterly* XVII: 40 (1969).

Mason, Leonard. "The Ethnology of Micronesia," in Andrew Vayda (ed.), *Peoples and Cultures of the Pacific.* Garden City, Natural History Press, 1968.

Mason, Leonard. "A Marshallese Nation Emerges from the Political Fragmentation of American Micronesia." *Pacific Studies* XIII: 1 (November 1989).

_____. "Unity and Disunity in Micronesia: Internal Problems and Future Status," in Hughes and Lingenfelter (eds.), *Political Development in Micronesia*.

Meller, Norman. *The Congress of Micronesia: Development of the Legislative Process in the Trust Territory of the Pacific Islands.* Honolulu, University of Hawaii Press, 1969.

_____. *Constitutionalism in Micronesia.* Honolulu, University of Hawaii Press, 1985.

_____. "The Micronesian Executive: FSM, Kiribati, and the Marshall Islands." Paper presented to the Conference of the Pacific Islands Political Studies Association, University of Guam, December 16-19, 1989. Typescript.

_____. "Micronesian Political Change in Perspective," in Hughes and Lingenfelter (eds.), *Political Development in Micronesia*.

_____. "The Pacific Island Microstates." *Journal of International Affairs* XXXXI: 1 (Summer/Fall 1987).

_____. "Three American Legislative Bodies in the Pacific," in Roland W. Force (ed.), *Induced Political Change in the Pacific*.

Metelski, John B. "Micronesia and Free Association: Can Federalism Save Them?" *California Western International Law Journal* 5 (Winter, 1974): 162-83.

Mihaly, Eugene B. "Neutralization of the Pacific Island States: a Proposal," in Hughes and Lingenfelter (eds.), *Political Development in Micronesia*.

_____. "Tremors in the Western Pacific." *Foreign Affairs* 52 (1974): 839-49.

Mink. "Micronesia: Our Bungled Trust." *Texas International Law Journal* VI: 181 (1971).

Morgan, William N. *Prehistoric Architecture in Micronesia*. Austin, University of Texas Press, 1988.

Moos, Felix. "The Old and the New: Japan and the United States in the Pacific," in Hughes and Lingenfelter (eds.), *Political Development in Micronesia*.

Murphy, Raymond E. *Geographic Studies in the Easternmost Carolines. Final Report*. Coordinated Investigation of Micronesian Anthropology, 1947-49. Pacific Science Board, National Research Council, 1950.

Murray, James N., Jr. *The United Nations Trusteeship System*. Urbana, University of Illinios Press, 1957.

Myers, Ramon H. and Mark R. Peattie. *The Japanese Colonial Empire, 1895-1945*. Princeton, Princeton University Press, 1984.

Nason, James D. "Political Change: an Outer Island Perspective," in Hughes and Lingenfelter (eds.), *Political Development in Micronesia*.

Robert R. Nathan Associates, Inc. *Economic Development Plan for Micronesia: A Proposed Long-Range Plan for Developing the Trust Territory of the Pacific Islands*. Part I. Washington, D. C., Robert R. Nathan Assoc. Inc., 1966

_____. *Economic Development Plan for Micronesia: Summary and Index*. Washington, D. C., Robert R. Nathan Assoc. Inc., 1966.

_____. *Socioeconomic Development Plan for the Northern Mariana Islands*. Washington, D.C., Robert R. Nathan Assoc. Inc., 1977.

Nevin, D. *The American Touch in Micronesia*. New York, W. W. Norton, 1977.

Nufer, H. *Micronesia Under American Rule: an Evaluation of the Strategic Trusteeship*. Hicksville, Newyork, Exposition, 1978.

O'Connor. "Micronesia, America's Frontier in the Far East." *National War College Review* 57 (1970): 73.

Bibliography | 231

Oliver, Douglas L., ed. *Planning Micronesia's Future: a Summary of the United States Commercial Company's Economic Survey of Micronesia.* Honolulu, University Press of Hawaii, 1951 and facsimile 1971.

Olsen, Dennis F. "Piercing Micronesia's Colonial Veil: *Enewetak v. Laird and Saipan v. Department of the Interior."* Columbia Journal of Transnational Law XV: 473 (1976): 473-95.

Overall Economic Development Stategy. Saipan, Commonwealth Development Commission, 1980.

Pacific Concerns Resource Center. "Memo Regarding Palau Plebiscite Irregularities and United States Involvement." Typescript, March 16, 1983.

Pacific Planning and Design Consultants. *Physical Development Master Plan for the Commonwealth of the Northern Marianas.* Saipan, Office of Transition Studies and Planning, 1978.

Palau Indicative Development Plan. Koror, Palau Political Status Commission, 1977.

Palau: Self-Determination v. U. S. Military Plans. Honolulu, Micronesia Support Committee, 1983.

Parmentier, Richard. "House Affiliation Systems in Belau." *American Ethnologist* XI: 4 (November 1984): 656-756.

_____. "Mythological Metaphors and Historical Realities: Models of Transformation of Belauan Polity." *The Journal of the Polynesian Society* XCV: 2 (June 1986).

_____. "The Sacred Remains: an Historical Ethnography on Ngeremlengui, Palau." Ph.D. diss., University of Chicago, 1981.

_____. *The Sacred Remains: Myth, History, and Polity in Belau.* Chicago, University of Chicago Press, 1987.

Peattie, Mark R. *Nan'yo: The Rise and Fall of the Japanese in Micronesia, 1885-1945.* Honolulu, University of Hawaii Press [Pacific Islands *Monograph Series*, no. 4] 1988.

Peoples, James G. "Dependence in a Micronesian Economy." *American Ethnologist* V (1978): 535-52.

_____. *Island in Trust: Culture and Dependence in a Micronesian Economy.* Boulder, Westview Press, 1985.

Perkins, Whitney T. *Denial of Empire: the United States and Its Dependencies* Leyden, A.W. Sythoff, 1962.

Petersen, Glenn. "Breadfruit or Rice? The Political Economics of a Vote in Micronesia." *Science and Society* XCV: 4 (Winter 1979/80): 472-85.

_____. "A Cultural Analysis of the Ponapaen Independence Vote in the 1983 Plebiscite." *Pacific Studies* 9: 1 (November 1985): 13-52.

_____. *One Man Cannot Rule a Thousand.* Ann Arbor, University of Michigan Press, 1982.

_____. "Ponapauan Matriliny: Production,Exchange and the Ties that Bind." *American Ethnologist* IX (1982): 129-44.

_____. "Ponape's Body Politic: Island and Nation." In *The Politics of the Evolving Cultures of the Pacific Islands.* Honolulu, Brigham Young University, 1982.

_____. "Ponape's Culture of Resistance." *Radical History Review* XXVIII (1984): 347-66.

Planning Legislation. Honolulu, Hawaii Architects and Engineers, 1968.

The Politics of Evolving Cultures in the Pacific Islandss. Proceedings of a Conference held February, 1982. Honolulu, Brigham Young University, Institute for Polynesian Studies.

Pomeroy, Roy S. "American Policy Respecting the Marshalls, Carolines and Mariana Islands 1898-1941." *Pacific Historical Review* 17 (1948): 43-54.

Price, Willard. *America's Paradise Lost.* New York, John Day, 1966.

Prince, Harry G. "The United States, the United Nations, and Micronesia: Questions of Procedure, Substance, and Faith." *Michigan Journal of International Law* II: 1 (Fall 1989).

Quigg, Philip. W. "Coming of Age in Micronesia." *Foreign Affairs* 47: 2 (1969): 493-508.

Ramarui, David. "Education in Micronesia." *Micronesian Reporter* XIV: 1 (1977): 1-10.

Rampell, Ed. "Remeliik Looks Ahead: Palau Edges Closer to Compact." *Pacific Islands Monthly* (April 1985).

Ranney, Austin and Howard R Penniman. *Democracy in the Island: the Micronesian Plebiscites of 1983*. Washington, American Enterprise Institute for Public Policy Research, 1985.

Reed, Christopher. "Stormy Waters Surround Palau's Power Problems." *The Guardian* (June 4, 1984).

Renahan, Thomas. "The Political Status of Micronesia: National Interest and American Strategic Interests." Ph.D. diss., Georgetown University,1976.

Republic of Palau. Senate. "Analysis of the 1984 Compact of Free Association." Typescript, 1984.

_____. Senate. "Memorandum re Major and Substantial Differences Between the Compact of Free Association Voted in February of 1983 and the Compact Recently Signed in May of 1984." Typescript, June 22, 1984.

_____. Supreme Court. Order Granting Summary Judgement in *Ibedul Yutaka M. Gibbons et. al. v. Haruo I. Remeliik et. al.* Civil Action no. 67-83. Typescript, August 6, 1983.

Richard, Dorothy Elizabeth. *United States Naval Administration of the Trust Territory of the Pacific Islands*. Washington, Office of Naval Operations, 1957.

Ritzenthaler, R. E. *Native Money of Palau* . Coordinated Investigation of Micronesian Anthropology, 1947-49. Pacific Science Board, National Research Council, 1949.

Rodriguez-Orellana, Manuel. "In Contemplation of Micronesia: the Prospects for the Decolonization of Puerto Rico Under International Law." *University of Miami Inter-American Law Review* XVIII: 457 (1987).

Rogers, Robert and Dirk Ballendorf. "The Marianas Option." *New Zealand International Review* IX: 9 (1984).

Rosenblatt, Peter R. Introduction to *Brooklyn Journal of International Law* VII: 2 (Summer 1981) [Issue on Micronesian Status Negotiations].

Rynkiewich. "The Ossification of Local Politics: the Impact of Colonialism on a Marshall Islands Atoll," in Hughes and Lingenfelter (eds.), *Political Development in Micronesia.*

Sahara, Tamotsu. *Land Classification Program Proposal for the Trust Territory of the Pacific Islands.* Honolulu, Land Study Bureau, University of Hawaii, 1967.

Sahlins, Marshall. *Islands of History.* Chicago, University of Chicago Press, 1985.

_____. "Poor Man, Rich Man, Big-Man, Chief: Political Types in Melanesia and Polynesia." *Comparative Studies in Society and History* V: 3 (1963).

Schwalbenberg, Henry M. "Marshallese Political Developments: No to Commonwealth." *Journal of Pacific History* XX: 1 (January 1985): 105-15.

_____. "The Plebiscite on the Future Political Status of the Federated States of Micronesia." *The Journal of Pacific History* XX: 3 (July 1984): 172-84.

Shuster, Donald R. "Elections, Compact, and Assassination in the Republic of Palau." *Pacific Studies* XXII: 1 (November 1988).

_____. "Elections in the Republic of Palau." *Political Science* XXXV: 1 (July 1983): 117-32.

_____. "Islands of Change in Palau: Church, School and Elected Government 1891-1981." Ed. D. diss., University of Hawaii, 1982.

_____. "The Last Trusteeship: Islands and Opportunities. A Personal View of the Republic of Palau." Paper presented at the Guam Association of Social Workers Conference, March 30, 1989.

_____. "More Constitutions for Palau." In *The Politics of Evolving Cultures of the Pacific Islands*. Honolulu, Brigham Young University, 1982.

_____. "Palau's Constitutional Tangle." *Journal of Pacific History* 15 (1980): 74-82.

_____. "The Politics of Free Association and the Politics of Violence in the Republic of Palau." Paper presented to the Pacific Islands Political Studies Association Conference, Apia, Western Samoa, May 23-25, 1988.

_____. "The Salii Presidency: Triumph to Suicide." Paper presented to the Conference of Pacific Islands Political Studies Association, University of Guam, December 16-19, 1989. Typescript.

_____. "State Shinto in Micronesia During Japanese Rule, 1914-45." *Pacific Studies* V: 2.

Smith, Donald F. "Diversity in Micronesia." *Current History* 65 (November 1973): 221-23.

Smith, D. R. *Palauan Social Structure*. New Jersey, Rutgers, 1982.

Smith, DeVerne. "The Ties that Bind: Exchange and Transactions between Kinsmen in Palau." Ph.D. diss., Bryn Mawr College, 1977.

Smith, Frances McReynolds, ed. *Micronesian Realities: Political and Economic*. Santa Cruz, University of California Center for South Pacific Studies, 1982.

Smith, Marjorie. "Resetting the Bones of Culture: the Beginnings of Micronesian Land Registration," in *The Politics of Evolving Cultures of the Pacific Islands*.

Smith, Patrick. "Memorandum re Interference with the Legal Processes of the Republic of Palau." Typescript, October 1983.

Solomon, Anthony M. "Report by the U.S. Government Survey Mission to the Trust Territory of the Pacific Islands." Typescript, 1963.

The Solomon Report: America's Ruthless Blueprint for the Assimilation of Micronesia. Berkeley, Friends of Micronesia, 1974.

Souder, Paul B. "Guam: Land Tenure in a Fortress," in R. Crocombe (ed.), *Land Tenure in the Pacific*.

Spoehr, Alexander. *Majuro: a Village in the Marshall Islands*. Coordinated Investigation of Micronesian Anthropology 1947-49, Pacific Science Board, National Research Council. Chicago, Natural History Museum, 1949.

Swartz, Marc J. "Personality and Structure: Political Acquiescence in Truk," in R. W. Force (ed.), *Induced Political Change in the Pacific*.

Talaleyev and Boyarshinov. "Unequal Treaties as a Model of Prolonging the Colonial Dependence of the New States of Asia and Africa." *Soviet Year Book of International Law* (1976): 169-70 [English summary, 177].

Tobin, Jack Adair. "The *iroij* system of the Marshalls." *Micronesian Reporter* XVIII: 4 (1970): 8-9.

_____. "The Resettlement of the Enewetak People: a Study of a Displaced Community in the Marshall Islands." Ph.D. diss. Berkeley, University of California, 1967.

Toyosaki, Hiromitsu. *Goodbye Rongelap!* Tokyo, Tsukijishokan, 1986.

Trumbull. Robert. *Paradise in Trust: a Report on Americans in Micronesia, 1946-1958*. New York, William Sloan Associates, 1959.

Trust Territory Planning Program, Final Reports (1968-73). Honolulu, Hawaii Architects and Engineers, 1969-74.

United Nations. Department of Political Affairs, Trusteeship and Decolonization. *Decolonization: Issue on the Trust Territory of the Pacific Islands* 16 (April 1980).

_____. Trusteeship Council. *Conditions in the Trust Territory of the Pacific Islands: Report of the Drafting Committee*. T/L. 1238 (June 3, 1983).

_____. Trusteeship Council. *Outline of Conditions in the Trust Territory of the Pacific Islands: Working Paper Prepared by the Secretariat* T/L. 1235 and T/L. 1235 Add.1, 4 (May 1983).

_____. Trusteeship Council. *Outline of Conditions in the Trust Territory of the Pacific Islands: Working Paper Prepared by the Secretariat.* (April 29, 1985). T/L. 1244.

_____. Trusteeship Council. *Report of the United Nations Visiting Mission to the Trust Territory of the Pacific Islands, 1985.* (October 16, 1985). T/1878.

_____. Trusteeship Council. Verbatim Record of Proceedings, 19 May-11 June, 1983. T/P. 1544-1560.

_____. Trusteeship Council. Verbatim Record of Proceedings. May 16-July 18, 1984. T/PV 1564-1580.

_____. Trusteeship Council. Verbatim Records of Meetings May 13-June 11, 1985. T/PV 1581-1598.

"United Nations Trusteeship—Law to Approve the Covenant to Establish a Commonwealth of the Northern Marianas Islands in Political Union with the United States." *Harvard International Law Journal* 18 (Winter 1977): 204-08 [Note].

United States. Congress. House. *Message from the President of the United States Transmitting a Draft of a Joint Resolution to Approve the Compact of Free Association.* March 30, 1984.

_____. Congress. House. Committee on Interior and Insular Affairs. *Approving the Compact of Free Association with the Federated States of Micronesia and the Marshall Islands.* July 15, 1985.

_____ Congress. House. Committee on Interior and Insular Affairs. *Approving the Covenant to Establish a Commonwealth of the Northern Mariana Islands in Political Union with the United States of America, and for other purposes. Report to accompany H. J. Res. 549.* Washington, 1975.

_____. Congress. House. Committee on Interior and Insular Affairs. *Reports on Pacific Affairs, 1965. Hearings Before the Subcommittee on Reports of Meetings of the First Congress of Micronesia Held at Spain and Sixth South*

Pacific Conference held at Lae, New Guinea. Hearings held August 5, 11, and September 7, 1965. Washington, 1965.

_____. Congress. House. Committee on Interior and Insular Affairs. Subcommittee on Territorial and Insular Affairs. *Marianas Political Status; Hearing Before the Subcommittee, April 14, 1975.* Washington, 1975.

_____. Congress. House. Committee on Interior and Insular Affairs. Subcommittee on Territorial and Insular Affairs. *Progress Report on Trust Territory Status Negotiations; Hearing Before the Subcommittee to Hear Progress Report on Negotiations Concerning the Future Status of the Trust Territory of the Pacific Islands, March 15, 1973.* Washington, 1973.

_____. Congress. House. Committee on Interior and Insular Affairs. Subcommittee on Territorial and Insular Affairs. *To Approve "The Covenant to Establish a Commonwealth of the Northern Mariana Islands, and for other purposes; Hearing Before the Subcommittee on H. J. Res. 549, H. J. Res. 550, and H. J. Res. 547, to Approve the "Covenant to Establish a Commonwealth of the Northern Mariana Islands in Political Union with the United States of America," and for other purposes, July 14, 1975.* Washington, 1975.

_____. Congress. House. Committee on Interior and Insular Affairs. Subcommittee on Territorial and Insular Affairs. *To Provide Authorizations for the Trust Territory Government and for the People of Bikini Atoll; Hearing, March 24, 1875, on H. R. 5192.* Washington, 1975.

_____. Congress. Senate. Committee on Armed Services. Subcommittee on General Legislation. *Northern Mariana Islands. Hearings Before the Subcommittee on H. J. Res. 549: Joint Resolution to Approve the "Covenant to establish a Commonwealth of the Northern Mariana Islands in political union with the United States of America", and for other purposes, Nov. 17, 1975.* Washington, 1976.

_____. Congress. Senate. Committee on Energy and Natural Resources. *Hearings on S. J. Resolution 286, A Resolution to Approve the Compact of Free Association, and for Other Purposes, May 24, 1984.* Washington, 1984.

_____. Department of State. *Despatches from U.S. Consuls in Ponape. Caroline Islands 1890-92.* National Archives and Records Administration.

_____. Department of State. *Trust Territory of the Pacific Islands Annual Reports to the United Nations on the Administration of the Trust Territory of the Pacific Islands, 1947- .*

_____. Department of the Interior. Office of Inspector General. *Report to the President of the Republic of Palau on Palau's Efforts to Obtain An Electrical Power and Fuel Storage Facility.* November 17, 1983. Typescript.

_____. District Court for the District of Columbia. "Complaint for Declaratory and Injunctive Relief," in *Laji Taft et. al v. United States of America,* Civil Action no 84-3708. December 5, 1984.

_____. Executive Office of the President. Executive Order 12569, October 16, 1986. "Compact of Free Association with the Pacific Islands."

_____. General Accounting Office. *Problems With New Responsibilities of Self-Government in the Northern Mariana Islands.* Washington, Government Printing Office, 1980.

_____. Office for Micronesian Status Negotiations. "Analysis of the Agreement Between the Government of the United States and the Government of Palau Regarding the Putting into Effect of the Compact of Free Association by the Government of Palau and Amending the Military Use and Operating Rights Agreement." July 1, 1983.

_____. Office for Micronesian Status Negotiations. "Compact of Free Association." May 1984. Typescript.

_____. Office for Micronesian Status Negotiations. "The Political Status Negotiations for the Trust Territory of the Pacific Islands and the Compact of Free Association." April 1984. Typescript.

_____. Office for Micronesian Status Negotiations. Text of cable from Ambassador Fred M. Zeder to Ambassador Lazarus Salii. August 1983. Typescript.

_____. Office for Micronesian Status Negotiations. "United States and Palau Sign Compact of Free Association." May 23, 1984. Typescript.

United States Survey Mission to the Trust Territory of the Pacific Islands Report. Washington, Government Printing Office, 1962.

Useem, John. "Changing Structure of a Micronesian Society." *American Anthropologist* 47 (1945): 567-88.

_____ *Report on Palau*. Coordinated Investigation in Micronesian Anthropology, report no. 21. Pacific Science Board, 1949.

_____. "Structure of Power in Palau." *Social Forces* 29 (1950): 141-48.

Van Cleve, Ruth. *The Office of Territorial Affairs*. New York, Praeger, 1974.

Vidich, A. J. "Political Factionalism in Palau." Coordinated Investigation of Micronesian Anthropology, report no 23. Washington D.C., Pacific Science Board, 1949.

Vincent, J. *America's Future in the Pacific*. New Brunswick, Rutgers University Press, 1947.

Von Uexkull, Jakob. "Report on the September 4, 1984 Referendum on the Lifting of Palau's Constitutional Ban and the Compact of Free Association with the USA." Typescript, 1984.

Vrevskii, V and V. Ivanov. "The Soviet Position on Questions of Normalizing Political Relations and of Developing Economic Relations in the Pacific Ocean Region." *Soviet Studies in History* XXI: 4 (1983): 87-115.

Washington Pacific Report I : 1 (October 1, 1982-seriatum).

Webb, J. *Micronesia and U. S. Pacific Strategy*. New York, Praeger, 1974.

Weisgall, Jonathan. "Micronesia and the Nuclear Pacific Since Hiroshima." *SAIS Review* V: 2 (Summer/Fall 1985): 42-55.

_____. "The Nuclear Nomads of Bikini Atoll." *Foreign Policy* 39 (1980): 74-98.

Willens, Howard P. and Siemer. "The Constitution of the Northern Mariana Islands: Constitutional Principles and Settings. *Georgia Law Journal* 65 (1977): 1373.

Woodward, Bob. "CIA Bugging Micronesia Negotiations." *Washington Post* (December 12, 1976).

Worthley, John A. "Legislatures and Political Development: The Congress of Micronesia." *Western Political Quarterly* 26 (December 1973): 675-85.

Yanaihara, Tadao. *Pacific Islands Under Japanese Mandate.* Oxford, Oxford University Press, 1940.

Zafren, Daniel Hill. *The Compact of Free Association—Foreign Policy Provisions: A Section by Section Legal Analysis.* Washington, Congressional Research Service. 1984.

Index

Island Trading Company of
   Micronesia (United States
   Commercial Company), 55
Kwajalein, 48, 61, 108, 126-27,
   143
Land alienation, 63
Micronesia, anthropological
   description, 47, 177-78; as
   only strategic trust under
   United Nations, 57;
   economic stagnation, 52-
   55, 59, 105, noted in
   Solomon report, 61;
   education, 64, 69-70; health
   care, 119; history before
   1945, 47-49; political elite,
   66, 70; self-government, 55,
   59-60; recommendations of
   Solomon report, 64-65;
   transition to trusteeship
   status, 49-60
"Micronization," 70
Micro-states, and membership
   in United Nations, 26-27
New Caledonia, 38, 146
Non-aligned movement,
   Bandung conference, 14;
   contradictions of position
   regarding Non-self-
   governing territories in
   1970s, 29-32; opposition to
   Belgian thesis, 14-15;
   opposition to status other
   than independence for
   Palau, 82
Non-self-governing territories,
   and Belgian thesis, 8-9;
   declaration regarding non-
   self-governing territories,
   5-7, 15; non-aligned
   movement on, 15-16.
Palau, as first nuclear free state,
   100; Coalition for Open,
   Honest and Just
   Government, 171, 173;

constitution, 108, 112;
   constitutional amendment,
   165, declared invalid by
   Congressional Research
   Service, 168; economic
   situation, 105; modern
   secular leadership, 181-82;
   and substances ban, 74, 99,
   103; role in constitutional
   convention, 72-73, 182-83;
   sovereignty, 81-82;
   traditional leaders, 130;
   traditional political culture,
   177-80; vote for separate
   political status, 77; women
   elders, 166, 169-70. See also
   Compact of free
   association.
Peace Corps, 69
Plebiscite, Roosevelt (Franklin
   Delano) on, 4; used by
   Trusteeship Council, 21-
   24. See also Compact of
   free association
Puerto Rico, 13
Referendum. See Plebiscite
Remeliik, Haruo (President of
   Palau),120-22, 181;
   assassination, 125; and
   IPSECO, 123-25
Republic of the Marshall
   Islands 106-08, 117, 143
Salii, Lazarus, 72, 74, 148, 152-53,
   156, 162, 165-66, 181; acts
   ultra vires, 136; as
   Palauan ambassador for
   status negotiations, 110,
   113; elected President of
   Palau, 129-30; and
   IPSECO bribe, 168; suicide,
   171
Self-determination, as principle
   in establishment of United
   Nations, 4-7; violated by